ADIVASI LIFE STORIES
Context, Constraints, Choices

ADIVASI LIFE STORIES
Context, Constraints, Choices

INDRA MUNSHI

RAWAT PUBLICATIONS

Jaipur • New Delhi • Bangalore • Mumbai • Hyderabad • Guwahati

ISBN 81-316-0044-0
© Author, 2007

Published by
Prem Rawat for **Rawat Publications**
Satyam Apts., Sector 3, Jawahar Nagar, Jaipur 302 004 (India)
Phone: 0141 265 1748 / 7006 Fax: 0141 265 1748
E-mail: info@rawatbooks.com
Website: www.rawatbooks.com

New Delhi Office
4858/24, Ansari Road, Daryaganj, New Delhi 110 002
Phone: 011-23263290

Also at Bangalore, Mumbai, Hyderabad and Guwahati

Typeset by Rawat Computers, Jaipur
Printed at Chaman Enterprises, New Delhi

For
my parents, who taught me
to respect people
and for
the adivasis of Thane, who taught me dignity and courage

Contents

Acknowledgements

The book has long been in the making and many people have contributed to it. Some find a mention here; others do not, but that does not diminish their role in the preparation of the present study. However, for my interest in sociology and, more specifically, in research, I am grateful to Surendra Munshi, my brother, who has been a teacher and more to me. For the hours he has spent with me encouraging and advising and improving my understanding, I cannot thank him enough. His comments have sharpened the focus of the study. Mariam Dossal nagged me into giving my research in Thane the shape of a book. She read through the drafts and gave me valuable suggestions. A.R. Momin offered useful comments on the proposal of the project, which I submitted to the ICSSR. To Nasreen Fazalbhoy, Ritu Dewan, Kamala Ganesh, Darryl and Zareen D'Monte, Helene Basu, Narendra Panjwani and Tilu, I owe much for a lively discussion and useful comments on the various drafts.

Shiraz Balsara and Pradip Prabhu made this book possible. They made their home available to me during the fieldwork in Thane, helped in the selection of interviewees, offered information on many issues. Their commitment to the adivasis has been a source of inspiration to me. Shiraz shared many a tiring hour with me during the transcription of the tapes. I could never bring myself to tell her how much I appreciated her involvement with my work. Other members of the Kashtakari family – Brian, Madhu, Meena and Priya – made my life easier in different ways during the fieldwork. Saunri and Kabir brought much joy and laughter to me during my long stay in Dahanu. I hope they will grow up in a better society.

I am most indebted to Radkibai, Babubhau, Ramabai, Dasma, Suman and Subhash for sparing time to share their life experiences with me. They displayed tremendous patience, a remarkable virtue of the Warlis, in sitting for days and replying to my questions. I am also grateful to the large number of adivasis whom I interviewed in the course of my fieldwork. This book really belongs to them.

I must also acknowledge with gratitude the information, insights and data made available to me by many government officials at different levels.

It was in the beautiful surroundings of Margret Blasche's home in Erlangen that I finalised two chapters of the book. I do not want to embarrass her by praising her hospitality. The discussions with Michael von Engelhardt and Heide Inhetveen forced me to answer many questions related to the methodology of life story research, despite the language barrier. To Fritz Schutz, I owe my fascination with the life history approach. The sensitive insights he had been kind enough to share with me almost two decades ago was my first introduction to the method, and I have still not forgotten it.

To the ICSSR, I am grateful for the scholarship which freed me from all teaching responsibilities at the university for two years to do full-time research. Thanks are also due to the University of Mumbai and the department of sociology for allowing me to do this.

I would like to thank the staff of the libraries of the University of Mumbai and the University of Erlangen-Nurnberg for giving me valuable assistance. I am also grateful to the staff of the Maharashtra State Archives in Mumbai.

My student, Rajni, was a vital link between me and my computer. Beena helped me with a hundred small things that had to be done till the end. I have appreciated their help. Prasad Gogate prepared the maps at a short notice and I thank him for his help.

I have appreciated the patience and interest with which Leela worked on improving the text. Rawat Publications deserve my sincere thanks for the publication of the book. Navjot designed the cover page and I appreciate the care and involvement with which she did it.

Thanks are due to my parents and my family for being very understanding throughout.

And above all, Vikram, who kept my spirit alive through the highs and lows of research.

FLIGHT OF THE EAGLE

Like the eagle that flies high
and with a keen eye takes a look at everything below;
Oh youth, you too look at your society
with the keenness of an eagle
and prepare to reach your goal.

Poor people with empty stomachs,
exploiters fill their godowns;
Why are you not angry, I ask you?
Our children are naked, our women in rags;
Why are you not angry, I ask you?

Those who exploit live in tall houses,
the poor live in broken down huts
Do not be quiet any more,
Prepare yourself, prepare yourself.

The footsteps of thousands of poor will resound,
the exploiters will tremble.
Prepare yourself to reach your goal.
The voices of thousands of women will ring,
the exploiters will tremble with fear;
Get ready to reach your goal.

Babubhau

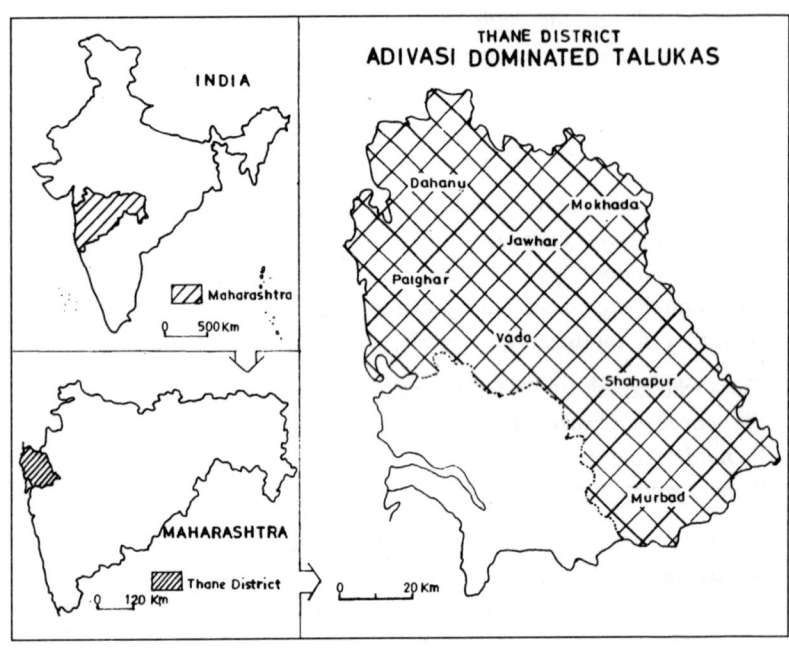

Introduction

This book is about the lives of the adivasis, also known as tribals, and the circumstances in which they find themselves, in one district, Thane[*], in Maharashtra, western India. I prefer to use the term adivasi because that is how they refer to themselves. The adivasis of Maharashtra who number 73.18 lakh, according to the 1991 Census, constitute 9.27 per cent of the population of the state, 10.8 per cent of the total adivasi population of the country, the largest in the country after Madhya Pradesh. Just three hours train ride from Bombay, renamed Mumbai in 1995, Thane district has a large adivasi population, the second largest adivasi population of the 35 districts of Maharashtra, 18 per cent of the total population of the district and about 13 per cent of the total adivasi population of the state. In Thane, they are largely concentrated in the talukas of Dahanu, Palghar, Talasari, Mokhada, Wada, Jawhar, Murbad and Shahapur. The adivasis of the district belong to the Warli, Kathkari, Kokna, Koli, Thakur and other groups. The Warlis are the most predominant among them and are believed to be the original settlers of the region. Out of the total population of 5,249,126 in Thane district, adivasis number 951,205 of which the Warlis are 413,823 [GoI 1991].

---

[*]   Till 1979 the district was called Thana after which it was changed to Thane. I have used Thane throughout the book except in Chapter 1, which deals with the colonial period. In the records of this period the name Thana is used. I have also used Bombay instead of Mumbai in this chapter.

The district forms part of the north Konkan region, a long fertile coastline of about 113 km, with the Sahyadri ranges in the east and the Arabian Sea in the west. The district borders the Ahmadnagar and Nashik districts in the east, Pune in the south-east, the state of Gujarat and the centrally administered areas of Dadra and Nagar Haveli in the north, Greater Mumbai in the south-west and Raigad district in the south. The Arabian Sea forms the north-western boundary. It is estimated that about 28 per cent of the district is hilly and upland. The plain regions are located in the Thane coast, accounting for 58 per cent of the district. The remaining 14 per cent comprise the midlands formed by various plateaus. Isolated hills dot the entire district. Agriculturally, the most important inland area is formed by two river valleys, Vaitarna and Ulhas, and is 40 per cent of the total area [Ambasta 1998: 43].

The soil near the beach is suitable for the cultivation of fruits, vegetables, flowers and spices. Large areas are under paddy cultivation with an intensive use of improved inputs like fertilisers and pesticides and higher irrigation levels made possible by the use of tube wells. This is the fruit-growing zone, the rich 'bundarpatti', coastal plains, where non-adivasis, especially Iranis and Parsis, have developed very lucrative horticulture. The most important produce is chikoo but plantains, mangoes, guavas, coconut, cashew and a variety of vegetables are also cultivated. The soil in the eastern region, mostly on the slopes, is red. It is brownish black on the patches of the valleys lying mainly between the coastal plains and the hilly slopes. The entire coastal belt with its creeks, wetlands, and mangroves forms a rich fishing area, which abounds with a variety of fish, crabs, lobsters and prawns. These find a ready market in Mumbai, in the rest of the country and even overseas.

The 'junglepatti', forested hilly area, lies to the east of the railway line at the foot of the Sahyadri range which provides an unbroken boundary running north to south in the eastern part of the district. There are also spurs running laterally to the main ranges. The terrain is hilly and uneven, with an alternation of desolate cliffs with wooded slopes. The hills are covered in tropical, moist, deciduous and semi-evergreen vegetation. The main species are teak, ain, hed, mango, shisham, apta, bibla, kalamb, savar, dhavada and khair. Wild game can be also found in the interior of the forest. But, as the Gazetteer reports, "most of the virgin forest cover has been destroyed over years, except perhaps in inaccessible steep slopes and higher elevations" [GoM 1982: 14]. The process of denudation of forest during the last two centuries is discussed in detail in the following chapters.

The two main rivers – Vaitarna and Ulhas – join the area on the west coast. The Vaitarna and its main tributaries, the Pinjal, Daherja and Surya pass through Shahapur, Mokhada, Wada, Jawhar and Palghar talukas. The tributaries of the Ulhas – Barvi, Bhatsa, and Kalu – pass through Murbad, Ulhasnagar, Shahapur and Kalyan talukas. Thane also has one of the biggest lakes in the state, Tansa, with a large catchment area, located in Shahapur taluka, a major source of water supply for Mumbai city [GoM 1981-82: 2].

The district is well connected to Mumbai, and of course, to other cities in India and the world. The Central and Western Railways which link Mumbai with the rest of India, as well as the Mumbai-Ahmedabad National Highway pass through the district, making it an important centre for trade.

Thane's history shows that it has been exposed to external influences since early times. Several waves of migrations and invasions have occurred, each leaving its impact on the economy and the society. The social diversity of the region is a testimony to its past. The district came under the successive rules of the Muslims (1332-1660 A.D.), the Portuguese (1500-1670 A.D.), the Marathas (1660-1800 A.D.) and the British (1800-1947) [GoM 1882: 703-704].

The Gazetteer of the district records that the Vanis from Gujarat and Rajasthan, the Parsis, Iranis and the 'bhaiyas' (as migrants from Uttar Pradesh are commonly known in these parts), entered the district at different states and settled down to lucrative business. By 1870s, the non-adivasis – Brahmins, Parsis, Vanis, Muslims and others – controlled most of the land, orchards, trade, moneylending and services.

The measurers adopted during a century and a half, after the British took over Thane in 1818 brought about significant changes. After 1860s, the British government systematically carried out a new forest policy in the country, bringing the forests under state control and this, to a great extent, affected the life of the people who had been depending largely on the forest for their survival. The rights of the adivasis to the forest were redefined and restricted. Shifting cultivation, which they claimed to have practised since "time immemorial" was more or less stopped and they were "settled" as cultivators. But by the end of the century, most adivasis had lost their land to the non-adivasi outsiders – the liquor contractors, the traders, the shopkeepers – who acquired control over the land of the adivasis and turned them into tenants and bonded labourers. Although many of them were reported to have been indebted and bonded to the higher castes even before the British rule, the process of land alienation and the conversion of the adivasi cultivator into a rent-paying tenant was sharply accelerated during this time. Commercialisation of agricultural and forest produce further deepened the exploitation of the adivasis by the non-adivasi landlord-trader-moneylender classes which emerged as a very powerful group in this region. High rent, unpaid forced labour and other forms of oppression including sexual harassment of adivasi women characterised the class relations between the landlord-moneylender-trader and the tenant and bonded labour.

After gaining independence in 1947, as a result of the tenancy legislations introduced by the government of India, certain categories of tenants were able to acquire ownership rights to the land they cultivated. A number of adivasi tenants became owner-cultivators, while others who had been evicted for one reason or the other, became agricultural labourers. Although exact figures are not available, rough estimates offered by the people familiar with the region suggest that not more than 35-40 per cent got land, and that too was only 40-50 per cent of what they had owned and cultivated before. At the same time, the overexploitation by the forest department, the near plunder by timber traders and the demand for more and more firewood and timber, led to further depletion and destruction of the forests, causing deeper erosion of the fragile survival base of the adivasis. The subdivision of the landholdings over generations as well as the destruction of the forests forced the adivasis to look for other sources of employment and livelihood.

The district has undergone rapid industrial development in the last four decades, but this development is restricted only to certain parts, for example, the Thane-Belapur-Kalyan zone. The talukas which witnessed this spurt are Thane, Kalyan and Ulhasnagar where modern industries are concentrated. Other talukas, Vasai, Bhiwandi, Palghar and Dahanu are developing industrially with a large number of small-scale units each employing less than 10 workers. The rest of the talukas, where adivasis are predominant, have had practically no industrial development.

The major sources of livelihood available to the adivasis at present are employment in orchards, popularly known as 'vadis', small-scale factories, brick kilns, salt pans, fishing boats and construction sites – sand digging and loading and unloading of trucks, all very strenuous and risky – and cultivation of encroached forest land. A large number of them have what they call "forest plots", the legal status of which is still uncertain. Most, including those who have had school education, need to migrate out seasonally to earn cash to supplement the income from agriculture, to "buy clothes, to pay to the doctor, to spend on children's education and to buy spices and other necessities of life".

Some adivasis are better off, "with enough to eat and a little left over", who have benefited from the government measures for "tribal development" and improved their land or started small businesses. About 5-10 per cent may be said to be 'khandani', who do not migrate out, whose children can go to school and who can afford to improve their land and remain in the village. Not more than 3 per cent are those who have improved their condition by entering the state administration or the political bodies at the lower levels. For example, the local members of legislative assembly, chairpersons of the zilla parishad, panchayat samiti, and those engaged in illegal trade, who have siphoned development funds to their private coffers form a so-called "creamy layer". Some have found employment as school teachers, forest guards, watchmen, multipurpose health workers, policemen and conductors or drivers in state transport. Very few, less than 1 per cent, have become involved, either independently or in partnership with big traders in the illegal trade of timber.

The large majority of the adivasis of this district,.85-90 per cent, must continue to strive hard to secure a meagre subsistence. While about 60 per cent of them, with small landholdings migrate for two to four months, the landless or those with very small plots do for seven to nine months in the year. They migrate in order to survive, 'jagayla', where the entire family migrates for long periods for low wages – as distinguished from those who go out for 'dhandayla', where only men migrate for shorter periods on higher wages.

I have endeavoured to reconstruct the process delineated above and used the life story approach to illuminate it. These broad social-historical processes which basically transformed the economic and social organisation of the adivasis, have largely shaped the trajectory of their collective life. The impact of these processes and the response and resistance of the adivasis to them, constitute the context which is discussed in some details in the first part of the book.

The second part of the book consists of six life stories of adivasi men and women, belonging to different age groups, even generations, as narrated by them. The life story is essentially understood as "narratives about one's life or relevant parts thereof" [Bertaux and Kohli 1984: 217]. These stories help see how the macro historical processes impinge upon individual lives, and how each individual in special circumstances, shapes his or her life. It is in the context of the extraordinarily difficult circumstances in which these marginalised people live and die, that individual life stories make sense.

It is generally agreed that individual life stories make the larger processes more vivid and comprehensible, and that "individuals' lives are the stage on which societal changes are played out" [Dex 1991: 2]. Dex elaborates the point that individuals' experiences reflect the structural facts that impinge upon them, shape and constrain their action. For example, market supply and demand factors, demographic changes and government policies, legislation and changes in the socio-legal framework influence individual experiences, making it "possible to explore and research social change through life histories" [ibid: 2].

Other scholars point to the significance of the cumulative effect of individual decisions, revealed through life histories, as an important source of social change. For example, "........decisions which individuals make to move or improve a house; to leave one community and migrate to another; to leave a job which has become intolerable or to look for a better one; to put the money into the bank, shares or a business of one's own; to marry or to separate; to have or not to have children. The changing patterns of millions of conscious decisions of this kind are of as much, probably more, importance for social change than the acts of politicians" [Thompson 1981: 298-299]. These myriad decisions cumulatively not only give shape to each life story, but can also constitute the direction and scale of major social change.

One can argue that individual trajectories are undoubtedly a part of the social trajectory of the collective, shaped by structural changes, but individually and collectively people also intervene in the processes which affect their lives, especially, those they find working against their interest. They respond, resist, challenge, undermine, manipulate and do everything to work the system to their least disadvantage. Within the boundaries and constraints set by the structures, largely shared by the collective, each individual makes a choice regarding the most important aspects of his or her life.

It is in understanding this dialectical relation between the social and the personal, the collective and the individual, the macro and the micro, that I have found the life story method to be of great advantage. A brief comment on the status of the method in social sciences may not be out of place here.

Although literature, history, sociology, psychology and anthropology have long used the method, and each tradition has evolved its own standards and perspectives on life story writing, only recently, has the value of the life story approach been recognised by sociologists. The method had been important in the work of W.I. Thomas and the Chicago School of Sociology before the second world war, but later it was ignored by sociologists when the survey method became dominant [Giele and Elder 1998: 19]. For long the aim of "human sciences" was objectivity, so human beings had to be reduced to objects. No science could be based on the "subject", the individual actor who was by nature unpredictable. So along with the individual, "subjectivity" – personal experience and consciousness – had to be abolished too. "...hence to study individual experience through personal accounts – subjectivity subjectively – was a double rejection of social science, an unforgivable provocation" [Life Stories 1985: 3].

As subjectivity became one of the core approaches to research in the field of women's history in 1980s, both oral history and feminism engaged themselves with spoken histories and life story became a theme of central concern within the oral history movement. The subjectivity of oral sources came to be recognised as a point of strength, a clue to changing consciousness rather than a weakness [Leydesdorff et al 1996: 6]. Oral historians were keen to introduce the missing voices of the underprivileged, while feminists wanted to reconstruct the past in order to give adequate attention to the contributions of women. "Both came very quickly to recognise personal feeling as an important focus of investigation, and to emphasise the significance of everyday patterns of behaviour and experience. Both moved on from discovering the value of qualitative research to challenging the traditional 'objectivity' of social science, emphasising not only the usefulness but the ethical imperatives of empathy" [ibid: 5].

In 1991, Bertaux still found the omission of life histories in sociology remarkable, considering what a rich source of information individual histories and, more so, family histories provided, for the reconstruction of social trajectories. The failure, according to him, could be blamed on the obsession with statistical representativeness and the fetish of statistics which was characteristic of a certain period in sociology from which it was with difficulty just emerging [Bertaux 1991: 85; Denzin and Lincoln 1994]. By 1999, the literature on life histories had grown immensely but scholars still found it to be "a rather underutilised source in sociological research" [Laslett 1999: 392].

The strength of personal narratives, which include life stories, as an analytical technique and source, was recognised for its ability to access motivation, emotion, imagination, subjectivity and action in ways less available to other sources [ibid: 392]. What was also less available with other methods was the introspection, reflexivity and the feelings aroused by the telling (and reading about) life stories, which could be a rich source of sociological insights. Scholars argued that life stories are not just another research technique, "They are engaging in ways that many of us have been taught not to be engaged, emotionally" [ibid: 401; Laslett 1990, 1998].

It is, however, the feminist and minority perspectives that have grown vigorously in the last decades in the field of biography and autobiography. Understanding issues of equity, power, social structure, agency, self definition and their inter relations, feminists believe, is enhanced by "personal narratives" of all kinds of lives of all kinds of women [Smith 1994: 299]. Feminist scholars see in the stories women tell about their experiences a challenge to the master narratives, which the latter find confining, distorting or oppressive. Women's stories are far more complex than the master narratives which are at best partial and simplistic [Romero and Stewart 1999: xvi]. They serve a political purpose of empowering women by breaking silence, talking back and making visible the complexities of their lives. Narrating their experiences gives women visibility in historical events, and "confronts research, social policy, and laws that, either ignore, distort or simplify women's lives" [ibid: xix].

By combining archival sources with field data, the study of historical processes and life stories, I have emphasised the need to bring together different approaches, different methods and different types of data. This is in order to empathically understand the changing world of a people, and how they cope with it. My purpose in writing this book is to understand how ordinary people live their everyday lives in extremely limiting and difficult social economic conditions; how they make their choices, manipulate their circumstances, resist and fight oppression and make sense of their lives. In recording the life stories of the adivasis who display admirable courage and dignity, I hope, in the words of Sidney W. Mintz, to "illuminate the immense human potential, often unrealised, that lies outside our reach because our social and economic system often destroys individual capacities before they can blossom" [Mintz 1974: xii].

References

Ambasta, Ashesh (1998): Capitalist Restructuring and Formation of Adivasi Proletarians, Agrarian Transition in Thane District (Western India) c.1817-1990, Ph.D. thesis, Institute of Social Studies, The Hague, the Netherlands.

Bertaux, Daniel (1991): "From Methodological Monopoly to Pluralism in the Sociology of Social Mobility" in Shirley Dex (ed) *Life and Work History Analysis: Qualitative and Quantitative Developments*, Routledge, London.

Bertaux, Daniel and Martin Kohli (1984): "The Life Story Approach: A Continental View", *Annual Review of Sociology*, Vol. 10.

Denzin, Norman. K. and Yvonnna S. Lincoln (1994): "Introduction, Entering the Field of Qualitative Research" in Norman, K. Denzin and Yvonnna S. Lincoln (ed) *Handbook of Qualitative Research*, Sage, Newbury Park, CA. For a good introduction to the method see Atkinson, Robert (1998): "The Life Story Interview", *Qualitative Research Methods*, Sage University Paper Series, Volume 44, Sage, Thousand Oaks.

Dex, Shirley (1991): "Life and Work History Analysis" in Shirley Dex (ed) *Life and Work History Analysis*, Routledge, London.

Giele, J.Z. and G.H. Elder Jr (1998): "Life Course Research, Development of a Field" in J.Z. Giele and G.H. Elder Jr (ed) *Method of Life Course Research: Qualitative and Quantitative Approaches*, Sage, Thousand Oaks.

GoI (1991): Special Tables on Scheduled Tribes, Census of India, *District Census Handbook*, Thane, Vol. I.

GoM (1882): *Gazetteer of the Bombay Presidency*, Vol. XIII, Part I and II, Thana, Government of Maharashtra, Government Central Press, Bombay.

— (1982): *Thane District Gazetteer*, Government of Maharashtra, Gazetteers Department, Bombay (Revised Edition).

— (1982): *Socio-Economic Review and District Statistical Abstract of Thane District, 1981-82*, Directorate of Economics and Statistics, Government of Maharashtra, Bombay.

Laslett, Barbara (1990): "Unfeeling Knowledge: Emotion and Objectivity in the History of Sociology", *Sociological Forum*, Vol. 15.

— (1998): "Gender and the Rhetoric of Social Sciences: William Fielding Ogburn and Twentieth Century Sociology in the United States", in Jeffery Cox and Shelton Stromquist (ed) *Contesting the Master Narrative: Essays in Social History*, University of Iowa Press, Iowa City.

— (1999): "Personal Narratives As Sociology", *Contemporary Sociology, A Journal of Reviews*, Volume 28, No. 1, January.

Leydesdroff, Selma, Luisa Passerini and Paul Thompson (1996): Introduction, in *International Yearbook of Oval History and Life Stories*, Vol. IV, *Gender and Memory*, OUP, London.

Life Stories/Recits de vie (1985): Editorial, Vol. I.

Mintz, Sidney (1974): *Worker in the Cane: A Puerto Rican Life History*, W.W. Norton and Company, New York.

Romero, M. and A.J. Stewart (ed) (1999): *Women's Untold Stories: Breaking Silence, Talking Back, Voicing Complexity*, Routledge, New York.

Smith, Louis M. (1994): "Biographical Method" in Norman K. Denzin and Yvonnna S. Lincoln (ed) *Handbook of Qualitative Research*, Sage, Newbury Park, California.

Thompson, Paul (1981): "Life Stories and the Analysis of Social Change", in Daniel Bertaux (ed) *Biography and Society, The Life History Approach in Social Sciences*, Sage, London.

Part One

Context and Constraints

I

Colonial Regulations and Collective Resistance

Early Years

In the early nineteenth century Thana was one of the most heavily forested districts in Bombay Presidency [Gazetteer 1882: 1-3]. Some of the early reports testify to this fact. The descriptions of Captain Dickenson in his reports on the inland parts of this collectorate show that "at the end of the Peshwa's rule the whole country was lying waste and unpopulated. That upto about 1850 wasteland was everywhere so abundant as to create a feeling of despair about the future of the district, that the increase of cultivation was so much desired that the poorest people were allowed to cut down as many trees as they liked merely for the purpose of clearing the land, and that wood itself was so abundant that everyone cut where and as he liked" [BFC Vol 1, 1887: 21].

Before the British took over the district in 1818, the adivasis – the Kolis, Bhils, Katkaris, Thakurs, Warlis and others – were dependent almost entirely on the forests for their survival. They practised 'dalhi' or shifting cultivation by burning down the trees, prepare the ground by crude methods, and after the crop was raised, abandoning the patch and taking up another by paying eight annas per acre. The same spot was seldom used before seven years had elapsed. For part of the year the adivasis lived on fruits, roots, berries, small game, etc. They managed to survive by raising a meagre crop, by sale or barter of forest produce and by occasional plunder of the more prosperous villages in the plains. The non-adivasi small cultivators, too, depended on forests for their agricultural and domestic requirements like timber, fuel and grazing.

During the second half of the century, the forests were depleted severely as a result of the demand for timber by the Royal Navy, the expansion of railways and the growth of urban centres close to Thana, particularly Bombay. In the absence of a system of supervision over the felling of trees, merchants exploited forests in the most reckless and wasteful manner [ibid: 24]. In 1841 Dr. Gibson, superintendent of the botanical gardens, made an inspection of the forest tracts of north Konkan and confirmed the alarming state of the forests. Colonel Jervis, the chief engineer at Bombay and a member of the military board, noted in 1843 that in large parts of Thana the teak forests had been destroyed and that only stumps and shoots were left behind [Stebbing Vol 1 1922: 114-14]. Although the reports were probably exaggerated with a view to emphasising the need for conservation, there was obviously some truth in them.

As part of their forest conservation policy, the British embarked on the programme of settling the "wild tribes" who numbered 380,000, or 45 per cent of the total population of Thana in 1872 [Gazetteer op. cit.: 60], in order to bring more land under cultivation and open out an additional source of revenue. Special incentives were provided, in terms of lower assessment, to the adivasis to give up 'dalhi', which was considered "wasteful", and to take up settled agriculture.

Several regulations were introduced between 1847 and 1862 to restrict the rights of cultivators and commercial interests, the merchants and contractors. From time to time, both the cultivators and the traders made numerous complaints against the restrictions [BFC Vol 1 op. cit.: 27]. As a result of Gibson's vigorous campaigns against the "destruction" caused by dalhi, it was greatly reduced in the district by the 1860s [Stebbing Vol 1, op. cit.: 220]. The preservation of the existing forests became the raison d'etre of the forest department. A detailed survey of forest lands was carried out at the initiative of N.A. Dalzell, the chief conservator from 1860-69.

As years passed, the policy of conservation was pursued zealously by the government and its officers. With the object of facilitating production of timber on a sustainable basis, for both revenue and imperial purposes, it was found expedient to pass a law, "to abolish all rights of the people and make government the only master" [BFC Vol IV 1887: 36]. The legal machinery was set into motion and the all-encompassing Forest Act VII of 1878 passed.

Restrictions of Customary Rights

Tensions between the forest department and the cultivators had been building up since the 1860s, but the conflict became sharper after 1882 when the provisions of the forest law of 1878 were enforced. The needs of the people came into conflict with the interests of the forest department. Under the provisions of the act, the division of government-held forests into "reserved" and "protected" was further systematised. In reserved forests the government held full rights of ownership and the produce were not to be used without official permission. Protected forests were also owned by the government, but had not yet been systematically surveyed with respect to the nature of the vegetation or that of the user's rights [Tucker 1979: 282]. Special forest boundary marks were erected to facilitate the "detection and punishment of forest crimes" [F. ADM. R 1887: 43]. Rules of conservancy were more strictly applied than ever before [RD, 104 1885: 207]. Above all, vast areas of unoccupied or wasteland, on which the villagers had previously depended to a large extent for firewood and farm implements, and for free lopping of 'rab' and cultivation by burning the seed bed, were incorporated in the reserved forests and administered by the forest department. The feeling among district revenue officials was that "there is too much taken up for forests and is scarcely enough left for cultivation" [RD, 138 1884: 118].

The hardships caused by the restrictions put on the collection of wood and on the use of grazing lands as well as the harassment caused by the forest subordinates, resulted in widespread discontent. The law was particularly harsh on the inhabitants of the non-forest villages. Both big landowners and small cultivators were distressed over the new arrangements. In their struggle against the forest department the former made common cause with the adivasi and non-adivasi cultivators, whose legitimate rights were seen as having been curtailed by the department in its pursuit of profits. The simmering discontent among the inhabitants acquired alarming proportions. Two organisations, the Thana Forest Association, which had some of the leading landholders of the district as its members, and the Poona Sarvajanik Sabha, a leading nationalist organisation, campaigned to have the forest laws amended and to repeal the repressive measures applied against the violators of the law. The matter got a lot of publicity in the local press. In 1885, a deputation consisting of influential persons from Thana and Kalyan, and eminent personalities like Kashinath Trimabak Telang, Dadabhai Naoroji, P.M. Mehta and others met Lord Reay, governor of Bombay, to acquaint him with the hardships caused by the act. The government was forced to appoint a special commission, the Bombay Forest Inquiry Commission, to study the situation in Thana and Kolaba districts [RD, 105 A 1885: 3]. The commission submitted its voluminous report in 1887.

Not only the dalhi system of cultivation, but all rights to the forest were progressively restricted with little regard for the prevailing custom. The commission reported that,

> ...upto the year 1847 or thereabouts, the people of this zilla have been in the habit as of right of bringing, cutting, removing, and using for any purpose whatever teak or any trees of any kind whatever unrestrictedly, uninterruptedly and peaceably from generation to generation, and that the unlimited exercise of this right of custom has never been upto then challenged. ... That the grazing, fuel and agricultural domestic and ordinary casual trading rights of the people over the jungles had never been seriously questioned until the time of the Forest Act which put a wholesale restriction on all of them and all of a sudden [BFC Vol 1V op cit: 36-37].

The commission observed that the governments which preceded the British had appropriated certain parts of the forest for imperial purposes and regulated cutting of trees by local residents in others. At the same time, the inhabitants were allowed to take all the produce they required for domestic and agricultural purposes from the public forests without hindrance [BFC Vol I op. cit.: 20-21].

But now elaborate rules specifying the nature of rights and the parts of the forest in which they could be exercised were introduced. While some parts of the forest were closed for the regeneration of "valuable" species, especially teak, grazing and collection of timber and other forest produce were permitted in the open portions of the forest. But the cultivator had to obtain a pass by paying a fee and then collect what he required from the forests. For this he would have to subject himself to the "whims and caprices of not less than half a dozen officers", to follow their strict injunctions, to follow a certain route for the removal of the material, to answer innumerable questions of a policeman whom he may chance to meet, and to do all this within the prescribed time limit [BFC Vol 1V op. cit.: 41].

The prohibition on moving and taking forest produce without a "pass", the commission observed,

> ... has come to many of these persons in the light of a death warrant and has practically placed the whole population of the hills at the mercy of the forest subordinates who have not scrupled to use their power in the most cruel and oppressive manner [ibid: 42].

Factors such as lack of clarity even among the forest officials with regard to the nature of "privileges" in the government forests [RD 97, 1891: 59] and frequent modifications of forest regulations increased the vulnerability of the poor.

The commission was very forthright in its criticism of the government for deriving revenue from wholly "illegitimate" and "improper" sources such as taxation, by means of fees, of the poorest classes and the sale by contract of a vast amount of grass and forest produce required for agricultural purposes. These prohibitions necessitated closer vigilance and forest officers often acted strictly. Prosecutions increased in number and the forest staff became little more than police officers [BFC Vol 1 op. cit.: 37]. A great deal of harassment of cultivators resulted from the fact that lands adjoining cultivated fields, or even situated in the heart of the villages, were reserved. They found it impossible to keep cattle away from the reserves, "which served as traps", for as soon as cattle entered them, they were impounded [RD, 96 1897: 37].

Major Grievances

The special grievances of the adivasi groups were insufficiency of 'shindad' tree-covered land, and land for tillage, the restrictions on removal of fuel, the prohibitions against cutting wood for building huts and cattle sheds and for agricultural implements, the reservation of mahua flowers and fruit, apta and tembhurni leaves, the restriction against cutting of bamboos, prohibition of dalhi, and insufficient supply of dry wood [BFC Vol II, 1887: 43].

One of the main grievances of the adivasis of the district was that dalhi had been prohibited. A number of petitions asking for permission to practise dalhi were submitted. For example, a petition to the revenue commissioner signed by the Thakurs, dated May 8, 1873 represented the plight of the adivasis:

> Wherever there may be some little ground on the hills, we prepare the same by sowing and burning it and thus cultivate the dalhis and maintain ourselves on the crops of nachni and vari that may be raised there. If we were to grow corn (that is impractical, since) it required a good ground and whence can we poor people get such ground? There is no hope at all of our getting it . . . . But now we have been prevented, we come to know that government has included our land for cultivating dalhis, within the forest limits. . . . . In short we are poor people. We maintain ourselves in the jungle by feeding on such things as roots. . . . . . But we certainly cannot live, and shall die, if we are not allowed to cultivate dalhis. This (we pray) may be considered [RD, 105A 1885: 125-127].

Grazing

One of the complaints of the people of Thana was that the inclusion of wastelands in the reserved and protected forests in 1879 had seriously affected their existing grazing arrangements.

During the course of the demarcation of forest lands, which was carried on from time to time between the introduction of the survey and the passing of the Forest Act of 1878, some free grazing areas were included in imperial resources and removed from the list of free grazing lands. The curtailment did not, the commission observed, cause much inconvenience or provoke complaint. The action taken in 1879 as regards the inclusion of grazing lands into reserved and protected forests was, in contrast, a matter of serious concern for the population of Thana.

Under the Forest Act, out of the 470,790 acres included in the forest villages, 401,566 acres or nearly 85 per cent were notified as reserved and protected forests. The area of the free grazing land thus included in forests of one or other description, viz., 401,566 acres, amounted to about 50 per cent of the total forest area of the district [BFC Vol I op. cit.: 32]. The new rules, it was observed, brought upon them a great hardship and reduced greatly the number of their cattle for want of pasture, thus preventing them from cultivating the ground [RD, 105 1887: 382].

The effect of the notification of the reserve gave the forest officers the right to prohibit free grazing. They often acted strictly, displaying very little tact. The two main complaints were: (1) large areas of the old free pasture had been wrongly included within forest limits and (2) the inhabitants of villages, having no forest within their limits, were no longer allowed to graze their cattle free, according to former custom, in the pasture lands of other villages [BFC Vol I op. cit.: 37]. The people of the so-called non-forest villages were particularly hard hit by the regulation.

The commission suggested that if the government conceded free grazing as a privilege, it should prescribe the limits within which it could be enjoyed considering both the area and the number and kind of cattle. However, at the time, it maintained, to restrict the number of cattle to be admitted for free grazing in the forest was unnecessary and inexpedient. For the total number of cattle, 306,040, kept by the residents of Thana, was not more than what was required for the proper cultivation of the area annually cropped.

This brings us to the issue of 'rab', which, as we notice, was closely related to the problem of grazing.

Rab

In local usage rab denoted cultivation by burning. An important feature of Konkan agriculture, rab was practised for cultivation of paddy as well as dry grains like nagli and varai. A seedbed would be prepared in March or April by burning layers of cowdung, tree loppings or 'tahal', shrubs, leaves, grass and clay earlier spread over it in different combinations. Clay was used to prevent the wind from blowing the ashes away. When the rains came in early June, the seed was sown and the seedbed ploughed lightly and harrowed. After an interval of 18 to 30 days the seedlings would be transplanted in the field.

The practice was a major source of friction between the people and the forest officials, who considered it "unnecessary", "wasteful", "unjustifiable" and an obstacle to forest conservancy. It was on the issue of the use of tahal that the forest department was most vociferous. The agricultural experts, however, asserted their views on the usefulness of rab in Konkan, given, one, the peculiarity of rain on the western coast, its intensity and continuity in early monsoon and its early cessation; and two, lack of water storage facilities in the Konkan. After carrying out experiments with other methods of cultivation, E.C. Ozonne, director of agriculture, concluded that rab greatly increased the yield, that "...the raiyat in rab areas was adopting the only ready means by which he could cultivate his rice crop with profit", and that "... in Thana loppings are absolutely necessary, because other rab material is not sufficient to meet the demand for rice, nagli and varai" [BCF Vol I, op. cit.: 221-236].

Before the introduction of the revenue survey in Thana, all the 'varkas', grasslands, except those reserved as state forests by former governments, were communal wastes. From time to time, portions of the communal wastes were appropriated for supplying loppings of trees and brushwood for rab. These were called shindad lands and were generally attached to particular rice fields. Other portions were utilised either for cultivation of hill grains, or for supplying grass required for rab and cattle. The remaining part served as common pastureland. However, assessment was levied only on the actual areas of the varkas land which was converted into separate occupancies transferable at the will of the occupant, with or without the rice land to which they were formerly attached. While some cultivators retained the shindad lands, many lost them. Consequently, the supply of rab material was greatly diminished [ibid: 101]. The senior forest officers attributed this to the reckless cutting of trees for sale by the 'raiyat', cultivator [for details see Munshi 1990: 439]. In all respects, the demand for rab kept increasing while the supply area was constantly decreasing.

The condition of government wastelands outside reserved forests was even worse than that of occupied lands given that there was no owner to check the reckless cutting of tahal and that there was more demand on resources than on occupied lands. The people made no attempt to preserve the trees on wastelands and cut them recklessly for tahal and fuel. According to the settlement officer, they felt certain that the lands would be taken into the forest after the demarcation was completed. In all the unsettled talukas, people cut trees recklessly in protected forests which, they feared, would sooner rather than later be made reserved forests. An additional factor, it was pointed out, to be considered in view of the growing scarcity of tahal supply, was the scarcity of firewood. Owing to the restrictions on the removal of firewood from the forest, the people had to fall back upon the trees kept for tahal [TWC, 1904: 13].

A very serious consequence of the inadequate supply of tahal was that even cultivable land could not be cultivated. The general rule was to cultivate as much as the cultivator could find rab material for [Note 1897: 11]. An important issue, which had a bearing on the decline in the supply of rab material, was highlighted by J.P. Orr, the forest settlement officer of Thana, in a communication to the collector of Thana in 1895. He emphasised the need to clear the teak trees (which the people may not touch) from the occupied as well as the government wastelands to stop the 'injaili' trees from being totally smothered. Preservation of injaili trees to which people turned for tahal and fuel was, therefore, urgently required. He suggested that for the propagation of injaili, both occupied and wastelands should be cleared of teak. Needless to mention that for its commercial value, teak was treated as a privileged species under the colonial rule, as it is at present.

Agricultural Implements

Agricultural implements used by the cultivators in the region were the plough, the 'alwat' used for levelling the ground after ploughing, 'tonka' used for the seedbed in the transplanting season, 'ghase', a kind of sledge on which the seedlings are drawn from the seedbed to the area of transplantation and 'baila' or the spear. Apart from teak, timber from the trees such as 'ain', 'khair', 'dhawda' or 'tivas' was also used. None of the implements lasted for more than three years and many had to be replaced after one year. The kind, shape and size of wood required varied for different implements. Whole trees were seldom required so the cultivators selected particular branches. The wood had to be flawless, without cracks or hollows [ibid: 12-13]. Through long years of experience, the cultivator acquired the necessary knowledge which was passed down from generation to generation.

By the government resolution of 1863, free grant of timber was allowed (within a limit to be fixed by the revenue commissioner) for agricultural implements, but only if the collector considered the circumstances of the applicant reasonable [BFC Vol I op. cit.: 109]. Alternately, the applicant was allowed a permit or a pass to cut such trees as might have been marked for cutting. The forest establishments were to ensure that the privilege was not misused. No important changes were made until 1880 when the whole question was reconsidered. The government then decided that free wood should not be granted in any circumstances for any purpose, without its prior sanction [ibid: 110].

The cultivator could obtain a "pass" by paying a fee and then proceed to the forest to collect what he required. For this, he would have to follow the strict orders of the forest officers and face harassment by the policemen. Or else, he could go to the depot, pay the price and get the supply ready-made. The cultivator was subjected to a great deal of trouble owing to the inconvenient location of the depots, non-availability of the required produce and restrictions and limitations on certain classes of wood and other forest produce. Above all, he had to pay rather than take what he needed [ibid: 41]. The large and impoverished population was practically compelled to buy from the government all the wood required to satisfy their innumerable needs.

An important matter, which aggravated the situation, was that teak, the most useful wood for agricultural implements, was kept out of reach of the cultivators. It could not be touched, not even when it grew on the rayat's 'malki' land or on the government's wasteland. The adivasis had been so affected by the stringent rules that they were on the verge of starvation. The commission reported:

> They have hitherto looked at the hills and jungles as their sole resource and means of subsistence. The prohibition contained in the rules against moving and taking forest produce without a pass has come to many of these persons in the light of a death warrant, and has practically placed the whole population of the hills at the mercy of the Forest subordinates who have not scrupled to use their power in the most cruel and oppressive manner. A large proportion of this vast forest population, numbering about a quarter million of souls in the zilla, is now reduced to the cruel dilemma of perishing by starvation or of appropriating wood and forest produce and being treated and punished as criminals [ibid: 42].

It was this situation that led J.P. Orr to make the suggestion to the collector of Thana, that as teak is largely required for agricultural implements, some provisions ought to be made by which the adivasis may also have it easily available [TWC op. cit.: 19]. For this it was necessary, in his opinion, to mark off a small teak reserve in non-forest woodlands near each hamlet. Once teak was cleared in occupied or wastelands, although the government retained the right over it after growth, the privilege of using it for agricultural purposes, and not for export, could be given to the people [ibid: 19].

Recommendations for the Improvement of Agriculture: J.A. Voelcker

An important voice at the close of the last century, which advocated closer attention of the forest department to agricultural needs, was that of J.A. Voelcker, consulting chemist to the Royal Agricultural Society of England. His recommendations for the improvement of Indian agriculture focused on better management of forests and are relevant even in the present.

Voelcker touched upon the fundamental issue in his comments on the role of the forest department.

> When it began to work, its chief duties were the preservation and development of large timber forests such as the teak forests

of Lower Burma, the sal forests of Oudh, and the deodar forests
of the Himalayas or the forest of the Western Ghats. Its objects
were in no sense agricultural, and its success was gauged mainly
by fiscal considerations; the Department was to be a
revenue-paying one. Indeed, we may go so far as to say that its
interests were opposed to agriculture and its intent was to
exclude agriculture rather than to admit it to participation in the
benefits [Voelcker 1893: 135].

The necessity of preserving the large forests which supplied
Europe with teak, provided timber for building purposes, railway
sleeper, furniture, etc, and were a "means of obtaining a large
revenue" [ibid: 140] was not questioned. These forests which
were mostly on the hills and mountain ranges, far removed from
the general areas of cultivation, were, in Voelcker's view, rightly
included in the reserved forests. But the reserved forests near the
cultivated areas, which could be made to serve agriculture, were
also being diverted from this end. As it happened, he noted, in
most instances the agricultural population did not see the
reservation of a forest and their exclusion from it as providing any
benefit to them. This was so because the department was guided
by the principle of growing only large timber for sale, and deriving
huge revenue from doing so. As a result, even those areas which
were not suited for timber, but only for scrub and grazing, were
taken up to grow timber [ibid: 143].

With specific reference to Bombay presidency, he pointed out
that the rab system could be the most useful aid to agriculture and
that the growing of trees which could be pollarded would do
much more good than supplying timber. He reported seeing in
Mahim, Bombay, cultivators lopping the trees around their own
fields, the twigs and leaves being utilised either for rab or directly
as manure for rice fields. Yet the trees were not ruthlessly
destroyed, for they were lopped only once in four years. Since in
wet regions the rab system had been proved to be the best for rice
cultivation, "it would frequently be very legitimate for the forest
department to work for the supply of rab instead of timber" [ibid:
144-145].

Voelcker did not mince words when he suggested that there
were other ends, which the forest department should serve,

besides growing timber and reaping huge revenue out of the forests. And, these were to provide for the agricultural community primarily, the facilities for obtaining what they required, viz, small timber, wood for implements, firewood, leaves, grass, or, wherever possible, grazing.

It was clear to him that the only way to increase the supply of wood to agriculture was the creation of new enclosures of land for growing wood, scrub, jungle and grass. Voelcker convincingly argued for the creation of fresh reserves on available land: for example, the wastelands belonging to the government, the waste-lands of villages, ravines, banks of canals and railway lines and certain types of lands under dry cultivation which might better be developed as reserves. He found it absolutely essential, in addition, to institute an agricultural enquiry to ascertain the requirements of each district in respect of wood, etc. A portion of the forest revenue could be set aside for the extension of reserves to meet agricultural needs. The results, Voelcker emphasised, "must not be gauged by financial considerations alone, but by the benefits conferred on the agricultural population, the keeping up of soil's fertility and the maintaining of the land revenue to the state" [ibid: 157-168]. In one word, the agricultural needs come before, not after, commercial and revenue requirements for the forest department.

In reality, however, the cultivators were truly "reduced to despair". In forest villages and even more so in non-forest villages, they were hard-pressed to meet the requirements of agriculture, grazing, timber for agricultural implements, material for rab and a large number of other forest produce for domestic needs. Moreover, they were exposed to the tyranny of petty forest officials as well as elaborate bureaucratic procedures which were beyond their comprehension. Even by the 1880s, a number of adivasis had lost their lands and become tenants and labourers to moneylenders and big landholders, the Marwaris and Gujarati Vanis, Parsis, Brahmins and others. The majority of them supple-mented their meagre income from land or labour, by the sale of forest produce, especially firewood. And, when this "privilege" was withdrawn in 1896, there was an open violent confrontation with the government. But there were other ways, less dramatic ones, in which the poor routinely resisted forest regulations and sought to reassert their rights to the forest. We will look at these in the following section.

Evasion and Confrontation

The resistance to forest regulations in Thana was marked by a combination of evasion and confrontation. The forest laws established new property rights, making "government the only master" and so challenged the arrangement sanctioned by customary law. Threatened by the new law, the cultivators sought in different ways, to reassert their rights to the forest and its produce. The defiance, at times, took an open and violent form. The 1896 upheaval was one such occasion. But the common form of resistance included unauthorised occupation of land, thefts, bribing and setting fire to the forests through which the poor, especially the adivasis, tried to re-establish their rights to traditional means of livelihood, challenging the claims of the government. We do not know what intention guided their resistance, given the lack of direct evidence. It appears to be, as James C. Scott points out while speaking about peasantry in general, "nearly always survival and persistence" [Scott 1990: 301], and as Hobsbawm succinctly puts it, "working the system to its advantage or rather to its minimum disadvantage" [Hobsbawm 1973: 13]. The Thana cultivators, too, were trying to ensure survival in the new system but, in doing so, came into conflict with the state.

Evasion

Non-compliance was an important strategy in the struggle for asserting some control over forest resources, or, in other words, for survival. In the new moral-juridical order these actions were categorised as "crimes" and "offences" punishable by law. The definitions of legal and illegal, right and wrong, fair and unfair, and just and unjust, had got somewhat mixed up and the poor were trying to cope with the confusion.

Forest regulations were evaded in a routine manner and this created major administrative problems. District officials reported an enormous number of cases of unauthorised cultivation of land, amounting to several thousands [RD, 27 1887: 44]. The demand for land was high because of the pressure of the growing population as well as the transfer of land from small cultivators, especially adivasis, to moneylenders and landholders [RD, 25 1882: 96]. As one official put it, the landless, like the adivasis, "who can't buy the land, steal it" [RD, 34 1884: 125].

People regularly committed theft of wood and other forest produce for agricultural implements, house construction, rab and sundry other domestic requirements. The strategy was to ignore forest guards and, when that became impossible, to bribe them into connivance. The guards, too, used the opportunity to extract from the helpless peasant in order to supplement their meagre income. The same story was heard everywhere: "For the last three years we have been paying the guard by raising subscriptions among the villagers. I pay six annas a year in three instalments", or "We never pay him anything as we are too poor to pay" [BFC Vol II op. cit.: 73, 34].

The fact that large-scale theft occurred was recognised by district officials, especially revenue officials, who viewed the forest policy with distrust and as detrimental to the interest of agriculture. In 1882 the assistant collector of Thana observed, "In the absence of (such) a low price thefts will still continue and in these wild parts they cannot be found out" [RD, 25 1882: 97]. In 1887, it was pointed out that stealing and cutting was rampant in the forests. Occupied lands intermingled on all sides with forest lands, and the occupants, when felling trees on their own lands, frequently stepped over boundaries and cut timber from government forest lands [RD, 38 1887: 43, 53]. In 1894 also "petty thefts" continued to be reported [RD, 48 1894: 24].

A matter of even greater concern for forest officials was forest fires, which continued to occur frequently in Thana district [RD, 151 1885: 65; RD, 42 1886: 19; RD, 39 1895: 172; RD, 39 1898: 147]. Although there was a reduction in the percentage of forest area burned from 14.6 in 1886-87 to 5.5 in 1892-93, it was still a cause of concern [F Adm R 1887: 55; Adm RFD 1894: 24]. There was a general agreement among officials that the fires were "not always accidental but due to mischievous or still worse motives". The commissioner of northern division, G.F. Sheppard, attributed the large number of forest fires in 1885 to the "irritation" felt by the people at the strict enforcement of forest regulations [RD, 151 1885: 65].

An important reason for firing the forest was believed to be "manufacture of dead wood". Headloads of dead firewood was allowed free to forest villagers for household consumption and to adivasis for both consumption and sale. It had to be made artificially since its natural supply in Thana was inadequate compared to the demand [RD, 138 1887: 55]. Forest fires, it was pointed out, were made to facilitate the finding of dead wood by removing undergrowth, hasten the death and fall of living trees and give the appearance of dead wood to freshly cut timber [Adm RFD 1885: 21]. Forests officials never tired of reporting that dead wood was manufactured wholesale for sale to dealers who set up timber depots at 'bandars', inland ports, and railway stations and persuaded forest villagers, adivasis and others to take it to them. The wood was bought for export, primarily, to Bombay [RD, 42 1886: 19; RD, 25 1891: 74].

The adivasis had long engaged in the sale and barter of firewood and other forest produce in coastal villages and towns. Given the restrictions on dalhi, and the subsequent loss of land, for many of them it was an important source of livelihood. The presence of timber dealers all over the district, ready to buy wood, provided an added incentive to augment the supply of dead wood and other timber by resorting to axe and fire. Besides, district officials often remarked that wood-cutting was a far more congenial employment to adivasis than agricultural labour or road making [RD, 104 1885: 228]. Obviously, by burning forests the adivasis were protecting their livelihood and at the same time giving vent to their resentment against the forest department.

The officials were very much exercised about the damage caused by forest fires. The general feeling was that if the privilege of collection of headloads of firewood for consumption and sale continued, the problem would persist. The forest department's strategy of increasing vigilance and meting out threats of punitive action including withdrawal of privilege was only partially effective in controlling the fires.

Not only forest fires, but the other "crimes", too, continued to occur and, in fact, increased. The figures of forest "offences" reported in the administration reports of the forest department do not, however, convey the magnitude of the phenomenon. A total number of 715 offences were reported in 1878-79, 571 in

1889-90, 1325 in 1892-93 and 1168 in 1898-99 [Adm RFD 1879: 53; F Adm. R 1891: 81; Adm RFD 1894: 57; Adm RFD 1900: 7]. A large number of offences went undetected, much to the despair of forest officials. The possible reasons for this were that the lower-level forest officials were neutralised by the adivasis through bribes and this undermined the efficiency of the forest department. Although some of the crimes were committed individually, bribing was widespread. In a sense, it was even sanctioned by the community as a strategy for survival, an important factor in its persistence over a long period of time.

Confrontation

In a dramatic move the government passed a resolution in 1894 discontinuing the privilege of collecting dead wood in the forests in one taluka. In July 1896, the order was enforced throughout the district. The privileges hitherto granted by the government in the reserved forests to adivasis to collect firewood free for sale and to others on payment of a fee, were withdrawn. Anyone seen fetching loads of firewood from forests after September 1896, was liable to a punishment of imprisonment for maximum six months, or a fine of Rs. 500, or both. The justification offered was that the privilege had been abused, resulting in the injury to the forests, and that the adivasis had "turned a concession into a trade" [RD, 116 1896: 23]. Besides, it was argued, the introduction of the coupe system in the late 1880s had ended the problem of unemployment of the adivasis, who now earned a livelihood labouring on the coupes.

The resolution was the culmination of a process of gradual abolition of people's customary rights to forests. A series of bad seasons, high prices of grains and the general state of poverty had reduced the poor to despair. The new proclamation prohibiting the adivasis from taking headloads and cartloads deprived them of the only means of making a livelihood. Little wonder that "the greatest excitement prevail[ed] throughout the district and that the people of each taluka held mass meetings and memorialised the government to have the obnoxious notification withdrawn" [QJPSS 1896: 15-160]. Thana witnessed much agitation during the following months. Nearly 4000 Kathodis, Thakurs, Katkaris and others were reported to have called upon the collector of

Thana in September and petitioned for a cancellation of the notification.

There were violent confrontations between the deputy collector and the people. The grievances of the people were no longer restricted to the question of firewood. They demanded that the palm-tree tax should be abolished, country liquor sold at one anna per seer, salt at one anna per 'paili', and husked rice at Rs. 1-4 per 'maund', and that the government should redeem the mortgaged lands of the raiyats from the 'sowkar', landlord-moneylender-trader, and restore it to them.

The adivasis, joined by other poor people, reacted spontaneously and violently when in 1894 the government further curtailed their customary rights threatening their very survival. It was an event, rather a constellation of events, which caught the authorities somewhat unprepared. As the collector was forced to admit, the government was "quite powerless in the presence of the storm", resulting in "serious loss of prestige to the government" [RD, 112 1897: 93]. The adivasis, the commissioner of central division, reported, had "for a while ousted the jurisdiction of the forest department" [Palande and Phalak 1958]. Above all, they succeeded in having the obnoxious notification temporarily withdrawn.

Notwithstanding the people's feelings of dissatisfaction and hatred towards it, the forest department had reasons to congratulate itself on its "success" in this district. In Thana, the revenue derived from forest produce, primarily timber, continued to rise over the years. In 1878-79, Thana showed a net profit of Rs. 42,493 [Adm RFD 1879: 33]. It increased to Rs. 89,953 in 1880-81; Rs. 1,27,645 in 1884-85; Rs. 2,77,659 in 1888-89; decreased slightly to Rs. 2,59,745 in 1892-93 and Rs. 2,63,851 in 1896-97 [RD, 25 1882: 36; RD, 27 1887: 44; RD, 40 1889: 20; Adm RFD 1894: 69; F Adm R 1898: 189].

The success of the forest department was achieved at the cost of the small cultivators, especially the adivasis. The adivasis' material world, and also their symbolic world, so intimately connected with forests, was greatly threatened. In the course of a few decades, adivasis were transformed from being, by and large, independent producers, although at a very low level of subsistence, to tenants and labourers. They were compelled to commit crimes and were exposed to the tyranny of landlords, forest contractors, forest officials and the new legal system. But they asserted their rights and articulated their grievances in a variety of ways, ensuring their own survival and making forest administration in Thana a difficult task for the government.[1]

Liquor Legislations and the Adivasis

References have been made to the grievances of the adivasis with respect to 'abkari', liquor, regulations. It would be in order here to look at the two legislations, the Abkari Act V of 1878 and the Mhowra Act (III of 1892), which affected the lives of the adivasis of this district significantly. The two legislations had the effect of blocking the major sources of liquor – 'toddy', the fermented juice of palm tree and 'mahua' or 'mhowra', a drink made from the flowers of Bassia Latifolia – by taxing the former beyond the means of the poor and banning the latter. The new system opened up an important source of revenue for the government. It also gave rise to a class of manufacturers for whom liquor manu-facturing became an extremely lucrative business. In an emerging market economy, liquor, too, could be had for money or even land and labour. But with given the persistence of semi-feudal relations of production, liquor became an instrument for exploiting the adivasis.

The main principles of the reform were that no toddy be drawn from trees except by permission and under licence, that for each toddy tree tapped tax under excise be paid and that liquor and toddy be sold in licensed shops with licences auctioned as before. These measures were to be introduced gradually over a number of years [Hardiman 1985: 189, Hardiman 1987].

The effect of the change on the adivasis was best summed up by a British official, F.S.P. Lely, assistant collector of Surat district. He launched a powerful critique of the official policy, highlighting the hardships it had caused the poor adivasi peasants and labourers in his district, ". . . . the prohibitive tax has only deprived the women and children of much of their already scanty provision of food, clothes and salt. . . . . It cannot be denied that a fair amount of toddy acts, if not as food, yet as compensation for the want of it. It cannot be denied that if not a medicine, yet it is properly believed to be such". Should a moderate, legitimate supply not be placed within the reach of the people, he rhetorically asked [RD, 9 1884: 215]. His comments applied to Thana as well.

The adivasis resisted the abkari laws by making and consuming illicit liquor. In spite of government measures to curb the distillation of illicit liquor, it was rampant almost in every village in the inland talukas where the mahua grew in abundance. The people discovered ingenious ways to escape detection. As the price of liquor went up, illicit manufacture of liquor became more and more widespread [for details see Munshi 1995: 2323-31; RD, 9 1891: 55; RD, 33 1884: 186; RD, 6 1883: 10].

In accordance with the instructions from the government of India, the Bombay government appointed a committee to further inquire whether the high rate of duty charged on legal spirit in the districts of Thana and Kolaba had not encouraged smuggling and whether the mahua flower was ever used as food in those districts. A committee consisting of three revenue officials of Bombay was appointed and their conclusions were, as expected, in conformity with the government's position. It was stated that the high rate of duty on the licit spirit was not the cause of smuggling in the two districts; that mahua was not a staple article of food of the people, neither was it generally given, in any appreciable measure, to cattle. Finally, that the only way to check the evil of illicit distillation was to bring the free traffic in mahua flowers under legislative control. They even proposed the cutting down of all mahua trees.

On the other hand, a large number of witnesses, the lower level officials as well as non-officials, stated that the flowers were used by the poor, especially by the adivasis, as food for men and cattle when their stock of grain was exhausted, especially during famine. The flower was eaten fresh or dried, by itself or mixed with grain flour and made into bread. Oil extracted from mahua seed was used for purposes of consumption as well as lighting. It was clear that the poor also bartered the mahua flowers for gram, rice or other miscellaneous items of grocery, on which they subsisted during the monsoon. It was also pointed out that formerly the peasants planted mahua trees in plenty as it was profitable but now given the changed circumstances, they were trying to fell the existing trees and sell them off [RD, 6 1883].

The adivasis were reported to have asked the Christians of Bassein taluka to abstain from liquor as a form of protest [RD 112 1897: 80]. Among other things, people demanded that liquor be sold at one anna a bottle and the palm tree tax be abolished. In one instance, it was reported in a local newspaper called *Arunodaya* that people had forced the acting deputy collector to give an order on a stamped paper for liquor to be sold at one anna a seer. With this order they went to a liquor shop and bought a quantity of liquor at one anna per seer and consumed it on the spot [*Arunodaya*, November 25, 1896]. By 1896 the storm had blown over.

The group that benefited from the new liquor laws was the Parsis. Parsi liquor shopkeepers were known to give liquor on credit and to demand labour and even land in return. In 1882, the Gazetteer of the district recorded the presence of Parsi landowners and liquor sellers in the interior villages. Frequent complaints were made against them by the adivasis that "these men press labour for the cultivation of their fields" [Gazetteer op. cit.: 247].

Oral testimonies from the adivasis reconstruct how the outsiders came and settled in their villages several decades ago, acquired a little land, opened liquor shops and often encouraged the adivasis to buy drink on credit. And after the debts increased, they would demand land or money. Since adivasis did not have the money, their lands were taken away and they were turned into tenants on their own land. In this way, the landlords acquired entire villages. These stories are very much a part of the collective memory of the people. Liquor had become an instrument of exploitation of the adivasis by the high-caste moneylender-landlords, particularly the Parsis.

The following story, popular among the adivasis, illustrates this cogently: a Brahmin had a daughter and he wanted to bring home a son-in-law. An adivasi was contacted. The adivasi agreed, but then he sat at home and did not do any work. When his wife asked him why he did not work, he said he wanted implements to work in the forests. He was given the implements. He cut a sandalwood tree and made a cupboard out of it. In the meanwhile, 'Jum', the god of death, wanted to take away the Brahmin. 'Kal' and 'Vel' (both words mean time) were sent as messengers to take him. The adivasi went to meet the messengers and asked them to go to the forest because the Brahmin was there. He then pushed them inside the cupboard and locked them in. Jum came in search of his messengers in the form of a Parsi. He started a liquor shop and began to offer a little liquor to the people free of charge. The adivasi took his father-in-law to the Parsis shop. They drank and then began to quarrel. The adivasi blurted out the fact about Kal and Vel. The Parsi gave them more and more liquor. He challenged the adivasi about the truth of having locked up Kal and Vel. The adivasi took him to the forest and opened the cupboard. Kal and Vel were freed. Jum then asked Kal and Vel to take the spirit of the adivasi along with the Brahmin's to the land of death. The adivasis believe that this is how death came to them.

The restriction on the availability of mahua and toddy, deprived the adivasis not only of intoxicants, which they surely were, but also of a source of food and nourishment. Besides, in seeing drinking as "immoral" and therefore needing to be curbed, the British overlooked the importance of toddy and of drinking in the adivasi culture. No amount of prohibition stopped the adivasis from drinking, only, as they put it, they drank stuff which was more expensive and of poor quality.

Tenants and Bonded Labourers: Struggle for Liberation

The lower rate of assessment introduced by the British induced a section of the adivasis to take up land for cultivation. Some were known to have become prosperous farmers. But the lack of agricultural implements, poor quality of soil, frequent crop failures and the rigid revenue demand made it imperative for the small cultivators – adivasis as well as non-adivasis – to turn to the moneylender for seed loans, consumption loans or money to pay revenue to the government. The alternatives were to give up the land and emigrate to Bombay or other large towns, or to enter into the service of the high caste landlords, the 'Pandharpesha'. Many adivasis leased land on a half-share or a contract basis from the big landholders, generally Brahmins, Prabhus and Kunbis [Gazetteer op. cit.: 530]. By the beginning of the 20th century most adivasis had been reduced to the position of tenants and labourers to moneylender-landlord-traders and forest contractors.

The moneylenders on whom the adivasi cultivator grew increasingly dependent, as mentioned earlier, were largely the Brahmins, Maratha, Gujarat and Marwar Vani who had entered Thana at different points of time. The Gujarat Vani came and settled down as grocers around the 18th century, but established themselves as moneylenders, landlords and mortgagees towards the end of the 19th century. The Vani of Marwar flocked to the district after 1835. They settled in the remotest villages in the district and carried on moneylending at such an exorbitant rate of interest that the borrower invariably ended up selling all his property, movable and immovable, in order to pay back the sum and the interest on it [ibid: 589].

Parsis, too, engaged in moneylending and shopkeeping. While some of them were reported to have entered Thana hundreds of years ago, many others came to the district in the beginning of the 19th century and set up liquor shops all over Thana as shown earlier. After the 1870s, as a result of the prohibition on domestic brewing and constant rise in the price of liquor, "illicit distillation" by adivasis and others became a widespread "offence" [RAED 1930: 17-18; RAED 1932: 18]. The new system, however, proved to be advantageous to the liquor shopkeepers who sold liquor on credit to the adivasis, against cheap labour, or alternately, against land.

The moneylender, although not a creation of the British rule, acquired great power over his debtor during this period, since the British judicial system made alienation of land a dangerously simple matter. Sales under civil court decrees were becoming frequent [Gazetteer op. cit., 309-10]. In several talukas of the district, the trend of increasing indebtedness and transfer of land from the cultivating to the moneylending classes was to be noticed [Brahme and Upadhyaya 1979: 211-13; RD, 21 1897: 37; TWC 1904: 18]. In 1881, T.D. Mackenzie, the acting collector of Thana, reported that there was a general consensus of opinion among his assistants that the condition of the cultivators was generally deteriorating. Land continued to pass steadily from the small cultivators to the hands of the moneylender class. In several talukas the process of alienation of land to the moneylenders and shopkeepers was to be noticed. The condition of the people, especially the adivasis, Mackenzie found, was "abject and squalid, of continuous ill health and a painful struggle to keep a miserable existence" [RD, 33 1884: 17]. In 1893, John A. Voelcker, observed, "In Thana almost all the land has become the property of the non-cultivators" [Voelcker 1893: 292].

The adivasis often complained that the sowkar not only charged a high rate of interest from them, but also cheated them in accounts. One such petition reads as follows:

> ...they have been paying their debts with interest for the last 40 to 50 years and still they are not free from them. In all parts the sowkars receive for the money lent by them to the ryots 'wadh' or compound interest. . . establish their claims in courts of law and take possession of your petitioners' estates, and cattles and every movable property. To go to court, . . . petitioners have no means, and besides they are in fear that in case they go to court, these sowkars may not help them in time of their difficulties with money . . . pray that the government appoint some person to examine the accounts of their debts and establish what they may be owing to these sowkars and what they have paid [RD 105 1887: 383].

Mortgage of labour was widely prevalent amongst the poorer Kunbis, Agris and the adivasis in the district before the end of the 19th century. The servants of many rich Brahmins, Vani and Kunbi moneylenders were almost all bound in writing to serve their masters for a period ranging from 12 to 15 years, in return for the money received to pay their marriage expenses. Through the borrower's carelessness and the lender's craft, the bondage often developed into life-long and, sometimes, hereditary servitude [Gazetteer op. cit.: 189, 310].

Accompanying the process of land settlement was that of commercialisation of agriculture and forest and its links with the larger colonial market. Timber, salt, rice, grass, firewood and fish remained major items of export from Thana throughout the British rule [Gazetteer op. cit.: 333]. The Bombay-Thana railway, the Bombay-Baroda and the central India railway, the coastal sea routes and the rapid industrialisation and urbanisation of Bombay and other towns provided the necessary infrastructure and market. Prices of rice, grass and timber increased with growing demand outside Thana. Because of the high profits from grass trade (for dairies in Bombay) with low investment costs, the landlords had a tendency to convert rice lands into grasslands [BFC Vol IV op. cit.: 123].

The first world war gave a boost to the traders. Prices of essential commodities, timber and grass rose sharply. The traders gained huge profits. Many landlords entered the grass and timber trade. Labour on grasslands and forest coupes was largely forced and bonded.

The Gujarat and local Vanis and the bhaiyas from Uttar Pradesh in the region controlled much of the grass trade in the district. Other leading traders were Memans, Khojas, Parsis and Brahmins who often combined trade with moneylending. In most instances the traders acquired control over the produce of the small cultivators, both rice and grass, through a system of advances. The bhaiyas were particularly dreaded for their ruthlessness and their lathi was the symbol of power both economic and sexual. And with the lathi they held the adivasis in total subjugation.

The number of agricultural labourers and tenants continued to increase over the years. The number of "tenants" increased from 20,943 in 1872 to 74,840 in 1881 and 2,08,331 in 1891. During that period, "farm labourers" increased from 28,907 to 1,01,485 ("farm servants and field labourers") and 1,31,182. In 1911, their number increased to 1,89,262 and there were over 2 lakh "agricultural labourers" in 1931 (census for respective years).

A study on tenancy in Thana revealed that in 1917 some 73,815 agriculturists held an area of 647,566 acres and 13,038 non-agriculturists 268,045 acres. By 1942, while the number of agriculturists had increased to 78,489, the area held by them actually declined to 433,898 acres. The number of non-agriculturists, too, had increased slightly to 14,677 but their area almost doubled to 469,528 acres [Hate 1949: 136]. The percentage of tenant cultivated area to total area cultivated showed an increase for the period 1916-17 to 1942-43 in all the regions of Thana. In the three predominantly adivasi talukas, the increase was the highest from 22 per cent to 68 per cent; in

Bassein 44 per cent to 51 per cent; and in the rest of Thana 31 per cent to 45 per cent [ibid: 138].

In a very revealing report published in 1939, D. Symington, a British civil servant, observed that the majority of the adivasis were tenants. "Eighty years ago they are reported to have been the owners of the soil but the land has long since passed out of their ownership into the hands of sowkars who are their landlords" [Symington 1939: 29]. He described the nature of the landlord-tenant relation in Thana in details. The tenants known as 'kul' all over the district were expected to pay the landlord a rent of about half the yield. The rentals, he observed, were far too high, and they did not leave the cultivator sufficient for his livelihood even for half the year. In addition to the rent, the tenant had to pay back to the landlord 'khavti', consumption loan of grains, made to him during the preceding year. The interest on grain advances was generally 50 per cent for about four months and was paid in grains [ibid: 32].

The tenants were, therefore, dependent on their landlords and not only for lands to cultivate, but also for their sustenance for nearly five months in the year. Their huts were scattered in the landlord's fields and he could at any time order them to be removed. Their share of the produce from the land lasted upto about March, after which they relied on casual labour, for about four annas a day, and on khavti, advances from their landlord. From the onset of the rains until harvest, these advances were their only source of sustenance. They were, therefore, in constant dread of the landlord. If the landlord became too oppressive, the tenant would run away, but only to find another master or to face starvation. There was no alternative but to comply with the customary demands of the landlords [ibid: 34-35].

Symington also reported the prevalence of forced labour, 'veth', demanded by the landlords from their tenants. Veth was demanded for as many days as the landlords required, even a fortnight or a month, for which the tenants were paid a maximum of one anna per day. If they refused, they were liable to assaults and beatings. These were common occurrences and usually carried out by the landlords/local agents. There were even rumours of men having been killed in the past.

The landlords often retained lands in their possession and cultivated them by forced labour. At critical periods of the agricultural season when the rains came, cultivators were forced to be on the landlords' fields at the cost of their own crops. Each house had to provide one person during the period when veth was required. In addition such persons could be used for domestic work or for polishing and loading timber at depots. "The landlords did not scruple to use the tenant womenfolk for their sexual gratification" [ibid: 36].

A large number of landlords who were also forest contractors forcibly employed their tenants on coupe work as a form of veth and paid them either one meal of rice, or not more than one anna per day. The tenants did not dare refuse for fear of eviction and consequent starvation. The only subsidiary occupation of these impoverished holders of small plots was collection and sale of some forest produce, making of catechu, charcoal burning or felling trees in coupes. At any instance, the wages were not more than three annas a day. Rs. 12 was the payment for carting. Even officers of the forest department would force the adivasis to neglect their own work during the agricultural season and do veth in the forest, under threats of fine and court cases [Parulekar 1975: 57]. For the Kathkaris who were generally engaged in charcoal making during the dry months, "maintenance dole" was the sole earning. This was a result of the high interest rates and the false accounts maintained by the contractors [Symington op. cit.: 42].

In 1940s a study conducted in Thana showed that most Warlis did not occupy any land. Only nine out of 100 families, the author stated, "can be classified as 'happy' in the sense that they are able to get food twice a day and can manage to meet their barest needs" [Save 1945: 221]. The study revealed that the labourers, too, were not free wage labourers, but bonded to the landlord in consideration of loans, which the former might have taken to meet marriage expenses. This system of pledging services in return for cash advances, generally known as the 'hali' system, was found to be prevalent all over the district. Those labourers were "reduced to the position of virtual serfs of Parsis, Brahmin and Bania landlords" [ibid: 240]. The wife also had to serve the landlord, at times as his mistress. Debt generally passed on to the children despite years of service. The rate of interest charged on the loan for marriage was as high as six per cent per month. They were permanent hereditary servants of the landlords and in no position to leave the service or seek any other occupation.

Many adivasis entered into bondage, sometimes for generations, against small loans they had taken from their landlord-moneylender to meet their marriage expenses. The meagre wages paid to the 'lagna gadi', married serfs, and the dishonesty of the landlord made it impossible for the former to repay the loan. The wife and children of the lagna gadi also became bonded servants of the landlord. Married couples were made to do all kinds of chores.

> They would sweep the house and yard, sprinkle water to settle the dust, clean the utensils, wash the clothes, draw the day's requirement of water from the well, help in the preparation of meals, pound and grind corn, clean the cattle shed, milk the cattle, light the lantern at dusk, look after the horse carriage, give the horses their food and water and press the master's body for him, carry whatever load the master chose to send with them over distances of ten miles and more, run behind their master's horse for miles when he went out for a ride [Parulekar op. cit.: 91].

This was the description given by Godavari Parulekar, the much loved communist leader of the Warlis struggle, discussed in the following pages.

Parulekar noted that while some landlords allowed husband and wife lagna gadi to stay together in one place, others separated them, sending the man to work in the town house and keeping the woman in the farm house. By sending the man away, the landlord made sure that he could enjoy the woman whenever he wished without any hindrance. Sexual abuse of adivasi women was so common that the progeny were given a special name, 'Watla', a special caste [ibid: 47, 91].

The helplessness of the adivasis to escape from the situation is clear in the following conversation between Godavari Parulekar and the adivasi lagna gadi. "How can you just stand by and allow your wife's honour to be violated? Why don't you run away?"

Their reply was, "'Where can we run to, Bai? They will only beat us up and bring us back" [ibid: 91].

It is clear from the foregoing account that from a low subsistence level, but a relatively independent existence, the adivasis became totally dependent on the landlord-moneylender-trader for their survival. The necessary precondition for the dependence and the bondage was the alienation of the adivasis from their means of subsistence: forest and land. Subsequently, they came to depend on the landlord for land, for khavti, for loans for marriage and other needs – in a word, for their very existence. As Symington observed, the adivasis had "no alternative but to comply with all his customary demands". When the demands became too oppressive, the tenants might run away, but in most cases they preferred to stay on and cultivate the fields which, in many cases, were the property of their forefathers, and to submit to the wishes of the landlords [Symington op. cit.: 34-35].

The instrument through which compliance and submission was enforced was physical violence. Instances of men being tied to posts and whipped or even killed by the landlords were not uncommon [ibid: 36]. Godavari Parulekar, who entered the district in 1945, reported instances of flogging, of sexual assault, of men being yoked to the plough or killed – even burnt to death or buried alive [Parulekar op. cit.: 46-53].

These experiences were still fresh in the collective memory of the adivasis when I did my first fieldwork in a village in Dahanu in the late 1970s. The stories were recounted to me in hushed voices in dark huts till late hours of the night. But even the blackness of the night could not hide the horror of the deeds perpetrated on them. The fear, even more the outrage, was only increased by my own realisation that their experiences were not entirely a thing of the past.

Warli Revolt

The entry of the Kisan Sabha, the peasant wing of the Communist Party of India, in Thana in 1945 provided the necessary organisation and ideology to the adivasis, in particular the Warlis, the biggest adivasi group in the district, to revolt against the oppression and exploitation of the landlords. The struggle was directed against the landlord-moneylender-trader-forest

contractor section and their musclemen. After two major conferences at Titwalla and at Zari in 1945, the Warlis refused to do
veth. About 5000 Warlis including nearly 500 women, attended
the conference in Zari and launched a unified agitation against
'vethbegar', forced unpaid labour. Dissenters were socially
boycotted, and within weeks the practice was done away with.
Drawing courage and inspiration from their action, the Warlis
spontaneously organised themselves and took a decision to
liberate lagna gadi. Processions were taken out, and, as it passed
by a landlord's house, the call given to the lagna gadi was "pick up
your scrap of cloth and your earthen pot, get free and join us". The
agitation was successful and hundreds of them were 'liberated'
[Parulekar op. cit.: 93].

The adivasis succeeded in regularising the rent for the land
they tilled. The slogan given was "don't pay any increase in rents
over the agreed rents of the previous three years. Refuse to pay
old arrears". They also got rid of all the burdensome demands
made on them by the landlords. It was decided that peasants
would not allow landlords to claim, as rent, any produce other
than paddy. Two issues relating to the rate of grass cutting and
felling trees in the forest were a source of conflict between the
adivasis and the landlords as well as the timber merchants. The
dispute was eventually settled in favour of the adivasis.

The heroic role played by the adivasi women in the struggle
deserves special mention. They experienced and bitterly resented
class exploitation as also gender oppression. Sexual harassment
and violence was the main component of gender oppression
perpetrated by the landlords and their musclemen, and by the
non-adivasi petty government officials, the police and forest
guards. The women participated actively in the struggle to end the
oppressive and humiliating feudal practices. They displayed great
courage in withstanding physical torture, molestations and
threats of rape by the police and the landlords' musclemen. They
gave shelter to the underground party members, were careful not
to give any information to the police, faced the police and carried
food to the men hiding in the forest. In 1980s, the few survivors
from the time of the struggle still recalled with great pride their
role in ending the most hated forms of oppression and
exploitation [Munshi 1986].

This phase of the struggle, more or less, came to an end in 1947, after heavy repression by the state. Large numbers of activists were arrested, prominent workers of the Kisan Sabha were externed from the district, and a state of emergency was declared in Thana. The Maharashtra Congress Committee appointed a sub-committee to enquire into the causes of the struggle. It brought out a report recommending immediate reforms in the system of land tenure in the region [Parulekar 1947: 90].

It is not my purpose here to critically evaluate the role of the struggle, which has been done ably by Saldanha [Saldanha 1984]. A recount and evaluation, of the development policies after independence and how they affect the adivasi lives is undertaken in the following chapter.

Note

1. Many good studies on forest policy and management and their impact on local communities in colonial and post-independence contexts have appeared in the last three decades in India. To mention only a few, Ramchandra Guha, *The Unquiet Woods, Ecological Change and Peasant Resistance in the Himalaya*, OUP, Delhi, 1991; David Arnold and Ramchandra Guha (ed), *Nature, Culture Imperialism, Essays on the Environmental History of South Asia*, OUP, Delhi, 1995; M. V. Nadkarni, *The Political Economy of Forest Use and Management*, Sage Publication, New Delhi, 1989; Mahesh Rangarajan, *Fencing the Forest*, OUP, Delhi, 1996; Richard Grove, Vinita Damodaran and Satpal Sangwan (ed) *Nature and the Orient*, OUP, Delhi, 1998; Marlene Buchy, *Teak and Arecanuts, Colonial State, Forest and People in the Western Ghats (South India) 1800-1947*, Institute Francais De Pondicherry, Indira Gandhi National Centre for the Arts, 1996; David Hardiman, "Power in the Forest, the Dangs 1820-1940" in David Arnold and David Hardiman (ed) *Subaltern Studies VIII*, OUP, Delhi 1994; Ajay Skaria, *Hybrid Histories, Forests, Frontiers and Wilderness of Western India*, OUP, Delhi, 1999; Ramchandra Guha, "Forestry in British and Post British India: A Historical Analysis", *Economic and Political Weekly*, October 29 and November 5-12, 1983; "Fighting for the Forest: Forestry and Social Change in Tribal India" in Oliver Mendelsohn and Upendra Baxi (ed) *The Rights of Subordinated Peoples*, OUP, Delhi, 1994; Madhav Gadgil and Ramchandra Guha,

Ecology and Equity: The Use and Abuse of Nature in Contemporary India, Routledge, London, 1995; Nandini, Sunder, 1997, *Subalterns and Sovereigns: An Anthropological History of Bastar 1894-1996*, Oxford University Press, Delhi.

References

Adm. RFD (various years): Administration Report of the Forest Department of the Bombay Presidency including Sind for the year 1892-93 (referred to in the text as Adm. RFD), 1878-79 (1879); 1883-84 (1885); 1892-93 (1894); 1898-99 (1900).

BFC (1887): *Report of the Bombay Forest Commission*, (referred to in the text as BFC), Vols I, II and IV, Government Central Press, Bombay.

Bramhe, S. and A. K. Upadhayaya (1979): A Critical Analysis of the Social Formation and the Peasant Resistance in Maharashtra, Vol II, Pune, Mimeographed.

Census of India 1891 (1892): Vol VIII, Part II, Government Central Press, Bombay.

— 1911 (1912): Vol VII, Part II, Government Central Press, Bombay.

— 1931 (1933): Vol VIII, Part II, Government Central Press, Bombay.

Census of the Bombay Presidency (1875) and Part II, (1872): Government Central Press, Bombay.

F Adm. R (1887): Forest Administration Report 1885-86, Part 1, *Forest Administration Report of the Bombay Presidency for the Year 1885-86*, (referred to in the text as F Adm. R relevant years), Part I, Bombay.

— (1891): 1889-90.

— (1898): 1896-97, Part 1.

Gazetteer (1882): *Gazetteer of the Bombay Presidency*, Vol. XIII, Part I, Thana, (referred to in the text as Gazetteer), Government Central Press, Bombay.

Hardiman, David (1985): "From Custom to Crime: The Politics of Drinking in Colonial Gujarat", in Ranjit Guha (ed) *Subaltern Studies IV*, Oxford University Press, Delhi.

— (1987): *The Coming of the Devi*, OUP, Delhi.

Hate, M.V. (1949): Farm Ownership and Tenancy, With Particular Reference to the Effect of Tenancy in Thana District, Ph.D. Thesis, Department of Economics, University of Mumbai.

Hobsbawm, Eric (1973): "Peasants and Politics", *Journal of Peasant Studies*, Vol. I, No. 1, October.

Imperial Census of 1881 (1882): Presidency of Bombay including Sind, Vol. II, Government Central Press, Bombay.

Munshi, Indra (1986): "Tribal Women in the Warli Revolt: 1945-47, Class and Gender in the Left Perspective", *Economic and Political Weekly*, Vol XXI, No 17, April 26. See also Vasantha Kannabiran, K. Lalitha and Rama Melkote (1990): *We Were Making History: Women and the Telengana Uprising*, Zed Press, London; Rani Dasgupta, "Tebhaga Ladaiye Krahsak Meyeder Bhumika", Communist Party Publication, Undated.

— (1990): "The Political Ecology of Traditional Farming Practices in Thana District, Maharashtra (India)", *The Journal of Peasant Studies*, Vol. 17, No. 3.

— (1995): "On Drinking and Drunkeness, History of Liquor in Colonial India", *Economic and Political Weekly*, Vol. XXX, No. 37, September 16.

Note (1897): Note on some Agricultural Customs of the Thana District (referred to in the text as ACT).

Palande, M.R. and N.R. Phalak (1958): *Source Material for a History of the Freedom Movement*, Vol. 2, 1885-1920, Bombay.

Parulekar, Godavari (1975): *Adivasis Revolt: The Story of the Warli Peasants in Struggle*, National Book Agency, Calcutta.

Parulekar, S.V. (1947): *Revolt of the Varlis*, PPH, Bombay.

QJPSS (1896): "Forest Grievance in Thana", *Quarterly Journal of the Pune Sarvajanik Sabha* (referred to in the text as QJPSS), 19, 1-2 (July-October).

RAED (1897): Report on the Administration of the Excise Department in the Bombay Presidency, (referred to in the text as RAED), Government Central Press, Bombay, Volume 21.

— (1930): Report from 1928-29.

— (1932): Report from 1930-31.

RD (various years): Revenue Department, Maharashtra Archives, Bombay, Volume 25 (1882); Volume 6 (1883); Volumes 9, 33, 34, 138 (1884); Volumes 104 part 1, 105 A, 151 (1885); Volumes 27, 38, 105, 138 (1887); Volume 40 (1889); Volumes 9, 25, 97 (1891); Volume 48 (1894); Volume 39 (1895); Volume 116 (1896); Volumes 96, 112 (1897); Volume 39 (1898).

Saldanha, Denzil (1984): A Socio-Psychological Study of the Development of Class Consciousness, Ph.D Thesis, Department of Sociology, University of Bombay.

Save, B.G. (1945): *The Warlis*, Padma Publications, Bombay.

Scott, James C. (1990): *Weapons of the Weak: Everyday Forms of Peasant Resistance*, Oxford University Press, Delhi.

Stebbing, E.P. (1922, 1923, 1926): *The Forest of India*, Vols 1-3, John Lane Bodley Head, London.

Symington, D. (1939): Report on the Aboriginal and Hill Tribes of the Partially Excluded Areas in the Province of Bombay, Bombay.

Tucker, Richard (1979): "Forest Management and Imperial Politics: Thana District, Bombay, 1823-1887", *The Indian Economic and Social History Review,* 16, 3 (July-September).

TWC (1904): Thana Woodland Code (referred to in the text as TWC).

Voelcker, J.A. (1893): *Report on the Improvement of Indian Agriculture,* Eyre and Spottis Woode, London.

II

Development Policies and their Impact in Independent India

Land Reforms and the Adivasi Poor

Organised militancy of the adivasis as well as the rise of a class of tenant farmer, who were economically powerful and were increasingly consolidating their political power in Thane as in large parts of the country, forced the government of India to legislate in the interest of the tenants. In Maharashtra, the Bombay Tenancy and Agricultural Lands Act of 1948 was the first important step to usher in land reforms. Subsequently, the Land to the Tiller Act of 1957 was passed and tenants became the legal owners of the land. However, the success of the act was, according to Dewan, tilted in favour of the larger tenants in Thane district. Agris and Kunbis, the poor tenants were either evicted and became agricultural labourers or continued to work as tenants and share-croppers, albeit, in a concealed form [Dewan 1990: 61]. Alarmed by the growing landlessness, the state promulgated the Maharashtra Lands (Ceilings on Holdings) Act 1962, followed by Act No. 21 of 1975, which in the case of Thane, like in the rest of the country, had limited success [Dantwala and Shah 1969: 12-18].

An important consequence of the tenancy act and the legislations that followed was the virtual disappearance of the absentee landlords, a large part of their land having gone to the tenants, and their place taken by a class of more enterprising, profit-oriented landlord-traders, who combined grass trade with horticulture and paddy cultivation. However, by and large, because of the ongoing movement of the adivasis and the enormous efforts of the Kisan Sabha, the act was implemented successfully in the adivasi-dominated talukas of Thane district. Although tenancy and share-cropping continued to some extent, in a disguised form, a large number of adivasis became the proprietors of small plots of land they formerly cultivated as tenants. Few, who enjoyed political connections, acquired relatively large plots. At the bottom rung of the ladder were the agricultural labourers who were evicted, by force and fraud, from the land they held as tenants at the time of the Tenancy Act of 1957, or did not benefit from the ceiling acts [Saldanha 1984: 342,350; Munshi 1983: 146-158]. Many lost their land because either their names were deleted from land records or they were made to surrender "voluntarily" the evidence of their having been tenants to the landlords. In some cases the landlords resumed their lands for personal cultivation. Their numbers continued to grow, from 118,227 in 1961 to 179,784 in 1971, an increase of about 52 per cent during the years when the legislation was being implemented. The persistence of land concentration in the district is clear from the following figures: in 1970-71, 64 per cent of the households held only 16 per cent of the land in fragments of less than a hectare. By 1985-86, the percentage of households had increased to 71, with an increase in the proportion of land under them to 24 per cent [Ambasta 1998: 287].

In spite of numerous protective laws, a large number of adivasis continued to turn to the landlord-trader for credit to tide over the "difficult period", the lean season which could stretch between three and six months or more, even after thirty years of independence. A committee under the chairmanship of V.S. Page appointed by the state government in 1976 to look into the problems of illicit moneylending and bonded labour, reported the prevalence of the Pale Mode system in the district covering about 25 per cent of adivasi population. Under this system, the interest charged by the moneylender, in the form of paddy or grass, worked out to nearly 1200 per cent [GoM 1975: 22-23]. Bonded labour was also found to exist even after the passage of the Bonded Labour Abolition Act in 1976. During the years 1982-85, a political organisation called Shramjivi Sanghatana, managed to release 496 bonded labourers in Wada, Vasai, Shahapur and Bhiwandi talukas of the district [Shramjivi Sanghatana: 5]. Another organisation, Bhoomi Sena, active in Palghar taluka, reported widespread prevalence of the bonded labour system. Typically for one quintal of flour worth Rs. 200, borrowed for 4-6 months, eight maunds of paddy worth Rs. 400 was to be returned [De Silva et al, 1979: 25].

Land transfers from adivasis to non-adivasis continued to occur in contravention of the provisions in the Maharashtra Land Revenue Code 1966. This was confirmed by a committee appointed by the government of Maharashtra in March 1971 to examine this alarming trend. On its recommendations the government enacted two laws in 1974-75: the Maharashtra Land Revenue Code and Tenancy Laws (Amendment) Act (XXXV of 1974), also known as the Invalid Transfer Act, which dealt with the illegal transfer of land from adivasis to non-adivasis, and the Maharashtra Restoration of Land to Scheduled Tribes Act (XIV of 1975), known as the Valid Transfer Act, which provided for the restoration of land to adivasis after April 1, 1957.

That the power of the rural and urban elite has rendered the laws largely ineffectual is evident from the following figures: by 1977, the total number of cases in which land was registered under them in the whole district was only 1530 and that in which it was ordered to be restored was 210; but land was actually restored only in 70 cases. In contrast, the number of cases of occupation of adivasi land by non-adivasi landlords found by Bhoomi Sena in Palghar alone was 800 [Munshi op. cit.: 212-214]. The Bhoomi Sena played a very effective role in pressurising the administration to implement the restoration acts. By 1993, the total number of cases registered under the laws in the whole district was 5801. Reasons for this include intimidation by rich landholders, inability of the adivasis to handle the legal machinery and the non-inclusion of important category of lands in the purview of the laws [Ambasta op. cit.: 288].

In spite of all the efforts, large-scale transfer from the adivasis to non-adivasis continues to take place. Because of the proximity to Mumbai, land prices in Thane are high. Rapid urbanisation and industrialisation and the interest of the urban elite in acquiring land in Thane for a variety of purposes, both commercial and non-commercial, have put a lot of pressure on the adivasi landholders.

According to a government official in Dahanu it is well known that non-adivasis, especially from Mumbai, buy land from the adivasis for commercial purposes like horticulture, forestry or building farm-houses, petrol pumps, residential buildings and hotels. The construction boom in Vasai, for example, has resulted in large-scale alienation of adivasi land. The land near highways and towns is very much in demand, but given the ignorance and desperation of the adivasis, it is bought at a price far lower than the market rates. In 2002, when an activist, Navleen Kumar, tried to stop the illegal transfer of adivasi lands, she was brutally murdered.

The last two decades have witnessed purchase of adivasi land by the city people in Kelve, Manor, Vikramgod, Jawhar and Dahanu and rapid growth of bungalow schemes, farm houses and resorts like Great Escape, Water Park, Silent Valley, Divekar's Natural Trails, Jungle Camp and others. Encouraged by this, the government even decided to create a tourism zone and, towards this goal, proposed the construction of Talasari Expressway. But strong timely opposition, from both the adivasi and non-adivasi, rich as well as marginal landholders, forced the government to stall the project, at least for the time being. Since land transfer from adivasis to non-adivasis is illegal, the constraint is overcome by showing the adivasi as a business partner on paper or by retaining the land in the name of the adivasi while acquiring the de facto control over it.

Driven by the compulsion of the present, the adivasis even go to the extent of selling their top-soil to the brick kilns or to other agriculturists jeopardising their own future. Planning for the future is a luxury they cannot often afford. Some transfer of land from poor adivasis to the better-off adivasis also takes place, who, taking advantage of the fact that adivasi land cannot be sold to non-adivasis, pay a lower price than the market price.

That alienation of the adivasi land continues for one reason or another is evident from the applications made by several organisations working in the district to the Expert Group on Prevention of Alienation of Tribal Land and its Restoration, constituted by the government of India. To cite only a few examples, Shanti Seva Mandal of Palghar taluka sent to the above authority a list of 142 persons, 95 per cent of whom were adivasis, whose lands were taken for construction of National Highway No 8, Mumbai-Ahmedabad Highway, during 1971-76. These persons were neither served notices, which is mandatory by law, nor had they received any payment of compensation till October 13, 2001.[1]

Even the alternate land given to adivasis in return for the land taken away are not registered in their names. It is noted by the same organisation that even after 20 years, lands given to the people of Kosbad Dapchari Pada, for example, are not put in their names. There, people are still struggling to get the lands registered in their names.

Another application dated October 11, 2001 made by the Kashtakari Sanghatana to the same committee shows that "despite the best intentions of the government land alienation, both de jure and de facto, continues in the tribal areas... cases of de facto land alienation are widespread and found in almost every village of the district". It reports on the alienation of adivasis in the district since 1940s upto the present in spite of the promulgation of the tenancy and the restoration acts. Though the provision of law required a regular inquiry in all such cases by the tehsildar in order to verify the "correctness" of the surrender, in most cases it was done perfunctorily. The landlords resumed possession of easily accessible and marketable lands. But in a large number of cases, particularly in more remote villages, the tenants' names were removed from the records, even while they retained possession and use of the land. As these lands in interior villages became accessible and marketable with the building of roads, the landlords sold them to third parties on the basis of the position in the records. Subsequently, the tenants were evicted by the new owners. In many cases the alienated land is given the status of non-agricultural land without proper inquiry, and restoration becomes almost impossible.

Non-recorded tenancy is reported in almost every village in the adivasi talukas of Dahanu, Wada, Jawhar, Mokhada and Vikramgad. Considerable tracts of land have been in possession of the tenants for one or two generations but their names have never been entered in the land records. The land appears in the name of the landlord, even while the tenant retains possession and use of land. In addition, tenancy lands in such cases where the landlords were widows, minors, (or temples) were not transferred or sold to tenants, although the land remained in their possession.

The other types of land alienation, mentioned in the application, include land acquisition for projects, roads and water bodies under the Employment Guarantee Schemes (EGS) and for a variety of services. Almost all projects in the tribal areas, whether irrigation projects or industrial estates or towns and market places, mean loss of land for the adivasis. "If all such alienated lands are totalled, it would be in the range of 3000 hectares if not more". The adivasi lands are being lost rapidly along national and state highways, for hotels, restaurants, petrol pumps, garages and so on. For many government- or zilla parishad-run services like primary health centres or Ashramshalas, adivasi lands are acquired without proper compensation.

The most recent acquisition taking place, the application notes, is that of adivasi lands adjoining the reserved forests. As most adivasi villages are in the forest areas it is natural that their lands are in the fringes of reserved forests. The declaration of such land under Section 35 of the Indian Forest Act, and its subsequent acquisition under the Private Forests Acquisition Act, 1975 have rendered a large number of adivasi farmers landless. In Dahanu division alone, there are 400 such cases.[2]

Interestingly, in response to a meeting held between the expert committee and the NGOs in Thane, the deputy sarpanch (grampanchayat, Hanumannagar of Palghar taluka) prepared a list of 270 adivasis whose lands/trees were taken by the irrigation department for the Surya project, Dahanu taluka (Kowdas dam) and Vikramgad taluka (Dhamani dam) in 1974-78 without issuing any notice or paying compensation. The persons concerned, it noted, are still struggling to get compensation for the land and the trees, but without success.[3]

Two specific projects, among others, the Surya Irrigation Project and the Dapchari Milk Project were responsible for most displacement. The former, in Jawhar taluka, acquired 1863 hectares from 10 villages for submergence and resulted in the displacement of over 5000 landed families. The latter, in which some 6,693 acres were acquired from 10 villages in Dahanu and Talasari talukas, rendered 696 land record holders or 2400 families landless. In addition, there were those families who held 'ek sali' plots granted to them by the government, those whose encroachments on forest land were regularised in 1962 and 1972, and the landless, raising the total number of displaced families to 10,000. Besides, a sizable amount of land was acquired for construction works connected with projects like canals, administrative buildings and staff quarters for which no records are available [Prabhu 2002: 279-280].

Ironically, several government-sponsored projects, of which there are many in the district, not only have hardly benefited the adivasis in any substantial way, but affected them adversely. They lost their land all over the district to big and small dams, to Maharashtra Industrial Development Corporation (MIDC), to Expressways and to overall urbanisation. In Wada, Boisar and around Ganjad, large areas are under MIDC. Rapid urbanisation in Vasai and around Dahanu has deprived many adivasi families of their land. They have also been displaced by small and medium irrigation projects in Jawhar, Wada, Mokhada and other talukas.

Two major projects in the region, the Bhatsa Multipurpose Project as well as the Surya project, mentioned earlier, provide a case in point. They were originally conceived to provide drinking water to the 'bundarpatti', and irrigation to the adivasis. The Surya project was to provide irrigation facilities to 92 villages in Dahanu, Jawhar and Palghar talukas. It was to prevent the migration of the adivasis for work and to benefit backward adivasi areas, by providing for a second crop, and was approved by the Planning Commission and the Central Water Resources Commission in 1975. But in fact, water was diverted to augment the supply of drinking water to Mumbai city, in the case of the first, and to the urban belt of Vasai taluka, in the second. In 1998, it was reported that with the help of a World Bank loan, the state government planned to spend Rs 268 crore to lay the pipelines and complete other constructions to provide the water of the Surya project to Vasai-Virar. A significant amount of water was diverted to MIDC, Boisar-Tarapur, Tarapur Atomic Power station, and Dahanu Thermal Power Plant of the Mumbai suburban electric supply (now Reliance Energy) at Dahanu. Out of the total of Rs. 149.9 crore earmarked for tribal development, about Rs. 130 crore was utilised for the project. Understandably, observes Lobo, "to the adivasis of Thane district, the transfer of their water resources is a state-sponsored loot of their collective resource as well as wealth earmarked for their development" [Lobo 1998]. Little wonder that people express their cynicism, "Don't ask for water. They will take your land to build a dam that will provide water for some other area. That's what happened to us. They took our land for a dam. We were left with no land and no water" [Martyris 2001].

Forest and Forest "Encroachments": Adivasis vs the Forest Department

After independence in 1947, the Indian government continued to view the forests primarily as a source of revenue. The forests in Thane, as elsewhere in the country, were overexploited by the forest department and private contractors for quick financial gains. Little concern was shown either for the agricultural population or for the long-term effect on the environment. After 1960, "production forestry" was promoted vigorously by the government. It called for clear felling of existing forests and replanting of fast growing and "economically valuable" species, in order to meet the growing urban/commercial and industrial demand. Forest Development Corporations (FDC) were established in different states to carry out the above programme. In keeping with its main aim, the FDC of Maharashtra (FDCM) succeeded in clear felling and planting, almost entirely with teak, 16,000 hectares in Thane region comprising Thane and Dahanu divisions, during 1974 and 1986. The revenue obtained from clear felling of the areas during 1974-75 to 1987-88 was about Rs. 67 crore [Munshi 1995: 93-97].

The efficiency and the speed with which the FDCM carried out the conversion neglecting the other more constructive objectives were severely criticised by a Technical Review Committee appointed to review the activities of FDCM. It noted with alarm that "in actual practice, however, only the natural forests of many kinds, qualities and species were made available; and of the plantations raised, more than 95 per cent were of teak; on the whole, the sheet anchor of the FDCM's land development plan has been the conversion of natural forests into teak crop by clearing and planting" without any guarantee of the success of these plantations [Technical Review, 1984: 5, 36]. The report categorically stated that FDCM's clear felling of natural forests for raising teak plantations appeared "technically unsustainable, economically temerarious, and environmentally perilous" [ibid: 43]. It also warned that overfelling would encroach upon the future supply of firewood creating a major problem in the region.

The ruinous effect of this policy in nearly 75 per cent of the forest area of Dahanu forest division was brought out by the state government's own assessment. The preliminary draft proposal for the revision of the working plan in Dahanu division which had been in existence since 1968, revealed that in the areas considered for clear felling and planting with "economically valuable" trees like teak and other timber species, almost all the areas covered under the working circle were degraded:

> ...old miscellaneous crops have been replaced by hacked, stunted and poorly growing monocrop of teak. Whereas old miscellaneous crops which consisted of fruit trees and other important species important in the socio-economic conditions of the tribals and the local people were, to some extent, meeting their needs of food, firewood, fodder and small timber, the stunted and poorly growing teak plantations are of little use to them either at present or in future. Had these plantations been successful, the economic value of these forests would have increased and then there would have been ample chances of giving part of the benefits to the local people in terms of employment and other allied opportunities. But as that has not happened the replacement of miscellaneous forests with open scrubs of teak has seriously affected the vulnerable tribal economy. Further, as teak does not allow other species to grow in the early stages.......the major varieties of local species have been forced to bid goodbye giving rise to strong speculations for ensuing ecological disaster (Draft 1988: 56-57).

It further noted that the

> entire emphasis during the period of the plan, has been on 'felling', ie, exploitation of the best material available, and the

prescriptions which embodied the care and protective operations, aimed at restocking of the exploited area, have been
ignored [ibid: 70].

Forests, as usual, were looked upon just as 'depots' which were
meant only for supplying large-sized timber for industries and
firewood for urban dwellers. The contribution of these forests
for maintaining the basic life support systems like air, soil, water
and energy for the people in general, and providing for the very
basis of sustenance in terms of food, houses and livelihood for
poor local adivasis in particular, were not given any weightage
[ibid: 82].

The felling activity of the corporation had, however, to be
called to a halt, when the government imposed a ban on clear
felling in 1986. Afforestation was now deemed necessary to
restore the ecological balance, to meet the requirements of fuel,
fodder, minor forest produce and small timber for the rural and
adivasi population, to provide livelihood to communities
traditionally dependent on forests and to increase the productivity
of forests to meet the essential national needs [FDCM 1987].
Ironically, the FDCM was one of the agencies to undertake the
large-scale afforestation.

The adivasis, too, have become instrumental in the
large-scale illicit trade that is going on. Their skill in harvesting
timber is exploited by the business groups. A majority of the
adivasis who engage in illegal felling and supplying of valuable
timber forest do so for a meagre sum. As one forest official
observed in a private conversation, many adivasi women supply
firewood to the restaurants and hotels along the highway in
return for food. Poverty and starvation compel them to engage in
the illegal activity. But large-scale organised felling, he
maintained, is carried out at the behest of the bigger business
interests against whom the forest department is totally ineffective
given the political patronage enjoyed by most of them.

The adivasis remove firewood and timber from the forest to
meet their domestic and agricultural requirements, which include
construction of houses and making agricultural implements for
fencing, thatching, cooking, etc. This is undoubtedly a drain on

the already depleted resources of the forests. The destruction of the trees that supplied them with their daily necessities has, of course, intensified the problem, as no effective and viable substitute to firewood, timber, rab material and other forest products for everyday use are available to them. Moreover, in the context of commercialisation of forests and high value of forest products, given also the breakdown of norms which regulated their relation with the forest, a small number of adivasis have also joined in the loot, begun to trade in timber, although on a small scale, and become willing partners in the theft of timber. I am told that building big wooden houses has become a new status symbol among the adivasis.

The forest department, the forest contractor and the FDCM have carried out the destruction ruthlessly. In addition, a large quantity of firewood and large size timber is illegally removed from Thane forests to supply the urban markets of Mumbai and the fast growing towns in the district. Towns like Palghar, Boisar, Dahanu, Manor, Bhiwandi, Vikramgad, Jawhar, Bordi and Talasari in Thane are well connected by rail and road with big cities like Mumbai, Surat and Nasik where a substantial demand for timber and firewood exists. Increasing number of brick kilns, saw mills, hardboard factories, furniture and plywood factories in Thane and hotels and restaurants along the Mumbai-Ahmedabad Highway require timber and firewood. Big builders and furniture companies also get their supply of timber from the Thane forests.

A close look at Thane forests reveals that at present they are greatly depleted, and their rich variety has been destroyed. The official records of the forest department show that in 1989, out of the geographical area of 9,558 sq. km. of the district, a total of 3,827 sq. km., or 40 per cent, was under the charge of the forest department. According to the satellite map, however, the actual forest cover in the district was about 36 per cent of the total land area. Out of this, only 23 per cent or 2184 sq. km. was "closed" dense forest with the crown density above 40 per cent, and the rest 13 per cent or 1247 sq. km. was open degraded forest with crown density between 10 and 40 per cent.

Pushed by the growing need for land as a means of subsistence, a result of both alienation and fragmentation of land with every generation, number of adivasis took over government and forest lands for cultivation. This was perceived as "encroachment" and it became a major source of conflict between the adivasis and the forest department. The organised resistance of the adivasis to the government offensive against the encroachers in 1959, led to a government resolution permitting encroachments which had occurred upto 1961 to be regularised. This was done in consideration of the fact that a large number of tribals had lost their land or were landless with few alternative sources of employment available to them. It is important to note that the government itself had actually encouraged small and marginal farmers to cultivate on government land in order to counter the food scarcity during and after the second world war [Bhuskute 1989: 2355]. Under pressure, the government again decided to regularise certain encroachments made upto 1972 except those on forest land in control of the forest department. Owing to tardy implementation, a large number of encroachments were not regularised. Adivasi agitations erupted all over Maharashtra especially in Thane, Nasik and Dhulia districts. In 1978, the government issued a resolution to regularise encroachments on government fallow land, grazing land and forest land between 1972 and 1978. But this implied that a significant number of adivasis who had been evicted earlier and were not in a position to provide evidence for having cultivated the land during the stipulated period were denied the benefits accruing from the government resolution (GR) [for details see Kulkarni 1979; Bhuskute 1989; Munshi 1995].

Dissatisfied with the outcome and the high-handed and callous manner in which the forest department tackled the issue – often terrorising the cultivators, evicting them and destroying their crops – the activist organisations in the district filed a public interest litigation in the Supreme Court in 1986 on behalf of 5192 adivasis of Thane, seeking regularisation of their plots which were under cultivation. The court ordered that no eviction or interference from the forest department would occur and, appointed an enquiry committee to look into the claims of the petitioners. The committee consisted of two government nominees and one independent member. The government nominees submitted a report in June 1992 and consequently regularisation of 1,694 out of 5,192 petitioners was ordered; the remaining 67 per cent were declared ineligible as there was no evidence that they had encroached before 1978. The independent member submitted a dissenting report in August 1992 questioning the methodology used by the other two members and argued forcefully for the acceptance of circumstantial evidence in cases where no proper government record existed [Saldanha 1992].

The report highlighted the fact that much of the encroachments in Thane district had taken place on wasteland or on clear felled forest lands already degraded as plantations had failed. A large part of the present encroachments had resulted from displacement due to development projects. The encroachers, for example, of several villages in Dahanu and Jawhar talukas were persons who had been displaced by the Surya project and other minor irrigation projects and who had no alternative to eke out a living. Most important, all the encroachers numbering 5,192, except 48, who had put their claims through the writ petition, were found to be landless or at best, marginal farmers whose land, other than that encroached upon, provided them subsistence, if at all, for less than half the year. With lack of employment opportunities in agriculture and non-agriculture, their only recourse has been to seek subsistence from an encroached plot of land. "Encroachments have taken place very definitely to meet their basic need, not their greed" [Saldanha ibid.: 13, 19].

On the basis of this report, another petition (dated March 6, 1994) was filed pleading that all adivasis included in the original petition be granted permission to cultivate the plots in their possession (without land titles) for a period of 15 years during which time they would cultivate the land as a means of livelihood and at once promote afforestation and protect forests. In response, the Supreme Court passed an order (dated March 7, 1995) directing the state government to appoint responsible officers in different districts to examine the claims of the adivasis, take a decision on regularisation in accordance with the given instructions and till then not to take away the land in their possession.

Subsequently, the union ministry of environment and forest declared 45,000 adivasis in Maharashtra and 1.5 million in India illegal encroachers on forest land. It passed an order in May 2002 directing all the states to remove encroachers from forest land by September 30. Protest rallies in several parts of Maharashtra, including Thane, Amravati, Gadchiroli, prompted the chief minister of Maharashtra, Vilasrao Deshmukh, to stay the eviction till the claims were verified. In the meanwhile, eviction notices were served and much harassment was caused to the adivasis all over the country.

The GR of October 10, 2002, did, however, bring some relief. It entrusted the task of verifying the claims to a taluka-level committee and a village enquiry committee. The latter is to consist of the 'sarpanch', head of panchayat, 'police patil', a government servant attached to police department, 'talati', a government servant to maintain land records, the forester and one senior citizen. They are expected to visit the encroached spot, look into both oral and circumstantial evidence and announce their decision in an open assembly. However, there are some problems. For example, in the areas where there is no organisation to inform the people and to ensure that the correct procedure is followed, people are ignorant, and therefore no claims are made, no enquiry held. There is no written evidence of the announcements made in an open assembly; the talati sometimes understates the size of the plots; there are several cases which do not appear in any list.

The enquiry is on in Thane. By a rough estimate there are around 30,000 applications of which about 70 per cent are found to be legitimate and from those cultivating forest land since before 1980. The forest department does not accept this and asserts its authority by undertaking plantations on these lands. Small battles between the forest department and the adivasis are going on.

In the meantime, the adivasis continue to cultivate their plots, and in a few villages, have succeeded in protecting the forests around their plots from the traders, the local people and the forest department. Examples of Jamshet, Aswe, Raitali and Ashagad villages, where the adivasis organised themselves spontaneously with little external guidance, to protect their forests provide substance to the argument that the involvement of the local people is absolutely essential for the preservation and maintenance of the natural resources. In fact, the regularisation of forest plots can conditionally be linked to the preservation of the forest adjoining them. The 'Jungle Bachao', save the forest, movement is discussed in greater details later [Prabhu 2001b].

My own research as well as that of others in the district points to large-scale "encroachments" in the adivasi areas. That the adivasis do not view these as such is significant. To them these are 'palat' which were already degraded when they began to cultivate them for subsistence. More important, cultivating the forest plots, in their perception, helps them conserve the forest around them. In the life stories that follow, some respondents allude to this.

Industrialisation and Regional Imbalance

Mention must be made of the fact that Thane district has achieved a phenomenal increase in industrialisation in the last four decades. Second only to Mumbai, Thane is the most industrialised district in Maharashtra. Its proximity to Mumbai puts it in an extremely advantageous position. It has easy access to a large national and international market by air and sea; it attracts entrepreneurs who, for a variety of reasons, cannot invest in Mumbai. It also attracts the ancillary units of large industries in Mumbai, given the vast reservoir of cheap labour available in the district. During the 1960s, the state, too, played a vital role in encouraging private investment by creating industrial areas in which it provided infrastructure facilities like roads, water and electricity [Ambasta op. cit.: 300]. In the last decades the industrial development in the district has also got a boost as a result of the appearance of a number of multinational companies/foreign collaborations.

By the end of 1970s, the result was evident. Agriculture and other traditional activities like forestry and fishery were responsible for only 11 per cent of the district's net domestic product (NDP), of which the contribution of agriculture and allied activities was 8 per cent. In contrast, the non-farm, primarily urban sector was responsible for generating as much as 89 per cent of the NDP, the dominant share, 58 per cent, being that of registered manufacturing, to which must be added the informal units which accompanied the industrial boom [Ambasta op. cit.: 307].

Significantly, the nature and extent of industrialisation show sharp regional imbalances within the district, for example, the extreme concentration of industrial development around the Thane-Belapur-Kalyan belt. One can see three distinct regions in the district. The first, more or less a suburb of Mumbai, includes Thane, Kalyan and Ulhasnagar talukas where a number of organised modern industries are concentrated. The second comprises the industrially developing areas of Vasai, Bhiwandi, Palghar and Dahanu, and the third, the remaining six talukas with almost no industrial development.

That the adivasi-dominated areas of the district were not touched by the effects of industrial and the accompanying overall development is well argued and well-substantiated by Ambasta. The seven talukas of Palghar, Dahanu, Talasari, Jawhar, Mokhada, Vada and Shahapur, which he calls the "adivasi talukas" have 75 per cent of the adivasi population and 63 per cent of the rural population in the district. The talukas of Jawhar, Mokhada and Vada are situated in the interior with no railway line or highway. Although Dahanu, Palghar, Talasari and Shahapur are more accessible, the adivasi tracts in these talukas, too, are in the interior, hilly, rugged and forested areas, to which the adivasis have been pushed over a long time by force of special historical circumstances. Thus, 63 per cent of the rural population resides in these parts, in which falls 66 per cent of the cultivated area of the district, mainly the relatively unproductive land. Although figures show that nearly 77 per cent of the net irrigated area falls within this area, the fact is that 5,800 of the 7,100 hectares of the net irrigated area falls in the coastal belt of just two talukas, Dahanu and Palghar, where adivasis are not present in large numbers. The coastal belt, as pointed out earlier, is highly productive with fruits, vegetables and paddy as its main commercial crops. Besides, four irrigation projects – two medium, in Shahapur and Jawhar, and two small, in Palghar and Dahanu – are located in this region. But the largest of the four projects, Bhatsai, accounting for 62 per cent of the total cultivable command created by these projects, is supposed to provide irrigation to the downstream plains of Shahapur and Bhiwandi and not to the adivasi-dominated area of the former taluka. The primary objective of this project, it must be remembered, was to meet the drinking water requirements of Mumbai, and "not for the water-starved villagers of the region through which the river Bhatsai flows".

In contrast, the area categorised as "other talukas" is predominantly urban, with 97 per cent of the total urban population of the district concentrated in the talukas of Thane, Kalyan and Ulhasnagar which together constitute 91 per cent of the total population of the district. They are followed by Bhiwandi and Vasai talukas with nearly half their population urban. These talukas account for nearly 90 per cent of the non-farm jobs, and more importantly, nearly 95 per cent of the jobs in the manufacturing units are done by workers inhabiting this region [Ambasta op. cit.: 299-311].

Ambasta further points out that significant changes have occurred in the occupational pattern, with a pronounced shift of workers toward the non-farm sector in the district. There has been a notable decline in the share of cultivators, from 49 per cent in 1961 to 28 per cent in 1981; the proportion of labourers has risen considerably in the non-farm sector, from 31 per cent in 1961 to 56 per cent in 1981. In 1991, the non-household manufacturing sector was the single category with the highest proportion of workers, a position occupied by agriculture until 1981. But the pattern to be found for all workers differs vastly in the case of the adivasis as the following data shows. Their proportion in agriculture and allied activities, 94 per cent, which was any how higher than all workers in 1961, fell marginally to 88 per cent in 1981, compared to the more notable decline of 44 per cent for all workers. So, even in 1981, only 11 per cent of adivasi workers were engaged in non-farm activities, as compared to 56 per cent for all workers [ibid, 305-306].

Most adivasis must therefore combine single crop, rain-fed, subsistence agriculture with work in industries, both traditional and modern, as casual labour, at extremely low wages and in poor conditions of work, precisely because neither can by itself ensure a reasonable standard of living. The adivasis constitute the bulk of the unskilled, cheap, and unorganised labour that staff the thousands of small manufacturing units and hazardous industries in the informal sector, which flout all norms of fairness and decency, as we will see in the following section.

Avenues of Employment

Almost every adivasi family has some members migrating out for work. Seasonal migration is even more from the interior villages where less work is available. The growing need for cash to pay for medicines, clothes and children's education as well as for food compels them to go out. The sources of employment available to the adivasis are agriculture, the vadis and grass cutting, the traditional industries that continue to survive (some of them having got a boost by the rapid urbanisation of the district as well as the continuous expansion of Mumbai) and the new ones which have sprung up recently.

Entire adivasi families migrate to Vasai, coastal Dahanu, Palghar and Wada to work on agricultural fields and the vegetable and fruit vadis during the peak season. Those with landholdings of their own must sacrifice them to work on others lands. Packed like cattles on small vehicles, they are transported to their place of work. There they work for long hours under strict supervision, with short breaks, for a daily wage ranging between Rs. 40 to Rs. 50 for men and Rs. 35 to Rs. 40 for women.

Salt manufacture, sand dredging, construction work, brick making, deep-sea fishing and small industries producing balloons, glass, liquor and buffing, are the main avenues of seasonal employment for the majority of the adivasis with some land or without any. The forest department provides some employment which has been substantially reduced since the ban on clear felling. For the collection of dry grass and the undergrowth which must be burnt to prevent forest fires or when an afforestation programme is undertaken, and pits have to be dug, and saplings to be transplanted, does the forest department employ labour. Similarly, construction of projects like large dams which necessitates clear felling of vast forest areas provides intensive employment occasionally. These "wage hunters and gatherers circulate along a wide variety of work places whether or not in agriculture or in home villages," as Breman succinctly puts it [Breman, 1996: 222]

The salt industry thrives in the coastal districts of Thane, Mumbai, Raigad and Sindhudurg. It is estimated that nearly 178 salt works, varying in size from 20 to 600 acres, are spread over 19,650 acres of land leased from the central or state government.

The industry extracts 1.5 lakh tonnes of salt worth Rs 9 crore annually. The bulk goes to the fertiliser and chemical industry, while a small portion is used for household consumption [Prabhu 2001a: 121].

According to the official statistics, 120 of the 178 salt works are in Thane district. Salt manufacture is carried on along the coast, the salt pans being located in Bhayander, Vasai, Nala Sopara, Mira Road, Kelwa, Palghar, Boisar, Vangaon and Dahanu. Most of the salt pan owners are Marwaris, Gujarat Vanis, Maharashtrian Brahmins, Marathas, Konkani Musalmans and Agris. Mainly teen-aged boys and very few women or girls work on the pans. They are recruited by the 'patil', owner of the salt pans, through the 'khatedar', leader of a work unit on salt pans called 'khata', who is a local adivasi. The patils come around to the villages in August, identify the boys and settle the amount to be paid at the end of the season which lasts from October-November to June. Small advances of Rs 200-500 are given to them. After Deewali in October-November, 10-15 boys who form a khata, are taken to the pans by the khatedar, where they live for nearly six months.

They put up little huts on the salt pans and live on the wetland, far away from a village. Much of the time, neither fresh water nor firewood is available close by. Small boys, even ten-year olds, are responsible for fetching water and cooking. Food which includes rice, spices and rarely oil is provided by the 'seth' employer. Boys fish in their free time to supplement the inadequate diet. Every week an amount of about Rs. 200 is given to each khata.

The working conditions are extremely harsh. Young workers have to work long hours in water without even the minimum protection, in the form of gumboots, gloves and goggles, which by law the owner is supposed to provide but as a rule he does not. The boys have to prepare the pans, build bunds and press the mud down to drag the salt from the pan, measure it and stack it. They are woken up even at midnight to repair breaches in the bunds.

Working long hours in salt water causes the skin on the sole and the palm to peel and swell making it very tender and painful. The glare from the sun causes irritation of the eyes, but the employer does not provide any medication for it. On the contrary, when a worker falls ill and has to return home for treatment he forfeits his wages unless he sends a substitute.

At the end of the season in June, the employer is supposed to calculate and pay the workers, in a lump sum, the money due to them after deducting the advance as also the wages for the days taken off by them. But this does not happen, without a struggle. Employers do not even pay the statutory minimum wages fixed by the government. In early 1990s, the Kashtakari Sanghatana, the Centre of Indian Trade Unions (CITU) and Lal Nishan Party took up the issue of the payment of minimum wages, but without much success. Around 1994, the Kashtakari Sanghatana decided to take up the issue again, involved the concerned government officers and with their cooperation managed to put pressure on some salt pan owners to pay the minimum wages. The agitation was intensified following the death of a young salt worker who committed suicide out of sheer desperation. A major victory for the workers came in 1997 when the matter of payment of the minimum wages, which was taken to the high court by the owners, was decided in favour of the workers. Three owners were jailed and others were absconding. Subsequently, nearly 285 workers of 15 salt pans were paid their wages for seven months. The total amount was Rs. 28 lakh and each worker received Rs. 7,000–11,000 [Prabhu op. cit.: 17].

The struggle for recovery of wages continues as more and more workers are deprived of their rightful income. The following case, one among many, shows the situation in which the salt pan workers find themselves trapped, pitted against a ruthless employer and a tardy bureaucratic and legal procedure.

In 2000-01, some 40 adivasis from the remote and backward villages of Gadchinchle and Dhabadi in Dahanu taluka, were taken by an owner of salt pans to work in Uran taluka in Raigad district which adjoins the Thane district. They were employed at a rate far below the prevailing minimum wage. The work lasted till the end of April or early May. The situation there was extremely bad with acute water scarcity, no proper food and a lot of abuse. When the workers protested, the owner asked them to leave threatening them with physical violence. The workers approached the Kashtakari Sanghatana which filed a complaint with the labour commissioner of Raigad. The employer was called and, after some negotiation, an agreement was finally signed. The employer consented to pay the workers at the rate of Rs. 55 a day, which was below the then minimum wage rate of about Rs. 87. The workers agreed to this unfair deal because they were desperate and it was anyhow more than what had been promised at the time of recruitment. When the date fixed for payment came, the employer did not turn up; instead, he sent legal notices to them stating that since they had not worked till the end of the season he had to incur financial loss for which they were responsible. The labour commissioner expressed helplessness and advised the workers to go to court.

As non-payment of wages was an endemic problem, workers from other salt pans in Raigad also approached the Sanghatana, which in turn, moved in the High Court of Mumbai a writ petition regarding the general condition of work in salt pans and prayed for the payment of wages in specific cases.

The process of hearing took about a year. The high court then directed the labour department to conduct a survey to assess the veracity of the issues raised in the petition and also appointed a project officer, integrated tribal development programme (ITDP), Dahanu, to inquire into the specific claims of the workers of the four salt pans. The project officer submitted his report verifying the claims of the workers and stating clearly that they had not been paid the wages due to them. The report was presented to the high court and the judge accepted it, but no specific order was given to make the payments; the petition was dismissed. Subsequently, the workers appealed to the labour commissioner, Raigad, the project officer, ITDP, Dahanu, and the collector of Thane to intervene and recover their wages in compliance with the report accepted by the court. However, not even a letter was issued to the employer for a whole year. During this time, three workers lost their children due to malnutrition and illness, one worker died of tuberculosis because he had no money for medication and food, and the wife of one worker was slowly going blind.

In 2004, the workers once again approached the high court with a fresh petition. The matter has been kept for final orders till the end of August. In the meantime, the workers have got fresh notices from the labour commissioner, Raigad, to present the proof of employment and claims.

The growing demand for mud bricks following the construction boom in the district as well as in Mumbai has resulted in the springing up of a large number of manufacturing units in several parts, especially in Thane, Ghodbander and Vasai. The labour on the kilns is provided almost entirely by the adivasis. Most of the time entire families of men, women and children migrate to the work sites. The method of recruitment, the conditions of work and the mode of payment of wages are described in detail by Suman. It is hard work, and the workers are often duped of their wages. Since the site of the kiln can be shifted, it is nearly impossible to trace an employer who has defaulted on payment of wages and is absconding.[4]

For the same reason, to feed the construction business, sand excavation is carried out extensively in the rivers as well as in the creeks. Sand is also sent to the water parks which have recently made their appearance in Mumbai. Labourers are recruited from the nearby villages for the two important tasks of collecting sand and loading it in the truck. The contractor makes a high profit. Even though the work is very strenuous, as Subhash explains in his narration, many young men accept it as the wages are relatively higher. They can earn Rs 100 and more a day. Instances of workers being cheated of their wages abound, though. No minimum wage exists to protect them. The relation between the worker and the employer is characterised by a good deal of primitive form of bullying and violence. I was informed that at present migrant workers from Uttar Pradesh are preferred to the adivasis, because they are found to be better workers and more important, they work continuously for long periods without frequently taking leave to visit their villages.

Construction work itself provides employment for a large number of adivasis. Groups of thirty to forty men and women from a village migrate to Mumbai, Lonavala, Vashi or nearer home to towns like Boisar, to join it. Entire families from all over the district migrate. Much of the time women prefer to accompany their men rather than be saddled with the total responsibility of work on their own field. Women are in demand since for every male worker, two or three women are required to carry the construction material.

The 'mukaddam', supervisor recruits gangs of twenty to hundred, pays paltry sums as advances, and then takes them to the construction site. The work involved is heavy – digging, laying pipelines or telephone cables or foundations of buildings. The minimum wage for construction workers is Rs. 118 but the wage agreed on by them is not more than Rs. 50 for women and Rs. 60 for men. In almost all cases there are several sub-contractors who often cheat them of their wages. It is almost impossible to trace an absconding contractor because no one knows his name or address. In such situations the principal employer is caught and pressurised to pay up. But typically, one sub-contractor sends the labourers to another, and yet another, and so it goes on till the labourers give up or a political organisation takes up the matter. The workers also lose out on the overtime they do, since no proper records are maintained.

Life is extremely hard for the workers with no proper shelter, no water and no fuel provided to them. Women, of course, have to bear the brunt of this because at the end of a hard day, it is they who have to fetch water and fuel for domestic needs, not to mention the molestation and harassment by the contractors.

I was informed about the horrific conditions in which a group of nearly 350 adivasi labourers lived in 1998 in Sewree in Mumbai, where cables were being laid for the Port Trust of India by the Cable Corporation of India. They had to live on top of garbage dumps, with just plastic sheets as their shelter, and without any fuel or potable water made available to them. Since the water available was polluted they had to buy potable water from their meagre earnings. Women would have to go looking for pieces of wood and even rubber for cooking. Although the labourers wanted to leave, they did not do so for fear of losing their wages even for the days they had worked. Accidents and even deaths occur, not infrequently, on construction sites. The employers do not bother to take any precautions and the employees cannot afford to.

A number of adivasi men work in the fishing sector. The boats are, in general, medium-sized and partially mechanised. The workers go as far as Ratnagiri in the south and Veralval in

Gujarat, in the north. They stay on boats during the entire season, which extends from August-September till June, with a short break in November when some of them return home for the Diwali festival. When the season ends they are paid a lump sum, already agreed upon by the boat owner and the labourer, the present rate being Rs. 7000 to Rs. 10000. There is no minimum wage. The boat owners often cheat the labourers of their earnings. It goes without saying that the job is risky, since accidents occur frequently. Many men just don't come back, their bodies are not found, and the circumstances of their deaths remain shrouded in mystery. In most cases the owner cannot be traced and the insurance money does not come. There have been instances of boats straying into Pakistani waters, and the men being jailed in Pakistan for three, four or more years. In 1991, a couple of boats disappeared following an accident in Gujarat. As expected, no proper investigation was carried out by the concerned authorities in Junagadh, Gujarat. And, because of no proper record of the persons working on the boat is kept, it is impossible to prove that a particular individual worked on a particular boat. If there are survivors, they bring back information, otherwise their families are left guessing the cause of their disappearance and continue to wait and hope for their return one day. Ramabai's is one such story.

Earlier, fishing was largely done by the Mangela community in Maharashtra and Gujarat. But as their economic situation improved, they began to recruit Dublas in Gujarat and Warlis and Malhar Kolis in Maharashtra to go fishing. Generally, most of the high risk jobs characterised by harsh conditions, hard labour and low wages, are done by the adivasis. In fact, the non-adivasis who improve their situation move out of such jobs, leaving them for the adivasis who are desperate enough to take on anything that can afford them a bare minimum level of subsistence. For example, the better-off Agris and Kunbhis have moved out of agriculture giving the adivasis the hazardous task of handling harmful pesticides and fertilisers without masks, or gloves or even information about the poisonous material. The adivasi labourers are totally unaware of the risks to which they are exposed.

Many small-scale industries have come up in Dahanu, Palghar, Talasari and Vasai talukas. In Dahanu, in the last twenty years, polluting industries like rubber, plastics, buffing and asbestos have made their appearance. These industries have come with big tax holidays under the backward areas development programme. Taking advantage of the benefits, I am informed, owners of several industries close down their units after declaring them sick so as to apply afresh for tax exemption for setting up new ones. Balloon manufacturing, of which the main centre is Dahanu, employs almost entirely, adivasi women and children in abysmal conditions of work, at Rs. 30-40 for an eight-hour working day. The work is in tin sheds, which become very hot in summer, with an overwhelming smell of rubber and with fine powder dust in the air that covers everything including the workers' bodies. I visited many of these units, but because of the menacing presence of the supervisor/owner, I was unable to talk to the workers. They spoke freely when I met them in their villages.

As a rule, I was informed, the workers in these industries receive less than the minimum wages fixed by the government. In addition, they are not made permanent, not given any medical benefit, not permitted to form a union, not paid for the weekly off and not provided with protective gear like gloves, masks, goggles etc. Manufacture in these units is carried out without any safety measures whatsoever.

In recent years, many industries like alcohol, paper board and balloon have moved into the interiors of Dahanu and other talukas (the industrial estate at Ganjad is an example) where virtually no rules against industrial pollution operate. The waste from the industries is often dumped into unlined open pits or in streams, polluting both water and soil, and thereby depriving the adivasis of clean water and of an important food item, fish. The local people have been protesting against these industries which have adversely affected their lives.

Two very modern and large industries, which deserve mention, are the Universal Capsules Ltd and the Dahanu Thermal Power Plant of the Bombay Suburban Electric Supply (BSES), both located in Dahanu. The former, set up in 1984, is one of a group of eight big factories, which manufacture everything related to capsules, including machines. This group of factories has the distinction of being the second largest unit of its kind (the largest is in the United States), with a market in India and forty-one other countries. Spread over twenty-five acres of beautifully manicured grounds and the whole manufacturing plant air-conditioned, the unit presents a picture of a sophisticated technological enterprise. As expected, therefore, it employs a small number of highly skilled, technical personnel. Out of a total of 400 persons employed, about 100 are technical, including engineers, about 100 managerial, 100 clerical and office staff. About seventy-five are on contract for work in the canteen and for gardening and other jobs not related to manufacture. Adivasis are employed in the last category, as and when they are required. About 15 adivasis, I am told, have been made permanent only recently, after having acquired the necessary technical skill through experience.

The BSES 500 MW thermal power plant, funded by the World Bank to the tune of Rs. 700 crore, has been in operation for the last six years. It occupies an area of about 820 hectares of marshy land and has an annual turnover of about Rs. 500 crore. The plant was established in order to supply power to north Mumbai although it could supply power also in Gujarat and elsewhere. It employs about 550 persons out of which only about 40 are adivasis. At the time of the construction nearly 3500 people were employed, but most of them were migrant labourers from Tamil Nadu, Orissa and elsewhere. Adivasis are employed on a contract basis for maintenance, gardening, cleaning drains, and most important, to fill the ash into sacks for disposal.

According to two environmental scientists, P.R. Arun and P.A. Aziz, it consumes about 8040 metric tonnes of coal each day and releases 76.4 tonnes of sulphur dioxide (SO_2), 4.7 tonnes of suspended purticular matter (spm), and 72.35 tonnes of nitrogen oxides (NO_X) every day...along with even more quantities of carbon dioxide (CO_2) and the ash slurries into the environment. "Such emission and effluents from the Thermal Power Plant contaminate air, soil and water and cause multifaceted impacts on the surrounding environment through multiple routes such as groundwater pollution... soil pollution... particular matter pollution... acidic disposition... radioactive pollution...and so on". "...Particular matter emitted during the coal combustion is called the fly ash and is contaminated with various toxic and radioactive elements" [Arun and Azeez, 2004: 19-20].

It is important to note that the plant was set up in spite of the Central Government Standing Committee's rejection in 1988 of the proposed site of the plant for the reason that it would impact negatively on the environment and the economy of the adivasis. Although it had been subjected to a large number of conditions they were blatantly and consistently violated, a fact noted by the ministry of environment and forests in a special inquiry [Dewan and Chawla 1999: 136]. Dewan and Chawla observe that "the BSES Plant's ongoing violation of the clearance conditions that sought to reduce pollution and protect the area is resulting in a decline in productivity levels and in the quality of agricultural commodities due to the effect of emissions, fly ash, coal dust, rising temperatures, etc. The increased air pollution and discharge of effluents is found to affect marine life leading to a decline in variety, quantity and quality. In addition, rise in sea temperature is severely hampering the breeding and spawning of fish" [ibid.: 157]. Arun and Azeez also conclude that the power plant is the single most likely source of pollution that is responsible for the precipitous decline of the yields from orchards, especially of chikoo for which Dahanu is famous, and the fishery sectors, affecting both the farmers and the fisherfolks. They suggest that as an immediate mitigatory measure, the plant should drastically reduce pollution by using state-of-the art pollution controlling devices such as flu gas desulferisation (FGD). In the long run, the plant should have to switch from coal to less polluting fuels like natural gas or to be shifted to another ecologically less sensitive location [Arun and Azeez, op. cit.: 30].

Many adivasis and Macchis are adversely affected by the plant. The ash from the plant has destroyed the plantations and the fields around. In addition, the hot water released by the plant kills the fish, so that small fishing on wetlands is no longer possible. A major agitation against the thermal power plant was organised by the non-adivasi women horticulturists of Dahanu. They fought in the court and through the media and brought together some adivasi peasants and macchis as well as political groups like Kasktakari Sanghatana, Shiv Sena and the Communist Party of India (Marxist) on the single platform of Dahanu Taluka Environment Welfare Association (DTEWA). Although the construction of the power plant was not stopped, an important consequence of the agitation was to have Dahanu declared as an ecologically fragile area by a government notification in 1991. And the high court appointed the Dahanu Taluka Environment Protection Authority (DTEPA) under Justice Dharmadhikari with several government representatives and experts to monitor the development of this region. But efforts are also afoot to denotify Dahanu, so that expansion of polluting industries can take place without any hindrance.

It is in the context of these processes which have been at work in Thane district in the last almost two centuries that the following life stories of adivasis make sense.

Notes

1. Letter dated October 13, 2001 to B.N. Yughandar, chairman, Expert Group on Prevention of Alienation of Tribal Land and Alienation, Government of India, signed by J. Mascarenhas, director, Shanti Seva Mandal, Manor, Palghar, Thane district.
2. Letter dated October 11, 2001, to the chairman, Expert Committee on Tribal Land Alienation, signed by Brian Lobo for the Kashtakari Sanghatana.
3. Letter dated October 13, 2001 to B.N. Yughandar, chairman, Expert Group on Prevention of Alienation of Tribal Land and Alienation, Government of India, signed by Anant Umbarsada, deputy sarpanch, grampanchayat, Hanumannagar, Post 'Shigaon'.
4. For a detailed discussion on the conditions of work in salt pans and brick kilns, see Jan Breman 1996.

References

Ambasta, Ashesh (1998): Capitalist Restructuring and Formation of Adivasi Proletarians, Agrarian Transition in Thana District (Western India) c.1817-1990, Ph.D. Thesis, Institute of Social Studies, The Hague, the Netherlands.

Arun, P.R. and P.A. Azeez (2004): Decline in the Yield of Sapota (Manilkara Sapota) from the Orchard of Dahanu Taluka: Causes and Concerns – An Ecological Investigation, Salim Ali Centre for Ornithology and Natural History, Coimbatore, May.

Bhuskute, R.V. (1989): "Tribals, Dalits and Government Lands", *Economic and Political Weekly*, October 21.

Brian, Lobo (1998): "Surya Project: Thane Adivasi's Waterloo", *The Indian Express*, July.4.

Breman, Jan (1996): *Footloose Labour Working in India's Informal Economy*, Combridge University Press, Cambridge.

Dantwala, M.L. and C.S. Shah (1969): *Evaluation of Land Reforms (with Special Reference to the Western Regions of India)*, Vol. 1, General Report, University of Mumbai, Bombay.

De Silva, G., V., S., Mehta, N. Raman (1979): "A Bhoomi Sena – A Struggle for People's Power", *Development Dialogue*, Vol. 2.

Dewan, R. (1990): *Political Economy of Agrarian Reforms in India – The Nexus with Surplus Extraction*, Himalaya Publishing House, Bombay.

Dewan, Ritu and Michelle Chawla (1999): *Of Development Amidst Fragility, A Societal and Environmental Perspective on Vadhavan Port*, Popular Prakashan, Mumbai.

FDCM (1987): Restoring Maharashtra's Degraded Forest Ecosystems: A Preliminary Assessment of Project for Wasteland Development, prepared by Forest Development Corporations Maharashtra Ltd., Nagpur.

GoM (1975): Report of the Committee on Problems of Illicit Moneylending and Bonded Labour, Government of Maharashtra.

Kulkarni, S. D. (1979): "Encroachments on Forest Lands, The Experience in Maharashtra", *Economic and Political Weekly*, November 10.

Martyris, Nina (2001): "In Dahamu, Its the Sarpanch Not the Budget who Matters", *The Times of India*, February 28.

Munshi, Indra (1983): Analysis of Class Structure and Class Relations in a Rural Unit in Maharashtra, Ph. D. Thesis, Department of Sociology, University of Mumbai, Mumbai.

— (1995): Where Have the Forests Gone? An Exploration into Thane District", in Indra Munshi and Manorama Savur (ed) *Contradictions in Indian Society*, Rawat Publications, Jaipur.

Prabhu, Pradip (2001): Salt Worker's Struggle in Thane, *Labour File*, The Information and Feature Trust, New Delhi, January.

— (2001): "The Greening of Haladpada-Shisne", *Humanscape*, Vol. V111, X1, December.

— (2002): "Land Alienation, Land Reforms and Tribals in Maharashtra", in Ghanshyam Shah and D.C. Shah (ed) *Land Reforms in India*, Vol. 8, Sage Publications, New Delhi.

Saldanha, Denzil (1984): A Socio-Psychological Study of the Development of Class Consciousness, Ph.D Thesis, Department of Sociology, University of Mumbai, Mumbai.

— (1992): A Dissenting Report to the Final Report of the Inquiry Committee Appointed for Thane District to Investigate into the Claims in Writ Petition No. 1778/86, Tata Institute of Social Sciences, Mumbai.

Shramjivi Sanghatana Vidhayak Sansad (undated): Rural Reconstruction, Especially in Tribal Areas of Thane District, Vidhayak Bhavan, Vasai, Thane District.

Technical Review (1984): Technical Review of FDCM's Activities 1974-1984, Nagpur.

Part Two

Choices

Doing Life Stories: Some Reflections

My contact with the adivasis of Thane district for more than two decades, during which time I researched different aspects of their history and society, made the present study richer. Familiarity with their myths, rituals, habits, practices, ways of thinking and behaving provided a better understanding of the collective as well as individual lives. In fact, familiarity with the history and culture of a community or a group ought to be regarded as a methodological necessity for doing life story research. As Reissman suggests ".....the context is multilayered, involving the historical moment of the telling, the race, class and gender systems the narrators manipulate to survive and within which their talk has to be interpreted.... The text is not autonomous of the context" [Riessman 1993: 21].

With the help of the members of the Kashtakari Sanghatana, mentioned earlier in the text, I was able to identify persons who would be willing to talk to me about their lives. Six persons, three women and three men, from the age groups, above 65 years, 40-45 years, and below 25 years, were selected out of fifteen interviews in order to cover a broad time span and range of experiences. Some interviews spread over three days, others a day and a half. Before starting the interviews, I explained my purpose to the respondents that I wanted to write a book about the story of their lives and circumstances. Most of them were willing and articulate, although hesitant because they did not know what they were letting themselves in for. As expected, all of them were narrating their life stories for the first time. In a situation where people know each other fairly closely, there is little need to narrate one's life story. Fragments of information about everyday experiences are constantly exchanged between relatives and neighbours. Knowledge about each other's life situation can be taken for granted and need not be repeated.

Many stories about experiences of work and hunger; events like illness, death of a dear one, marriage; natural occurrences like a drought or a famine; social events like a religious festival and the routine inconsequential happenings of everyday life add up to a story. It is not surprising that they do not narrate their stories in a chronological order. Most adivasis, especially the older ones, do not structure the events of their life or other social events by calender time.

Given their lack of knowledge of numeracy and also from sheer habit most of them, except those who have received formal education, use markers of time other than the calender and the clock. Given also the fact that most of them now have something to do with modern institutions, they demonstrate a need to order some aspect of their life in a linear temporal form.

Without exploring their notion of time further, it may suffice here to say, the adivasi view of life of human beings in their natural as well as supernatural world is a non-linear one. The cycle of human lives is only a part of the other, larger cycles of time. The continuity of the past, the present and the future in a repetitive mode is the essence of existence. Ancestors are a part of the living and death is not the end of life. Growth and decay, birth and death, times of scarcity and plenty make up a whole.

Inhetveen makes an interesting observation about the underlying notion of time in the narrations of German farm-workers. The absence of a linear chronology in women's biographies and their preference for presenting memories as a patchwork quilt is because all existing time scales are reworked into cyclical forms. Natural rhythms, generative cycles, liturgical traditions all have a strong revolving effect on work and leisure time, social and spiritual time, biological and biographical time [Inhetveen 1990: 109].

The six life stories included here were selected for the quality of their narration, and to represent a wide variety of experiences. Only one of the interviewees, Radkibai, asked me to tell her my life story, after she had completed narrating hers, which, of course, I did. The interviews were recorded, transcribed and translated from Warli into English, and finally organised in the form in which they appear here. I often played the tapes back to them to their sheer delight.

It may be of interest to discuss briefly the interviews that were not included in the book. Apart from one elderly man who agreed to speak when I first approached him, but refused to do so subsequently, all the others readily agreed to an interview with me. But given the circumstances of some of these respondents, I was unable to probe sufficiently into their lives to reproduce a life story that would do justice to them.

Some of them were not good narrators, and could not talk about their lives in the details that I would have liked them to do. One man was too nervous about "doing" the interview "correctly", and throughout the interview kept asking me if he was all right. He had spent the previous day and night at the police station, in connection with a murder that had taken place in his village over land, in which his nephew was implicated. His nervousness could partly be explained by this fact. Another man, a salt pan worker, talked only about his work and life at the salt pan. When I met him, he was trying to recover the wages due to him from the salt pan owner. He was so preoccupied that he could not talk about anything else. Nothing seemed to bring joy to him. When I spoke about festivals like Holi and Diwali, he dismissed it with the comment, "we don't do anything special on those days, there is no money to celebrate anything". The feeling of how irrelevant my life story project was to his life, prevented me from demanding more time and emotional energy from him. I could not bring myself to burden him with the task of going through his life and making sense of it.

It was quite clear that in general the interviewees did not regard their lives as of any value or interest to others, and probably even to themselves. Their response to me, "what is there to say", or "what can I say" or "it is like that only" conveyed this. They could not understand why an educated, urban, middle class woman could be interested in their life stories. But, although the interviews evoked many painful memories, put the respondents in a difficult situation of confronting their past and themselves, their experiences, actions, decisions, the one positive effect of the interviews probably was to enhance their self-esteem and self-confidence. I do not know if their willingness to narrate their life stories was partly because they hoped I would help in solving some of their problems. They did not say so. But this motive cannot be discounted totally, as most researches show.

With specific reference to reminiscence by the elderly people, Coleman observes, "by putting people in touch with their past lives, and by confirming to them that their lives have been interesting and valuable, it is hoped to maintain people's sense of self-esteem" [Coleman 1991: 131]. That someone was interested in knowing about their lives, ready to listen to them and to understand their predicament, and that the narration was done "well", to my satisfaction seemed to bring comfort to them. One respondent, whose life story is not included here, said in a voice almost choked with emotions, "do write and tell the world who live in palaces and who live in huts". On one of the young men, who had experienced a great deal of emotional and economic insecurity in his childhood, the interview seemed to have had a therapeutic effect. At the end of the interview when I asked him if it had been too painful to talk about the past experiences, he replied enthusiastically, "no, I have never talked about these things to anyone, one can't even tell one's friends these things. I hadn't found a person to whom I could say these things. It feels good." Empathy, the basis for doing life story research, must be regarded as a strength rather than a weakness of the method.

The narratives appear in a question-answer form. All the narrators demanded me to ask them specific questions to which they would provide answers. "You tell me what you want to know and I will give you the information", all of them said. Underlying the statement is the commonsense suggestion that not everything about a life can be told, and that a story can be told in many ways with very different foci, depending on the interest of the person who elicits it. Many of them looked nervous at the prospect of having to reconstruct the story of their lives and looked to me for help in doing it with them. A lot of information was, however, also supplied not to any direct question. After the initial interaction, they directed the narration as much as I did. Often my questions were a take-off from their narration. Clearly, the life story was produced in the interaction between them and me. I allowed them to talk, even repeat what was obviously of importance to them at that point of time and I listened. I have tried to reproduce the stories in their own words, not altering the meaning or interjecting the text with my own interpretation, in order to retain the power and poignancy of the narration. I have also tried to retain, as much as is possible in translation, the flavour of the language, the suggestions, the expressions, the way they wished to communicate their feelings and experiences. Only repetitions or unclear diversions, of which there were many, have been dropped. In saying this, I do not wish to underplay the importance of my own role, or the role of the researcher in general, in the production and reproduction of the stories.

For the hermeneutic perspective, in fact, the interaction between the researcher and the interviewee is at the centre of the life history project. If, Corradi argues, life history is not a copy of life, then with the help of hermeneutics, it can be defined as "a re-appropriation of the past taking place in a specific research situation. This is an interactive situation, it is based on dialogical interaction between the researcher and interviewee." It is seen as a dialogical relation, and the interviewer as an active part of this mediation, his or her presence and questions elicit the occurrence of the mediation, and "the common language of both participants is the terrain in which the re-appropriation takes place". If this definition is accepted, then, Corradi suggests, two important points follow: one, the researcher can stop checking life histories against what "actually happened" and stop looking for truth or falsehood, in the interviewee's narrative, and two, the interviewer's presence can be seen as productive, rather than as one that distorts the narrative [Corradi 1986: 3].

The issue of objective truth or falsehood of the narratives may be viewed in the light of following considerations. Except in the case of deliberate distortions, against which the researcher can take some precautions, it is important to recognise that the past is represented as it is experienced, perceived and remembered. Therefore, some core facts notwithstanding, there are many truths from many perspectives. Inhetveen highlights the point succinctly, "Experienced realities are realities which have been perceived by the senses, filtered by interests, and systematised and interpreted according to reconstructed criteria. They are all true. The different stories of single individual which are related to a certain event; the story that will be conveyed by future generations in their memories of village life; the political functionary's document which passes on a truthful account of the rural situation to those above" [Inhetveen 1990: 112].

In addition, central to life story research is the fact that the researcher trusts the respondent who is the best source of the individual story. The former can check against certain facts, make use of other sources to an extent, but the respondent remains central to the story. A related question raised by Engelhardt is, how authentically does the biographical account of the "present I" reflect the experiences of the "past I" [ibid: 114]. The mediation of the "present I" in the narration of the past is inevitable. Every narrator reflects on the past in the course of the narration. It does not, however, reduce the authenticity of the narrative. The expressions, the body language, the tone of voice, the emotions, the frequent use of expressions like "I remember it well", "I am telling you the truth", "this is how it was" are further confirmations of the authenticity of the narration.

The question of memory and the gender differences in memory is important to the practitioners of the life story approach and has been in discussion over the last 20 years [Leydesdorf et al 1996: 1-4]. It was generally felt that there were gender differences in the way men and women remembered. Given that, by and large, men dominated in the public sphere and women's lives focused on family and household, it was only common sense to expect that these experiences should be reflected in different quality of memory [ibid: 2]. On the basis of research in France, Bertaux-Wiame, for example, found that French men and women narrated their stories very differently, men used the equivalent of "I", placing themselves at the centre of the narration, whereas women used "one" or "we" [Bertaux-Wiame 1981: 257]. Recent research finds the fundamental speech differences in respect to reporting remembered experience between boys and girls, girls make much more extended use of direct quotation, dialogue and reported speech while recounting their personal stories. Boys typically simply summarise the remembered conversation. But these differences, we are told, seem to emerge extremely early in life, and are, therefore, difficult to explain as a result of sociali-sation [Leydesdorf op. cit.: 3].

My own research supports the observation that women by and large are more inclined to use dialogues and reported speech than men who tend to give the gist of a conversation or a speech. The narrations by the adivasi women that follow indicate this, the mode being, "he or she said" and "I told him or her". I have reproduced most of these reported conversations in the text.

There does not, however, seem to be a fundamental gender difference with respect to the use of "I" or "one" and "we". As a matter of fact, the collective "one" or "man" and the plural "we" are used by most of the interviewees. The individual "I" is so often submerged in the collective "one" or "we" that I frequently had to ask the respondent whether he/she was talking about his/her experience or the experience of the adivasis in general. And, their reply to my question was "this is the story of all the adivasis", or "this is true for all the Warli-adivasis". In the course of the narration it was difficult to point where the "I" ended and the "we" began, so smooth and frequent was the transition from one to the other.

The collective memory of a shared past among the older respondents as well as the persistence of a Warli-adivasi identity may explain the frequent use of the plural form. This identity is embedded in the largely shared cultural norms and practices, shared material conditions of existence and work experiences and a network of social relations. It is also rooted in the perception of "we" adivasis, the poor, backward and oppressed in opposition to "them" non-adivasis, the rich and powerful, and continues to survive despite significant changes in their conditions of life as well as the emergence of a relatively better-off and more powerful adivasi strata amongst them. It is difficult to generalise about the gender differences in memory and it may, in fact, be necessary to consider age, class, ethnicity as well for understanding the form memory takes. Research done in different social milieus would greatly contribute to this.

Interestingly in my research the two persons who used the distinct "I" form predominantly were a man, Dasma, and a woman, Ramabai. The latter could not identify with the other Warlis or adivasis. She was conscious of the fact, and expressed in her narration that the other adivasis did not share her condition of existence. She seemed to be on the margin of her society. Her poverty prevented her from interacting with her people or participating in social events. Her special circumstance had deprived her of land and home and she was not and did not feel rooted anywhere. Her story reveals that she felt alone in her struggle for survival in her social world which seemed to have turned hostile, where even the kinship network has nearly totally broken down. Brothers, sisters, son, sons-in-law, brothers-in-law, nephews have turned strangers even enemies, with the single exception of a cousin who provides some support. In contrast, Dasma has a stable family life. He shares a lot with his wife. He is by and large content with his children. He also has a few good friends whom he can trust. But, overall, the clan members are a source of trouble to him, and he does not feel a special bond with the extended kinship network. He has interests which are a source of fulfilment and joy to him. It is probably this circumstance that explains Dasma's use of the term "I" and "I and my wife". His long stay in the city has probably also contributed to his individualism.

The study of lives necessarily involves recognition of the fact that every life, and every individual is both unique and universal, particular and generalisable. This makes the life story project difficult but fascinating. While unique experiences of particular individuals enhance our understanding of the group experiences, it also elicits, as Benmayor and Skotnes point out, humility about the inadequacy of generalisations as well as a realisation that few individual lives actually conform to the master narrative [Benmayor and Skotnes 1994: 15]. Every life belongs to a time and a place, it is embedded in and shaped by a particular society at a particular historical time, and yet it may transcend time and place. In literature, one can see the universal in the particular, how individuals think and behave in a particular situation becomes a statement for human condition and human predicament. In individual experience, literature reveals the universal experience of humankind, and that, of course, is the greatness of literature.

As James M Freeman in his pioneering study of an untouchable in India observes that a life story transforms the lifeless abstractions of behavioural science into vivid personal accounts. For example, "Abstract discussions of the concept of stigma provide a necessary basis for generalisation but the high-caste tea stall boy's humiliating caste insults of Muli bring the concept of stigma to life in a way that no abstraction can convey. His history stands as an indictment, not merely of the caste system as an Indian phenomenon, but of stratified systems of inherited inequality everywhere, which invariably produce effects similar to those described by Muli" [Freeman 1979: 396].

The strength and the uniqueness of the life story approach are to highlight the particular and the general in every life. Every story is a different story, and one can only agree with Denzin that the meaning of life study inquiry is in the discovery of "the difference that sets the subject apart from others, yet joins her in the common epoch she shares with other ordinary people" [Denzin 1986: 16]. The six adivasi stories presented here reveal how each of them lives his/her life differently from others, within the shared social-economic context of their past and present. They are unmistakably stories of the Warlis of Thane district, an economically and socially marginalised group, poor, with the exception of a small minority, semi-literate and illiterate, oppressed and exploited, hemmed in by the forces of change and development, displaced from their means of livelihood over a long period, and in the process of gradually moving out of their villages to urban and semi-urban centres for employment. Notwithstanding the differentiation among the Warlis, they speak the same language, eat the same food, share a universe inhabited by the Wagh dev – the tiger god – who is the village god, Kul dev, the clan god, Saunri, the spirit of the forest, the ancestors who must be propitiated and kept happy, the gods and goddesses, Kansari, Hirva, Himai, who must be worshipped on special occasions, the "bhutali", witch, who can bring harm and must, therefore, be kept under control. They share a love for the forest and land, and for toddy and dance. They also share a concern for the plight of the majority of the adivasis, an anxiety about their own future and that of their children, aspirations. They express anger against the government, bureaucracy, forest department, and the employers, whom they hold responsible for their condition. And, of course, like other human beings, they love, fight, cheat, oppress, enjoy and go on with the business of living.

One cannot make sense of their choices and constraints unless one knows their social position in the larger society, what it is to be an adivasi, to live in a particular district with its specific geography and history and culture, without knowing legislations, policies, political and cultural influences, and all that affects their lives in significant ways. A researcher can only try to do so.

Yet, each one of them lives life differently, drawing from the resources, both material and non-material, available to him or her. Although they largely share the broader social-economic and cultural context, yet the specific location of individuals, especially in terms of access to resources, gender, family and kinship network, greatly affect personal experiences, behaviour and choices. Besides which, of course, there are the chance occurrences that shape the trajectory of life in crucial ways.

Babubhau and Radkibai, both in the sixties, belong to the same generation, they share certain experiences and memories, but the trajectories of their lives and the meaning they give to their lives, are very different. In spite of the pressure from her husband as well as other men of the community, Radkibai chose to be a political activist. The Kashtakari Sanghatana has been an important influence in her life, in channelising her life in a particular direction. She has always fought against all forms of domination and oppression and this is a source of high self-esteem and confidence. Her political work as well as her relationship with other political activists gives meaning to her life. She is remarkably different from most women of her generation in this regard. For the younger adivasi activists, especially women activists, she is a symbol of fearlessness and defiance and enjoys a degree of prestige in the community. At the same time, men of her community resent her for her courage and enterprise and many people dislike her for her sharp tongue which does not spare anyone.

Babubhau, on the other hand, is a very sober and sensitive man, an important Christian leader in his village. The Christian priests and the education he received through them has had considerable influence on his life. He values his education. He is reflective and cautious in his comments and opinions. But most important, he loves to work on his land and trees and this is a source of immense satisfaction to him.

A life story includes experiences of the past and expectations of the future. While all the respondents express anxiety about the future, one finds much more despair among the younger people. One reason for this could relate to the experience of the past and the other to the view of the future. Radkibai and Babubhau's generation has seen worse times, hunger, exploitation and domination, but they have also seen them end to some extent. The memory of the adivasis' revolt in 1945-46, led by the Kisan Sabha, the peasant wing of the Communist Party of India, against the system of 'khand', rent; veth, lagna gadi, is very much a part of their lives. This probably gives them some hope of a change for the better. The younger people do not even have this resource to draw from. I was surprised to find that Suman and Subhash, around 19-22 years old, and many other young adivasi boys and girls who gathered around us at the time of the interviews, did not know about the practices mentioned above nor did they know about the revolt. They were hearing about them for the first time from the older respondents, or from me in our informal interactions. Ramabai, too, hadn't heard about Godutai or about the conditions prevailing at that time.

The other important fact could be that the older respondents do not have much of a future left. Babubhau talks about it, Radkibai does not, but both of them are aware of their advanced age. They are concerned about the future of their children. But the younger respondents have their own lives and their children's to worry about. While the expanding market and rapidly increasing exposure to other lifestyles create more and more needs and aspirations, desires, the employment opportunities and wages available fall short of their fulfilment. There is also a growing realisation among them that education, at least the education available to them, does not guarantee a better life. Twenty years ago, the adivasis often expressed hope that education would pull them out of their poverty and backwardness. In fact, they repeated it parrot-like as though it were a political slogan. But one can clearly see a growing disillusionment with education. Degrees don't get one good jobs and good salaries.

Unlike Radkibai and Babubhau, Suman and Subhash have worked as migrant labourers in non-agricultural occupations. Suman is a steady worker while Subhash is not. Subhash can afford to take life easy given that his father has some land and they are not too badly off but more importantly, because he does not have a wife and children to support. He has had school education, but like many other young men of his generation, he has left studies and cannot get a "good job", but nor can he settle down to agriculture. Subhash is not physically very strong, he often fell ill during the fieldwork in which he assisted me. He loves to attend weddings in his village and the neighbourhood, and to drink and dance, which in fact, he does. He talks very enthusiastically about these experiences. Like many adivasi boys of his age, he wears western clothes, watches films, and has been in Mumbai and other towns near Dahanu.

Suman has not had the kind of exposure to "modern life" that Subhash has had and this is not only because Subhash comes from a better-off family, but also because of the gender difference between them. Adivasi boys are much more influenced by the urban lifestyle than the adivasi girls. There is a lot of joy in Subhash's life, whereas Suman can all talk about is the hard work that she has to do when she migrates out to the brick kilns. She is anxious about her life and that of her son. Suman is not politically conscious whereas Subhash is, largely because he belongs to a family, which has been politically active. But as his narration shows, he is not very focused in his views or actions. Suman does not see a way out. Subhash allows his mind to wander in dangerous directions. But in a strange, yet significant way, both see their lives as adversely affected by bhutali, attribute the miseries in their lives to the mischief done by bhutali. Suman suspects that the illness and subsequent death of her husband, a major turning point in her life, was probably caused by a bhutali. Subhash accuses his aunt of being a bhutali, and being responsible for his inability to concentrate on anything, to study and work consistently. An otherwise soft-spoken and pleasant young man, the passion and hatred with which he talks compulsively about his aunt, is almost frightening.

Ramabai is different from the others in the overwhelming feeling of hopelessness that she communicates. Her husband's death 10 years ago meant a loss of land and home for her. Molested, and accused of being a bhutali, the ultimate gender oppression in the adivasi society, she decided to leave her husband's home after his death. Ten years later she has no doubts about the correctness of her decision. In spite of her destitution, she is ready to forego her share of the land and the house but she does not want to go back. Her life is joyless, a relentless struggle to make ends meet, with not even hope to provide momentary relief. Not only has her support structure collapsed, she has also lost faith in human relationships. "No one helps". In contrast, Dasma's life is relatively secure. He has managed it well. He has given up drinking. There is enough food to eat. He has an interest in Bhagtai. He has happy memories of the past, and there is still a lot of joy and laughter in his life.

An important aspect of the collective life of the Warlis has been the forest, and it may be interesting to explore the respondents' relationship to the forest. They reveal very different attitudes towards the forest, but it is also clear that with each generation, their bond with the forest is weakening. Radkibai's feelings for the forest are translated into deliberate efforts to save the forests from its enemies, both adivasi and non-adivasi, to protect and regenerate it. In her scheme of things, she belongs to the forest and the forest belongs to her. She is of the forest, moves in and out of it and cannot accept boundaries that restrict her movement. Any attempt on the part of forest officials to do so can only invite terrible hostility from her. She often spoke like the leaders of the Kashtakari Sanghatana, repeating almost verbatim, but not without conviction, their views on the issues related to the forest.

Babubhau relates to the forest like an artist relates to his environment from which he draws his sustenance and inspiration. When in the forest, he is in communion with nature, at peace with himself and his surroundings. Forest is a part of his being.

This intensity is lacking in Dasma's or Subhash's or Suman's relationship with the forest. Although Dasma spends a lot of time in the forest, collecting herbs, the quality of his relationship is very different from Babubhau's or Radkibai's. Dasma has lived away from the forest for long periods of time, and survived. Ramabai has no contact with the forest, a fact, which could only have deepened her experience of essential alienation. She has nowhere to go.

Suman is away from the village most of the time. Her contact with the forest is, therefore, reduced to occasional visits. Subhash visits the forest more frequently. But like Suman, for a picnic, to go out with friends, to eat, drink and have fun. Both of them like to go to the forest, but unlike Radkibai and Babubhau, they donot belong to the forest, nor is the feeling that it belongs to them as strong.

We will now turn to the life stories, starting with Radkibai, the most fiery of them all.

References

Benmayor, Rina and Andor Skotnes (ed) (1994): "Migration and Identity" *International Yearbook of Oral History and Life Stories,* Vol III, Oxford University Press, Oxford.

Bertaux-Wiame, Isabelle (1981): "The Life-History Approach to the Study of Internal Migration" in Daniel Bertaux (ed) *Biography and Society: The Life History Approach in the Social Sciences,* Sage Publications, London.

Coleman, Peter G (1991): "Ageing and Life History: The Meaning of Reminiscence in Late Life", in Shirley Dex (ed*) Life and Work History Analysis: Qualitative and Quantitative Developments,* Routledge, London.

Corradi, Consuelo (1986): Dialogical Interaction and the Foundations of Life Histories, 1986, Paper presented at the XI World Congress of Sociology, New Delhi, August 18-22.

Denzin, Nerman K (1986): "Interpreting the Lives of Ordinary People: Sartre, Heidegger and Faulkner" in *Life Stofies/Recits devik,* Vol 2.

Freeman, James M (1979): *Untouchable: An Indian Lifestory,* George Allen and Unwin, London.

Inhetveen, Heide (1990): "Biographical Approaches to Research on Women Farmers", *Sociologia Ruralis,* Vol XXX, No 1.

Leydesdroff, Selma, Luisa Passerini and Paul Thompson (1996): Introduction, in *International Yearbook of Oval History and Life Stories,* Vol IV Gender and Memory, OUP, London.

Reissman, Catherine Kohler (1993): *Narrative Analysis Qualitative Research Methods,* Vol 30, Sage, London.

III

Radkibai:
"Where must this destiny come from?"

Radkibai was called Radki, which means cry-baby, because as a child she used to cry a lot. I was told and it was evident from my interaction with her that she is a fighter. She has always had a sharp tongue, she has spared no one, the elders of the village, her brother, husband, and of course, the officials and all men in a position of authority. Some years ago when Radkibai felt oppressed by the family, she built a hut for herself on a hillock close by and began to live there on her own. Gradually, her sons and a few others also came and built their own huts around hers, and slowly a small hamlet came into existence.

She is a capable and courageous woman, who, given her difficult circumstances, has had to struggle to bring up the family. She is also physically strong, capable of hard work. At the age over 65, she is still mentally alert, physically fit and in high spirits.

She came for the interview brightly dressed, her hair oiled and combed, ready to hold fort. She was articulate, had a good memory and was most willing to talk about herself and the adivasis. It was the most difficult and yet the most interesting of all the interviews precisely because Radkibai spoke a lot and with an exuberance, going into details, repeating conversations, acting out situations, which was difficult to translate into a script. She had answers to all my questions, never at a loss for words, and was ready to give her views, opinions and suggestions.

She was the only one among the interviewees who showed her impatience and irritation when I repeated a question, or did not quite follow her response, or asked for a clarification, which she thought self-explanatory. She was also the only one who, at the end of the interview, asked me to tell her my life story.

Radkibai is the oldest and the first woman activist of the Kashtakari Sanghatana. Given her temperament and her life-situation, it is not surprising that she proved to be a very efficient worker, taking on the sowkar, the forest official, the police, the government official as well as the men in the Sanghatana who tried to keep her out. Without demanding anything in return, she worked for the Sanghatana loyally till she could, and as one activist of the Sangahtana put it, "when physically she couldn't work any longer, she just faded out quietly, without demanding anything in return".

Tell me about your life from the very beginning, events, experiences and whatever you consider important.

Let us first look at what we need for our 'sansar', life-world, we need land, cattle and other things.

My father had no land, my grandfather had no land. They kept on taking loans and they were indebted to the sowkar and that is how the land went. If you borrowed one rupee you had to give back two. If you borrowed one measure of rice you had to return two. That is how whatever rice was produced was taken away. If we could not pay up, we were beaten and dragged to the sowkar's house. Beaten, that whole generation disappeared. They became disabled and helpless. Under these circumstances they died early, they could not live long. I often asked my mother why my father died so young. He suffered a lot of oppression, he went through a lot of suffering. We were very young when my parents died. They died of disease. When one is poor and one falls ill, then one dies.

The sowkars took away the land, the grinding stone, bullocks, they even took children, sons, when they grew up. They would say, your son has grown up now give him to me as a 'khedya', young boy around the house to do odd jobs. See how they humiliated the adivasis. The adivasi who was really a cultivator drowned in debt and ran away from one village to another. Then how could he keep his land?

There was a lot of suffering all around. The worst was 'veth'. My father and mother did veth. I also did veth. Veth means that you don't get anything for the work you do. After working for many days do you know how much you got? One anna or something like that. You had to get it out of the seth.

The foresters would also make us do veth. Do you think they planted the forest? No, the adivasis had to do it. Even the 'village patil', headman, had to do veth. I did veth for the 'sarkar', government, and for the sowkar. When we grew up and went to work for the Parsi, he gave us only one meal a day, no wages. Even now you can see the big house of the Parsi in halad pada. He doesn't live there any longer. When the adivasis became conscious, the seth ran away. He didn't come back. Now our children have rice fields and we have to pay some money to the government.

If you didn't have money in those days, seth would give you money to get married. Once you were married, you could not be with your husband. The seth would send the husband away on the cart and ask the wife to go into the house and spread cowdung on the floor. And, then he would go into the house and say, since I have given the money for the marriage, he is not your husband, I am your husband. I am going to use you first. And the woman realised that there was no point in resisting or getting angry. I heard older people talk about it. They felt angry about it. But, what was the use of getting angry, they had nothing, so they would have to go back to the seth for an advance. So they had to learn to live with him. You had to negotiate the relationship with him.

My father worked as a carpenter and as a labourer, and my mother did 'mazoori', daily labour. One of the things she did for the seth was winnowing the rice. Of course, she kept the rice for them and brought the husk and the broken grains for the children. There was no food at that time, you see. Then when we grew up we went to do mazoori.

We had cattle, bullocks and cows, and because we didn't have any land we used to give the bullocks on rent. Earlier the rent for the bullocks was one 'mann' (approximately 40 kilograms) of paddy, then it became one and a half manns and now it is three and a half manns.

How many brothers and sisters were you? Did any of you go to school?

We are two now. I have a sister. I had two brothers, both of them died. Only two of us are left. From the time we were very small, our mother would ask us to fetch water, send us for work. And because we were so small, people would ask in surprise, how will these little ones transplant? They would refuse to employ us. But once we began transplanting, we were very fast and efficient. We knew how to remove seedlings and to transplant. We worked in the fields of the adivasis who had a little land. My sister was just a little younger than me. She used to look after the younger siblings, tend the cattle, but as she grew a little older she began to work. My brothers also used to work. The older children got one anna for mazoori, the younger ones got one paisa. They used to give us thick grained rice or jowari, no food.

We did not even know what a school was. There was no school. Today we feel very bad that our mother did not send us to school. But she did not know what a school was, whose it was. The moment we grew a little big, we were hung on work.

When we didn't go to work, we used to go to the forest. Even if we were alone we used to take our bag and go to the forest, and bring home a leafy vegetable called 'dodhada' and a fruit called 'kakad'. The kakad had to be crushed and mixed with dodhada while cooking, otherwise dodhada would cause a lot of itching in the throat. The forest was very large at that time. I would take a stick and dig out 'kand', a root, which you have to clean with ash. From the time we were very young, we used to bring it. We would bring the kand, eat it and fill our stomach. We would also bring leafy vegetables, boil it, mix a little rice with it and eat it. Because there was no rice, you see. If you felt hungry you could eat something from the forest. In fact, some of these roots and tubers were known as sowkars of the forest, meaning that when people took loans and gave away all their produce to repay the loans, they had to fall back on the forest for survival. There were many riddles and songs about the forest. I don't remember those songs now.

There was enough food in the forest. There was as much food in the forest as there was hunger among the adivasis. We used to go to bathe in the forest streams, to eat fruits and berries and sometimes we would take 'daru', liquor also. Even now women plan and go. They go together for Holi. Now the adivasis have got a little land, but there are not that much leafy vegetables now, and even the roots and tubers have disappeared. When there was hunger there was plenty. In one year, I remember, there was nothing to eat, so we only brought food from the forest and ate it. You could bring vegetables from the forest, but to cut and bring wood was difficult. Sometimes the foresters stopped us from taking firewood, but we answered back. We did not listen to them. There was flowing water in the forest. We did not see wells those days. Now we have wells.

Did you see the British people? Who were there before the British came?

I did not see the British, but our father's father and other old people told us about the British raj. That is how it has stayed in our ears. They told us this and that. They told us about an army that came on horsebacks. People were frightened. Children were hidden in a particular tree and warned, even if your earring is pulled off your ear, you must not make a sound. The old people who couldn't run were put on a shelf, their bodies were covered with ash. The army would poke at them and say this is an ash pumpkin. The old people, of course, didn't utter a sound. This is what our forefathers told us. Now we tell these stories to our children. You may laugh but this is how our people suffered without uttering a sound. I was not there, I have no memories but the stories I have heard from the old people are there with me. These stories were not floating in the air, when one wanted to get information like you are talking to me now, one would get these stories.

Of course, adivasis were there, and it was their raj. Now that we have become conscious, we say to the sowkar, Marwadi, Parsi or whoever, we are the 'rajas', kings of the forest. It was our raj. That is what we say now. Earlier people didn't say so, because they were cowards, they were frightened. Because our raj was there, we have been talking about it since our forefathers' time. After all, if our raj didn't exist, how would we have known about it? We would not have known about it. Like we know about the British raj because it was there. Parsis, Marwadis, Musli, Konkan

Muslims, Vani, Brahman came and destroyed our raj. They destroyed everything. They are the ones who pushed us deeper and deeper into the forest and made us destroy the forest. Otherwise, if we had our lands from before we wouldn't have destroyed so much, we wouldn't have eaten away the forest so much. Because of this, we managed to barely survive. That is how adivasis were impoverished.

They gave us advances, they cheated us and that is how our land became theirs. If there was a mango tree on the field, it became theirs, even if the adivasi had planted it. When the land went to the Parsi, he would take all the mangoes from the tree. Once the children got hold of one mango, even before they could finish eating it, the sowkar came on his tonga and said now what should I do? Beat you or will you pay a fine? I have heard of these things from my father. People did not say anything, if anyone spoke, they would be taken and beaten. After all we had to live there. I don't remember the name of the person who told me the story about the mangoes. He has died, but the story has remained like a knot in my stomach. It is my memory.

Once my brother went to a seth for some jowari, because he and his children were starving for a day and night. We used to take a loan of jowari, for every kilogram we took, the seth would take two or three in return. We used to cook jowari into a watery gruel so that it could be made to last. The seth asked him to cut grass for him. This was the practice, when you went to ask for a loan, the seth would ask you to do some work for him, without wages, of course. My brother could have said I will come back tomorrow to work, today my children are hungry, I am hungry. But he is the weak type. The moment he showed some hesitation, the seth said take my umbrella and go to work. I told the seth in front of everyone, why are you making him work, he is starving. I told my brother, he is not the only one seth, we will go to someone else. The seth began to abuse me. I said, are we your lagna gadi? He is hungry, suppose he dies, what are you going to do? I am going to the police station and I will tell the police that he is making my brother work although he is starving. Then the seth let him go. I borrowed some rice from someone and made 'kaneri', watery rice gruel, for the children and sent my husband to get some roots and tubers.

Another time a man in the village had died. The sowkar came to recover his loan and he was demanding that the woman should pay him back his rice. He was a Marwari from Amboli. I confronted the sowkar and told him, if she gives you the rice, what will she eat. We will see what you can do. This I did because I remembered what Godutai had said about not cooperating with the sowkar. At that time the Sanghatana was not there. The woman paid back the rice little by little.

In those days you took something to eat and you gave away your land. We would give the land because at that time adivasis had a lot of land. But slowly, little by little all the land went. The adivasis would take a loan, and the seth would weave a web around us like a spider. The seth would say, pay back my loan, and because the adivasi had nothing, the seth would say, do you have a field, give it to me. And then the field would go. Then the adivasi would take more loans, and the seth would say, do you have a cart and bullocks, and the cart and bullock would go. Then the adivasi would take more loans, and the seth would say, do you have a daughter, give her to me to wash my utensils. Then the adivasi would say, I need another loan, I have nothing to eat and the seth would tell him, why don't you come to work in my vadi, bring your children and build a house there? Then the seth would use his wife and the man would work hard the whole day and fight with his wife in the evening because the seth had used her. Then the eldest son would say, father and mother, now our loans have gone very high, we won't be able to repay. Let us find some village near by and somehow run away. The seth has taken away everything. This is everybody's story, every adivasi' story and it is a true story. In this way the adivasis were kept on running and lost everything to the sowkar.

Tell me about your marriage

I told you that my parents died when we were very young. Someone in the family decided that they should bring a 'gharorya', a man who stays in his parent-in-law's house, for me. But I did not want to get one because we had no land. Under pressure, I agreed to a gharorya. I laboured and laboured in my father's house and then I was married and my husband had no land. His father had no land. Whatever land he had, had gone to the sowkar. Because the old people suffered, the effect of the suffering has come down to the generations to this day. If someone's father managed to keep the land, the son has it. If someone lost it, it was lost to the future generations as well. Today those who have the land get drunk and put down those who don't have any. Those whose father and father-in-law didn't keep the land have to live by doing mazoori. You get grains and money from the land because your father kept it for you, you don't get grains and money from your head because you are intelligent.

My husband's brother also went as a gharorya to a Patara family; his father-in-law had land. My father-in-law was also a gharorya to the Bodle family. And my husband came to the Gowari family. Pataras didn't give land to my brother-in-law, they gave him the right of use it, but not the title. I fought for the land from the Gowaris, and that's how I got some land which I am still cultivating. Till today, I fight with the Bodles that had you given my father-in-law land, which you should have given since he was a gharorya, we would not have been in this condition, we would have had some land. If there is a quarrel somewhere and they can't resolve it, they call me.

I was the one who got the brothers and the sister married, and as they got married, they began to live separately. I stayed in my parental home. Then my brothers began to fight with me saying, now you should go to your husband's house, he has a house. So I gathered the 'Pancha', village elders, and told them that my brothers want to send me to my husband's house, and what am I supposed to eat there, wood? My brothers did not inherit any land from my father, but they got a share of the family land. When some uncle or grand uncle died, a part of the land came to my brothers. The Pancha asked them to give a share of the grain, rice and nagli from my parental home to me. I took my share of grains, goats, cattle and my gharorya and went to live in my husband's house.

My husband had no cattle, no land. He used to play the drum in the 'tamasha', a musical event. He would go here and there with the tamasha party. There would be nothing to eat at home. I began to slowly earn for my family in my husband's house. We also began to cultivate the forest plot.

We had four children by then, but we had not passed through the rites of marriage. Gopal Bodle was getting married so we decided to go through the marriage rite as well. My husband sat in the 'mandav', an enclosure, got drunk and then came home. He did not know anything about the payments to be made. The Panchas came home and asked what we wanted. I said, if we put 'halad', turmeric, and tie the 'gathi', auspicious black beads, it is all right. Then they told my husband to say "Ram Ram", and he went on saying, "'Ram Ram Ram Ram", making a fool of himself. He couldn't speak properly.

We did not borrow from the sowkar. We just borrowed small amounts from the other adivasis. My husband and I had earned a little. When you have just 'halad gathi', a cheaper way to get married by putting turmeric and auspicious black beeds, the expenses are quite small.

My sister also went from my brother's house to make her life with a man. Like me, she too did not have a proper marriage, just went through the minimum formality. Her husband had some land. He is dead now, she has her children. Now she has also given a plot to her son. But if you go and ask her questions like you are asking me, she will not speak or she will keep saying I don't know. She will even be confused about telling you her name and the name of her village.

I had 12 children in all, of which eight have survived, four sons and four daughters. The girls are married and have gone to live with their husbands and I brought wives for my sons. It was difficult when the children were growing up. I used to bring home one kilo of paddy after a day's work, pound it and make kaneri and feed my children. And until I got my next mazoori, I had to make it stretch. There was no question of eating rice or 'bhakri', unleavened bread. My eldest son Vitthal used to say, no matter where you come from, you just make kaneri for us. By drinking kaneri only, they became very thin. That's how I raised my children, since there was no rice. Both my husband and I used to earn some grain as mazoori and bring some leafy vegetables from the forest. As I told you, there was forest at that time. Then it was completely destroyed. Now it is regenerated again. The adivasis are conserving the forest. The forest officials did not conserve it. Because the forest officials did not protect it, the thieves robbed it.

The traders were involved, our adivasis were also involved. Now the traders have been stopped, and the people have decided to let the forests grow again.

My children went to school. One of my sons works in a bank in Kalyan. My daughters didn't go to school, but sons went to school. My eldest son was not able to study much, he studied a little. Now he has learnt the skills of a mason. He is still doing that work. Next two sons did not learn any skills, so they migrate as labourers and do construction work.

Did your husband oppress you?

No, not much. I was smarter than my husband so how could he oppress me? He was not a big drunkard. Earlier he didn't drink but when the daughters got married, either they came as guests or invited him as a guest and gave him to drink. I did not take my husband's nonsense for too long. He didn't beat me much, but he was trying to acquire the habit, didn't I tell you what I did? One day he took an axe and threw it at me. I picked up a stone and banged him on his head. So he brought Gopal Bodle who told me, whatever he is, good or bad, you must not beat him. He is a man. So I said, what should I not do? He should beat me and I should just take it? He came as a gharorya and now that I stay in his house, I sell fish and support myself. Does he give me anything? Whatever you want to say Gopal, better think and speak. If he hadn't beaten me why would I have beaten him? I used to sell fish and bring things for him to eat. Once I even got goat's meat for him. After that my husband went with Gopal Bodle in anger, and I stayed there. For a long time it has been my policy that if anyone hits me, I will hit him back at least once.

Just like there was oppression from the seth in the past, now there is oppression from my husband. Once my husband drinks daru he gets very oppressive. The men drink daru on their way from work and they come home shouting for the wife, asking her to give him rice, fish or meat or vegetables. She gives whatever is there. They don't want that. They want something nice, like dry fish or potato or anything that tastes nice. If she is not able to give her husband something tasty, he throws the vessels and asks her to go to her father's house. But if he doesn't give her any money and spends all the money he earns on drinks, then how will she buy good food? But he starts chasing her out. I don't want you in my house, you are a rascal, he says. She goes out of the house but after he goes to sleep, she comes in but sleeps in a place where she can't be seen. When he wakes up in the morning and the drink has gone down and he is sober, he calls out to his son, where is your mother? The son would say, last night you abused her, beat her so she has run away. He would say, when did I do that? When did I fight with her, beat her? She has gone away for no reason at all. She is a rascal. If the woman confronts him, he doesn't beat her, but if she doesn't, he beats her and tells her to go to her father's house. If she has a father she goes to him and cries. If she doesn't have a father where can she go? She has to stay with her husband even if he beats her.

If she complains that he finishes off all the money he tells her that it is my money, it is not your father's money. But she also works, she doesn't sit at home. She brings firewood, collects cowdung, she does the rab, sows and transplants when there is rain. Even when there is no rain, there is plenty of work for her. After she comes home she has to cook, clean, wash, worry about her husband who will come home and ask for curry. Women work more. Men only do one kind of work, but women have to do 36 chores like collect fodder, cook and work through half the night. When the man comes from work outside, he lies down and relaxes. He doesn't help the woman at home. Women look after the children also. They are very oppressed.

The young and newly married don't drink and do not harass their wives. But as they grow older they drink and ask for good food and oppress their wives.

Do you remember Godutai? How old were you?

I remember Godutai and I was quite big by then. At that time the Kashtakari Sanghatana wasn't there. She had come to teach us about the sowkar. The sowkars used to take a lot of khand those days. She chased away veth. She told us you don't have to pay khand to anyone, you don't have to do veth for anyone. Now there is no veth. Land was given to the tenants, people got land on ownership. She would call us for meetings and teach us. Of course, I went for the meetings. There used to be very big meetings, lots of women also came. There was a lot of fear at that time. People would talk among themselves. The police used to come. These things happen now with the Sanghatana. What the 'Lal Bauta', Red Flag of the Communist Party, did was to stop the khand and veth, and even to this day they say, what have you Kashtakaris achieved? We stopped the khand and veth. They would beat us because we became Kashtakari. Now we have a lot of problem with them.

But Godutai did good work. I didn't do any work at that time. I didn't become an activist, others were activists. At that time I didn't know very much about anything. I used to go only to listen. I learnt from Godutai that we don't want the Parsis, we mustn't give anything to anyone, we are all adivasis and we are the kings of the forest. The sowkar used to ask for chicken, vegetables, pulses and women and we were not to give anything. Lagna gadi was also slowly stopped. Our condition improved a little. Those who didn't get any land, they took the forest plot later, but she didn't do anything about that, we took it ourselves.

Even when Godutai was there, the foresters used to come to our house and demand food from us, but this she did not stop. She stopped the oppression of the sowkar, but she didn't stop the oppression of the sarkari functionaries. They continued to take and eat from us. She didn't do anything about the police and the forester. The foresters harassed us. Suppose you had a wedding in the house and wanted wood for the mandav, he would ask for a chicken. And if we needed wood for a house, even a small pole, the forester would catch us. This has happened to me also.

We were very poor, our house was very small. If they had taken our house, we would never have been able to build it again. People used to give rice, chicken, pulses and the forester would give them permission to take wood from the forest. But I never had any of these things so I never built a big house. I used to borrow little money to give the forester some daru. Yes, I did such things. How could we not? We would need some little bit of wood, he would not let us bring even that. There was no problem in for bringing food from the forest. But if you were caught taking firewood or the bark of a tree, you would have to give something for that, money or rice. The better-off gave bribes and brought things. For the poor it was not possible.

Once my husband was caught. He was taking wood to my daughter's house because she needed it to build her house. She asked her father to bring some wood for her. The bullock cart owner, my husband and two other labourers were there. Others ran out of the forest, but my husband did not run. They caught him and abused him, you old man, whose wood are you stealing? Is it your father's wood? They beat him. When I heard about it, I borrowed some money from Vangad and went with him to the forest. They called us in the next morning. My husband was in the lock up. They had given him food. I gave them some money, and they gave us back the bullocks but kept the cart. Next, I got my husband released by giving them money. That is how I brought back my husband. Then I went back for the cart, but some Lal Bauta persons had taken it away by force without my knowledge and returned it to the owner. They didn't do it properly, the way I had done. So there was a lot of confusion over the cart and a case of dacoity was filed against the owner of the cart. The forest ranger asked me to stay out of it.

I have heard that you used to drink a lot? Is it true?

Yes, I used to drink a lot. Women also drank a lot. But then after I started working for the Sanghatana, I became aware and I stopped. See, it is like this, you work hard the whole day and then you take a little intoxication in the evening. Then the little becomes more. Somebody would come and ask, Radkibai, do you have some daru? I would say, come on. Once you began drinking, you moved from one person to another to drink until you got so drunk that you began to fight and damage other people's houses. That was the way I was. I drank a lot, every evening. That's whom you call a drunkard.

Of course, I would feel good. Like we drink tea now. If you don't get it you feel the urge. We used to get black jaggery on credit from the shopkeeper, and made daru for sale and to drink. If you had some money left over from the sale, you could buy some black jaggery with that money, but if you had drunk it all, then you had to get black jaggery on credit. Sometimes we would go even ten times to get credit. After all the aim of the shopkeeper was to drown people in debt.

At that time there were few toddy shops, now there are more. The toddy shops used to be far away, not in every village. If you didn't have money, why would you go so far for toddy when you could have daru at home. Now much more toddy is available. We used to have mahua also. Some people had mahua trees on their fields, otherwise you could get it from the forest. I used to make daru from mahua. I still make it. I have a lot of mahua trees around my house. We would dig a pit somewhere in the forest and distil liquor there. If the forester saw us, he would catch us. People used to make daru on the sly in the forest. If they made it at home, the police would catch them. People would run helter skelter if they heard that one policeman was in the next village. Then the police would enter the house and take away even the eggs. Now they make it at home. My husband was caught once because the police found daru at home. My daughter and I had to get him out on bail.

Now-a-days women go to the shop to buy black jaggery for liquor, to make a little money to buy some necessities. If they don't sell liquor, they won't be able to buy anything. Women have no other business. Some people work in the vadis, others go as construction labourers and they get wages of 40 or 50 rupees. With the money got from selling liquor, they buy salt, chillies, dry fish and all that you need for your everyday life. They hide the liquor from their husbands.

It is very difficult to get everyone to stop making liquor. Even if the Sanghatana stops women from making liquor, in the next village – may be a Lal Bauta or a Congress village – it may be easily available. Unless everyone decides to stop, it won't work. If you make liquor it is oppressive, if you don't make liquor, it is also oppressive and we feel that we have no money to buy our bangles or blouse or hair oil. What is the point of stopping if the others don't stop? In the early days of the Sanghatana, we had stopped making liquor, we had broken our pots. But men would go and drink in the next village and come and create problems at home. They would go for weddings and drink. In adivasi weddings daru and toddy are absolutely essential and not in small quantities. If there is no toddy or daru, then people don't even give gifts to the newly wedded couple. As the practice of gift giving has been there since the time of our forefathers, if the gift is not given there would be quarrels. And for the gift to be given, there has to be toddy and daru. The musicians need toddy, the 'suhasins', married women who perform important rites at weddings, have to be given their drink for the work they do. Not just weddings, every occasion and ceremony requires drinks. For tying the 'zoli', naming ceremony, building a house, you have to give daru and if someone doesn't drink daru, then you have to give tea. And all this activity never gets over. And since adivasis have many children, unlike you people, there are many celebrations and weddings. You need daru to negotiate for a bullock, a ploughman, a cowherd, a baby sitter. This is the custom among the adivasis.

It will be good if it stops, but everyone doesn't do it. Earlier generations died of drinking. And if you stop drinks in the villages, then you will find liquor shops in the market places and in towns.

People are hooked on to it like you get hooked on to cigarettes. Generations have been drinking, what reason can there be? You get into the habit. If the father drinks, the son drinks, if the mother drinks, the daughter drinks. It is such a vice that even if you offer mutton, they will say we don't want mutton, we want daru.

How did you become an activist of the Kashtakari Sanghatana?

I have been with the Sanghatana right from the start. I remember Pradipbhau and Nickybhau came to my house and talked about collecting one rupee a month. That was our first dialogue. I thought they were collecting money for religious education. I didn't know anything about religious education because I hadn't received any. Pradipbhau was from the mission. And because of that other people would not involve themselves with him. That is why they used to go house to house talking to people. Then they called us for a meeting and talked to us about daru, that it is a vice and because of it we keep falling lower and lower. They gave us education and held meetings and camps. Pradipbhau came with the message to us and what we heard we kept it in our ears. After that many people reduced drinking. Men and women. Even I used to drink a lot but stopped later. Those who took the message reduced it, but those who refused to listen, they continued to drink as before. Young people don't drink daru nowadays, because they have heard that it increases our expenses and causes illness. They ask themselves why do people who drink die young. Some people have it written in their fate to die young but we take the bottle and write our fate to die. They also told us why does the adivasi who sweats and toils have nothing and the sowkar who does no work have plenty of food. Wherever you go you see people have closed their houses with thorn bushes and migrated for work. When the situation gets bad to worse you are forced to go.

Seeing this situation they began their work. Those who participated in the camps went and spoke to other villagers. We united and pushed forth with courage and did away with oppression, with courage we drove away the foresters. We had a lot of problems with the Lal Bauta, like they would forcibly take our people to their meetings, beat up our people. We still have a lot of problems with them.

We became aware. The first thing we did was to stop giving chicken to government servants like the talati, police or forester. The second decision taken unitedly was to cultivate the forest plots. Because the adivasis don't have any land what do we do, we cultivate the low-lying land and protect the forest on the high lands and the slopes. The adivasis are bound to cultivate the forest plots because they have no other support for survival. So the forest is also protected because they can keep an eye on it when they cultivate their forest plots. Otherwise, the forest would not be protected. That way people can cultivate and eat and increase the forest. So we started this struggle. People made fields by building bunds on flat lands, where rain water stays, and on the slopes they planted, protected and allowed the forest to regenerate. Almost everyone has taken forest plots. Earlier some people had their fathers' land, but that has also got subdivided among four or five sons. So they also had to resort to forest plots. The government says, don't have more than two children, have an operation.

I went with others from village to village and had discussions with the people. The first issue we took up was of the forest plots. We asked the people to make applications for the plot. Wherever in the villages we went, we heard the same story. For example, a woman told us, wherever you have come from, sit down, but this evening there is no food I can offer you. If you don't have land how can you give us rice, we said. There would be food in the forest like leaves, roots and tubers, which we would eat and move on. Once a woman told me that our father has lost the land document, the record of rights. We told her that there must be some proof of their land in the land record office, Pradipbhau will guide you. That is how one by one people began to come.

Where else could we go? We used to seek out relations and acquaintances and go to their villages. We would go to the villages where I had given my daughters in marriage. We used to say the same thing, come to our meeting and you will understand everything. Come and listen to this man. I used to sell fish at that time. So I went from place to place and talked about the Sanghatana. I would sell fish during the day and come back in the evening and participate in the discussions. One evening Nickybhau met Gopal Bodle and asked him, who is this woman who goes around with a basket on her head and talks about the oppression of the sowkar? And Gopal Bodle told him, she is my brother's wife, she is like that only. She is a tough woman.

We were harassed by the forest department. I moved from village to village to educate women. I taught the women not to run away and drop their head loads when they came face to face with the forester. I told them to tell the forester that if you don't let us go with the wood, we will throw the wood on you and bury you under it and burn you. Now there is no harassment. The adivasis have protected the forest, now the forester doesn't come.

Slowly they took me into their organisation. The sowkars used to cheat the adivasis, take rice from them and not pay for it. So we took out a procession against them. They were forced to pay money to the adivasis. I spoke in the meetings that if we fight the sowkar alone, they will immediately silence us. But we must confront them unitedly, whether it is the seth or the government servant asking for chicken and daru, tell them, you get a salary, you are doing a job, you say, you are the sarkar, but you are our servant. Where do we get a salary from, we have to make things like daru to earn money. Now if a government servant asks for money, we make a thief out of him. This is the kind of education I give. Now they are a little bit subdued.

About seven years ago, there was a meeting in a village and I had collected the people there. The meeting was going on when we heard the sound of a vehicle. We said these must be the timber thieves. Let us all go and see. Just as we came out we saw the truck and we stopped it. Our men took out the air from the tyres. We asked the driver and the labourers to climb on top of the wood on the truck and sit there, so that none of them could run away. Within a short time the seth came on the scene, he had gone to bribe the forester to allow his truck to pass. The seth had come to see why the truck hadn't reached the gate. He asked, what happened? What happened? I took out my slipper and gave him a hard one on his cheek. None of us had touched the people in the truck, we had just kept them there. The seth began to shout "arre, arre, arre". So I said, what are you saying 'arre, arre' for? What do you have in the truck? Then we beat him up, he was bleeding. In the meanwhile, we asked him to go and wash himself since he was bleeding profusely. Then we thought of a story that when the police came, we would say that he fell off from the truck and injured himself. Then I told seth, now we will apply charcoal on your face and make you ride around on a he-buffalo. He pleaded, bai, you can blacken my face, but please don't put me on a he-buffalo. We told him that we are going to tell the police that he is a timber thief and a rapist. We recounted all the incidents of molestation and rape by him and beat him as we recounted the stories. He kept saying, forgive me. Until sunrise we kept him there.

The police came in the morning, and we gave our statement to the police that he is a timber thief and that he had gone ahead to give a bribe to the forester. The forester also came in the morning, pretending to go to the cashew plantation. I confronted him, oh, you are going to collect cashew seeds after taking a bribe. Are you blind that you can't see that this wood is stolen. Go and sit on the truck with the other thieves. Is your job only to get chicken from the adivasis? And we beat up the forester with our slippers. Later the same year when he came to a village and saw us there, he told the people, I am not coming to your forest plots. These people will beat me. I said, why should we beat you, we beat you then because we had caught you in the act of stealing. Now have this kaneri (not chicken) and do your work in peace.

The seth was frightened, they are frightened and that's why theft had reduced considerably. Earlier, there was a lot of theft of timber, they would hire labour, cut trees, get trucks and sell the timber. The adivasi would be left just with whatever little wages they were given. That is how the forest got finished by the seth sowkars. We were also involved in cutting, chopping and filling the trucks. The trucks were taken at night. Of course, we knew what was happening, but we couldn't always catch them. That day we saw them and caught them. Now we don't allow them to cut trees. The original forest is finished. There are only short stumps. But now we have taken up a programme of forest protection to make it grow.

The forester ate up a lot of money those days. They were in partnership with the seths. The seths wouldn't ask the Sanghatana people to cut. But in fact, the adivasis only cut the trees for labour. The forester showed the way to the seth and the seth paid him money for it. That is how one stomach filled another. The forester would take his salary as well as eat the bribe.

How did you begin the forest protection?

We began by protecting the forest around the forest plots but there is a continuous threat of it being cut by others. During the day women protect the forest and at night men do it. It is about five years since we have been protecting the forest. Forest protection is going on in many villages where the Sanghatana is. People go together to the forest and take stock of what is cut and catch the thieves. Now the forest department is digging trenches, etc., and telling us to do this and that. One day they came to our houses and asked us to go to the forest with them. They proposed joint forest management. So I told them, the forest that the adivasis have protected looks good, but show me the forest you have protected. Now you want to participate in the management of our good forest, which is your part of the good forest? Whom did you consult? They had consulted Radka, who belongs to the Congress Party. I told him, now it is fine that you call them to protect the forest along with us, but later on you don't know what they will do. Of course, it is a wrong policy.

We have a slogan that we will not cut the trees and we will not let go our plots. We sing it like this.

We adivasi women
beautiful women
of the green hills,

We toiling women
live in the hills
and valleys,

We live in the forests
listen to this
song of ours,

Tarfa, Gauri, Kaundi
dances are ours
Waghoba, Chedoba
are gods of ours,

We are Himai Hiroba's daughters
we are adivasi women
beautiful women
of the green hills.

We grow nagli, varai on our plots. If we do not protect the
forest immediately surrounding our plots the sarkar will not give
us our plots. People are basically cultivating the lands that were
barren to get something to eat. Because we go regularly to the
forest to cultivate, it also gets protected.

We don't cut any living trees now. If someone wants to
replace a piece of wood in the house then he is allowed to take a
dead tree. Women go into the forest to collect dead leaves,
firewood, etc. If someone chops live wood, then we catch her.
Women still bring all their requirements from the forest only. For
fuel, they bring dry wood, nobody is allowed to sweep the leaves.
In summer during a particular time the villagers declare it open to
sweep the dry leaves for rab. Men and women and even children
participate in the protection of the forest.

Everyone including women, all the plot holders and also
those who don't have a plot decide about the forest because
everyone needs wood. Women and even children are part of the
meeting where decisions about the forest are taken. If a
policeman comes to the village, and asks, who is the leader of the

Sanghatana here, the child replies, I am the leader. Earlier, if the children saw a policeman, they used to run. Now they say that they are the leaders.

Did you face problems as an activist of the Sanghatana?

Some people used to tell my husband why do you let your wife move about. They used to say all kinds of things and my husband used to get upset. But I kept on fighting with my husband and working. I used to explain to him that the Sanghatana is good for us, so why should we listen to what people say. I have discussed with people and agreed to become an activist. People would tell my husband we don't send our wives, why should you send your's. I used to answer, you should also send your wife or may be you like all the harassment by the foresters and that is why you don't send your wife. Whatever we gain from the struggles is also your gain. It is not just for us that I am going around. We are struggling against the harassment of the sowkars, the foresters, you must also do something or is it that you just want to sit back and eat from the gains. You also collect firewood and sometimes wood for your house. Remember you are able to do all this because of our struggle. I used to go and get the wives of those who spoke to my husband and tell them to unite. The villagers also tried to put hurdles but I would explain to them that we all stand to gain. Unless we unite nothing will improve. If you have to fight the seth-sowkar alone they will immediately silence you.

The activists of the Lal Bauta have beaten up a lot of our activists. Only I was not beaten. They would keep a watch on the paths we used to take. I used to enter the village at night and I wouldn't go on the known paths, I went through the forest. We, the activists didn't fear being eaten by a tiger or a bear. If we had a torch we were frightened to switch it on. As we reached the Kashtakari villages we would switch on our torches. We did not fear death, even if they kill us it is alright, because even now we are suffering. Pradipbhau had prepared us that there would be a lot of problems. We took an oath on Kansari, goddess of grain, that even if two or three persons die, more youth will join in.

Pradipbhau used to ask me to organise people in the villages, because I can't do that, he would tell me. He asked me to lead the demonstrations because I spoke so well. Then I would tell my husband, see, if we had land we would have cultivated it, but we have no land. And we don't know how to deal with the forest department, so this way, we can get the forest land. It will be useful for our children. Don't listen to what other people say. Then we managed somehow.

My husband didn't attend meetings or demonstrations earlier because there was no one at home. When the children grew up and we got a daughter-in-law, then the three of us, my husband, son and myself started attending meetings. I once participated in a camp and I gave my word that even when I am moving with a stick in my hand, I will do this work. I will not leave the Sanghatana. It is true that when the Sanghatana started, my eldest son said something. When your eldest son says something you must listen. But that did not affect me or my work. For example, when my youngest son told me the Sanghatana is like this and that and you must not move around, he was in contact with an old Vishwa Hindu Parishad (VHP) activist called Appa. This man used to ridicule my son saying your mother moves around with the Sanghatana. I told my son, the Sanghatana doesn't belong to any party. How is it that nobody told us that by uniting we can remove the oppression of the sowkar and the police and that we have a lot to gain by coming together, that we can also fight for our rights. I refused to buckle under.

I have encouraged my daughters to attend camps and meetings, particularly Lahani. She is an activist at the village level. She gets women together, mobilises them for meetings and demonstrations. Whenever I have an opportunity I teach her something. I talk to the other daughters also, although not as much as I do to Lahani. I tell them that others will give you a road or a bore well, but remember your unity is your only one security. Like we have united in Shisne, you should unite in your village. If you unite, then your children will also unite. You must teach your children. What will you do if outsiders come to your village? Lahani is very clever and she has a lot of children.

I have been to Mumbai, Pune and also to Delhi. In Mumbai we have had meetings and demonstrations. In Delhi, Pradipbhau showed us the books about adivasis, when they were the kings of the forest. But now a days the adivasis soil their hands in mud from finger tips to elbows, their legs rotting from the foot to the knees to cultivate grain, and yet after a few months, you see their houses sealed with thorns when they go to the city to survive. Why must this happen? They toil hard and yet there is nothing in their house.

How are your children doing?

I have got them all married. We did not go to any seth. There are adivasis who do not have money but have a little rice to spare. We borrowed from them. My sons were working, therefore they were in a position to borrow from the adivasis. Except for one daughter who did not have a proper marriage when she went with her husband, the others had proper halad-gathi marriages. Recently I have got this daughter married also. For the boys we had to pay to the villagers according to the practice, we had to give rice to the girl's father.

My daughters do cultivation and mazoori. The eldest daughter and her husband work on the land and she also takes basket of fish on her head to sell in other villages. My second daughter has had a lot of problems with her husband, he is a big drunkard. Now his brother-in-law has taken him on a fishing boat. But there in nothing to eat in her house, no one to help her with work on the land. She comes and cries to me. She is also selling some fish now. How can Lahani help her? She has so many children of her own. I help her with some jowari, I know her husband will come in the rains.

One daughter's husband is handicapped. He beats her. This boy had come to my village to look for a wife. He came to my house and asked my daughter to bring him a bottle of daru. They drank together and exchanged a few words. The boy went back and sent word that he wanted to marry my daughter, but my daughter didn't want to marry him because of his handicap. I insisted that since she had spoken to him she had to marry him. She went to the forest with a rope and wanted to hang herself. I didn't care. I called the boy and asked him to chop wood, he did it. I asked him to climb a tamarind tree and bring tamarind, he did it. He could plough, he could cut grass, only he couldn't cut rice because you need both hands for it. He could do everything else, fetch water, kill chicken. And he had a lot of good land. I thought he is born handicapped, but he must also live, and besides he can do all the work, so I gave my daughter to him. How did I know what kind of a person he was, could I see what was in his stomach? I once called him and beat him. What to say, everyone beats his wife.

We have no land so my sons have to go out to work. Each of them has four or five children. Two of my sons migrate to Goregaon (a suburb of Mumbai) to do construction work, or digging work for contractors. One goes to different villages to build wells, wherever he is called. He stays there for a few days and comes back. He stays close to my house. Sometimes they are away even during the festivals, because they have to repay the money. Sakharam works in a bank in Kalyan. You know what a bank is, where they take money from people. Now he has become a 'saheb', officer, he does this and that with papers. His family has gone there. He has three children. His wife doesn't work. She has to look after the children. He used to stay with me, now once in a while he comes to visit me. None of the children are with me. I am alone.

I told you about this Appa, they got him this job. I didn't spend any money for it. I am not the one to go throwing money here and there. Now a days you have to pay money to get a job. Sakharam was studying in a mission school. Then this Appa said, this boy is very intelligent, we must get him in the VHP hostel. He selected him from among many students and had his papers transferred. I went looking for my son and finally went to the VHP hostel. I stood quietly outside a big room where some big people were discussing something. I knew what they were saying. They were talking about my son, saying he is very intelligent as if he is from a high caste. Then they must have spoken to Sakharam. They must have spoken about me to him. When they finished talking I intervened, how could you do such a thing without even asking us? I am his mother. I have come to ask you why you have kept my son somewhere.

I live in the village. Once I had gone to Sakharam's house. But I came back earlier than planned. I remembered my home. I don't go there. Now Sakharam comes to the village sometimes, shows me his children and takes them back.

My grand children visit me sometimes. They are small. Except for one girl who looks after the younger siblings, the others go to school. One of my grand daughters has been married to a boy who works on the fishing boat. Now many adivasi boys work on the boats. The boats belong to the Mangelas. During the rains they give the boys an advance and then take them on the boat after the rainy season is over. The monthly wage is decided mutually, my boy gets 2000 rupees a month. But, of course, it is a dangerous work, cyclones and other things are there. Many don't come back. Because it is dangerous, it is given to the adivasis. My grand daughter comes to see me sometimes.

What do you think about 'bhutali'? Do you believe in it?

There are bhutalis. I have heard about the bhutali since I was a child. When the husband is there the woman is not called a bhutali, after the husband goes, she is called a bhutali. When people fall ill, they say that someone has cast 'bhuta' on them. She must be old, young women are not bhutalis. Even if she has a husband it is always an old woman, someone who has already had children. We can't see a bhutali, the 'bhagat' tells us about her presence. Of course, she says I am not a bhutali because she knows that if she admits it, she would be beaten and even killed by people. But if you put her to test, she starts shaking all over. For example, if I am put to test, I will lie down quietly because I am not a bhutali. Some women, when confronted, get agitated and admit to being a bhutali and that is how people get convinced.

There are more bhutalis now, because boys go to school and don't learn the 'bhagat vidya', the knowledge necessary for medicine man-cum-priest. The old and experienced bhagats have died so the bhuts, evil spirits, have increased. There are very few bhagats now. In the past, when there were bhagats they used to identify the bhutalis and frighten the potential bhutalis.

Also, earlier the village patil and the 'karbhari', the village master of ceremonies, had more control over the people, they resolved the village quarrels. But now their authority has diminished. Whenever there is some discord between the people, they practise bhut on each other. And basically you can't catch a bhutali because the sarkar doesn't believe in bhutali. The bhagat doesn't tell the name of the bhutali because if he does so, there would be a quarrel and he would be taken by the police. He would get into trouble. So the bhuts have increased, that's why you find that death has come more to men, while there are many old women around.

It is oppressive for those women who are identified as bhutali, not for all women. When I come across such a woman, I try to make her understand that I cannot see whether you are a bhutali or not, but why do you fight with people. Why don't you tell them I am not a bhutali. There was an attempt in my village of accusing me of being a bhutali. So I challenged them to take me to the bhagat, but no one was willing to do so.

There used to be big bhagats who did divination and also gave jungle medicine. They would see what was wrong with the body and knew what to do. They would do bhut and give you medicine to tie on different parts of the body. I have seen such bhagats. Medicine was available in plenty. Chicken and daru would have to be given to them. We did not know about doctors those days. The forest is gone and the medicine is gone, now there is little, not like before. When a bhagat dies, he becomes a 'vir', ancestor and he has to be installed as an ancestor. If you don't install your ancestor, someone in the family may fall ill or even die. So one has to find out where the ancestor wants to be kept, it is usually under a tree on his own field.

Only men are bhagats, but women do have some knowledge of medicine. When someone falls ill women are asked to bring jungle medicine and give it to the patient, that's how they have got the knowledge. Some of them got it from their husbands. Of course, ordinary women know what to give the children when they are ill. When we go out to work to fill our stomachs, we know what to take with us, because there the bhagats are not around. We have learnt these things through difficult times.

Whether there is bhutali or not, now a days everyone goes to the bhagat and the doctor, even if the bhutali has affected them, they need to go to the doctor. But the doctors take a lot of money.

How do you manage now?

I cultivate my land. My sons help. You see my son in Kalyan does not have an independent house in the village, he sends money to employ labourers at transplantation time. The son in Kalyan earns but he has a wife and three children. He has many bills to pay, he has to buy food from the market, he has taken a room on rent so he has to pay a bill for that, he has to pay a bill for water, electricity, children's snacks and for rations. The moment he gets his salary, he has to pay at least seven bills.

The young people don't drink, they realise that if you feel hunger you must work. But now adivasi children have studied up to 10th and 12th and yet they don't get jobs. We often discuss that the children of big people, even if they have studied less, get jobs. Why don't adivasi children get jobs. They get jobs because their fathers spend for them. It is true the missionaries helped the poor to study, for example. Johnbhau's son has become a doctor. But how can we talk about improvement?

For example, if a child goes to school, the teacher tells him to bathe well, dress well. Otherwise, the teacher doesn't let them sit in the class. Soap and oil we can manage, but where does one get clothes from? Very often there isn't enough food even.

One has to struggle to educate the children and after that you have no money to bribe to get a job. Then what is the use of spending on their education? Children who have done their 10th and 12th go for doing earth work of digging and carrying the mud on the road. Even then, they don't always get work. Those who get the contracts for government works are the local political lackies, and they don't give proper wages. Money you get in these jobs doesn't last for two days.

Children are always asking for something, they ask their fathers to get them a job, but that costs money. Even to get a small document there is no money. Yes, there is less oppression, but when you see that money is spent on education and there are no jobs, that is also a kind of oppression.

Where there is less forest and there is no protection, women tend to head load firewood for sale and that is a problem. There is the problem of corruption, the problem of high costs, the problem of having to pay money to the doctor. We don't get credit easily. And, if you manage to get credit from a shop, sometimes it is difficult to even pass that way, because he may call you and you don't have the money to pay back. I take credit from a shop, and I avoid passing that way because I know the shopkeeper would fight with me.

Let me tell you, adivasi life is full of problems. Everybody is more or less the same. I told you before that there are some who have enough food to loan a little food to the really poor, till their crop is ready. But there is no one who has a lot of land or a lot of money. In that sense we are all equal. Those who have a little, help the others. Everyone works for a living. No one is really rich, they cultivate and the food lasts for a year, but no one has surplus. If someone had lot of money, he wouldn't work himself to the bone. We cannot find a single adivasi sits at home and eating, there is no one like that. No adivasi has rest.

Even if we leave and go, even if we go to Mumbai, the adivasi of tomorrow will find it hard to get to eat and drink. Where must this destiny come from? We soil our bodies in mud, we tire ourselves to the bones, and yet, we cannot support ourselves.

But I have told you everything about myself, now you tell me about your life.

As mentioned earlier Radkibai spoke willingly, clearly, in fact, with a flourish. Her remarkably clear memory of the oppression by the landlord, forest officer, government officials, and her own resistance to it, can be explained by her ideological orientation which has sharpened her perception of the past events and the memory of it. Not many of her age would be able to recall so vividly and so passionately.

It is evident from the narration that she is a very confident woman, with a high degree of self-esteem. It is also clear that she wants to project herself as a strong, capable and courageous woman. In the course of the conversation, when I happened to mention the big libraries in Mumbai where a lot of books about the adivasis of Thane district are kept, she promptly replied that she had seen the libraries in Mumbai. And that Pradipbhau of Kashtakari Sanghatana, whom she holds in high regard, had read them all, and even familiarised her with the contents, conveying to me that she was not impressed.

Radkibai did not talk about the problems she had had with the male members of the Sanghatana who tried to keep her out of the organisation. I came to know about it from a woman activist who has known Radkibai ever since she joined it. Even when I asked Radkibai about it, she avoided replying to my question. It was either too unpleasant for her to recall, or more importantly, in my view, because she did not want to show herself as having been dominated and even humiliated by the male activists.

To join the Sanghatana has clearly been a very important decision. It is a turning point, which seems to have influenced the greater part of her life. Her narration revolves a great deal around it, her experiences, her views and her opinions are shaped and influenced by it. She seems to have sublimated her anger in her political work. The Sanghatana has obviously given what she considers, a meaningful direction to her life. In spite of her withdrawal from it, she is still emotionally engaged with it. She is in close contact with its founding members, whom she respects and loves very much and visits regularly. She has no complaints, no resentment, no demands and no expectations from the Sanghatana.

She has always been very independent and continues to be so. I was told that she gets her sons, daughters-in-law and grand children to work on the land and pays them something in return. Her son in Kalyan sends her money for cultivation, but takes away paddy in return. She is a source of support and strength to her children, especially her daughters, towards whom she is very caring. For example, when one of her sons-in-law was implicated in a police case, she arranged money and legal help and managed to get him out of it. She still helps her children, whenever they need her. With a lot of confidence still left in her, Radkibai seems to be still capable of handling any situation. Radkibai, like the others of her generation has suffered, but unlike them, not silently. Like most other women and men of her age, Radkibai's life is woven closely with the forest. Much of her narration is about resisting or fighting with the forest officials or about forest conservation by the adivasis. She is extremely happy about the forest protection undertaken by her people with the support of the Sanghatana. It is a source of satisfaction for her. She believes in bhutali, and offers extremely valuable sociological insights into the phenomena, that bhutalis are generally old, widowed women, past the reproductive age, without sons or male support. She also recognises the oppressive character of bhutali, she herself has been accused of being a bhutali. I was told that a strident, quarrelsome or talkative woman is often accused of being a bhutali. Radkibai confidently challenged her accusers to prove it. Given the fact that she is not a bhutali, she would only have proved them wrong. But her accusers did not want to invite trouble by taking on this difficult woman and at the same time, not to disturb their universe where fear and accusation keeps women under control.

Most of the time Radkibai offered an explanation for her actions and appeared comfortable with the explanations. On two occasions when there was a trace of doubt and regret, as though she needed to justify it to herself, was when she talked about hitting her husband, "if he hadn't beaten me, why would I have beaten him. I used to sell fish and bring things for him to eat. Once I even got goat's meat for him." And when she talked about forcing her daughter to marry a handicapped man, who drinks a lot and beats her daughter, she said, "I thought he is born handicapped, but he must also live, and besides he can do all the work, so I gave my daughter to him. How did I know what kind of a person he was, could I look inside his stomach?" She is acutely conscious of gender oppression, and in her own life she has challenged it, even though she has been criticised and ridiculed for it.

She also avoided talking about the visit to her son's house. I was told that she had returned earlier than planned because she was humiliated by him. He had told her that she embarrassed him. There is a lot of pain and hurt which she tries to hide behind her tough exterior.

For all the confidence, there is despair over the condition of the adivasis, and she is tormented by the inexplicable, "where must this destiny come from?"

IV

Babubhau:
"Without the forest there is no beauty"

Babubhau, approximately 65-years old, is a remarkable contrast to Radkibai. He is an extremely sober, dignified, gentle and a soft-spoken man. He has had some education and that shows in the narration. He was articulate, spoke willingly about his life and views, in a measured tone, with emotions but without anger or resentment. As is clear from his narration, he was extremely cautious, always qualifying his statements with "I think so", or "this is so in my village". He was concerned not to misrepresent, or exaggerate or generalise. As different from the others, he was much more reflective in reconstructing his biography, and seemed often just to be thinking aloud, trying to make sense of events and his own actions. He laughed often during the interview and seemed to be at peace with himself. He is a much-respected man in his village.

Where did your forefathers come from?

I was born here in Nagzari and so was my father. My grandfather's father had land near Uplat that is on the border of Gujarat. From there my grandfather came to my present village, Nagzari. His other brothers went to Bhilad in Gujarat. They are still there. He came because of the sowkar's oppression. Over there they were cultivating on khand. They might not have been able to pay the khand or might have had other outstanding debt they could not pay. So they came here to escape the sowkar's tyranny. That is what I have heard from my grandfather. Since my grandfather was a forest guard, he cultivated some land in the forest.

In the earlier years all the lands were belonged to the adivasis. They lost it because they borrowed money. Most of the time that's how the land went out of the hands of the people. When our people went to borrow money from our landlord who lived in Mumbai, he used to say, I am the man who got the land by cutting the necks of the adivasis, so I am the seth. That's how the sowkars took the lands of the adivasis and gave it to them to cultivate on khand.

The khand used to be rice paid to the sowkar. I don't know the exact proportion, but I know this that after paying the khand, there was hardly any rice left for us to eat. If there was a drought, if the rains didn't come in time and you couldn't pay full khand, then it would be carried over to the next year when there was better yield. But we used to grow nagli, vari, urid, tur, which we could eat. That is why we held on to the land.

And that is how we were able to sustain ourselves. Then, there was the forest and we used the vegetables from the forest. Of course, the other option was to do mazoori. What else could we do?

The forest was very thick at that time. In summer you could get the bitter varieties of food, and in rains there were plenty of leafy vegetables and shoots. There were also a lot of animals, deer, wild boar and tigers. The tigers were not a threat to the people, but they used to eat our cattle. In one month seven of our cattle were eaten. Of course, other people also lost their cattle, bullocks and so on.

My grandfather and father did a little bit of cultivation and mazoori. They took land from other people on khand and cleared a plot on the 'gurcharan', community grazing land, something like the encroachment plot people cultivate in the forest now. But this was not in the deep forest. Therefore, the foresters did not object much. If you gave them one or two chicken they would let you cultivate. But there was no permission to cultivate in the deep forest. There were a lot of restrictions then. In those days they were very strict. But after Independence, the law has become softer so the jungle has been destroyed.

Tell me about your childhood

We were seven children in all, three sisters and four brothers, sisters are elder to me. We, children went to school. I studied up to the fifth class and my youngest brother completed the seventh and became a teacher. My sisters were not educated. I and my three brothers studied in a mission school at Talasari, run by Christian fathers and lived in a boarding there. My father had become Christian. We had to walk 10-12 miles to come home. I came home once a month. Except for my youngest brother, all of us left school before completing the fifth class.

I liked school. The older boys would sometimes tease us. The teachers used to beat us, but I enjoyed studying. I liked subjects like geography and was good at it. I used to get 80 per cent marks. But in mathematics I got zero. That is why I gave up studies. I got fed up and gave up. What could I do? I simply could not understand maths. So I ran away. Then my father gave up saying this boy is not going to study so there is no point of beating him. My younger brother had a clever head so he completed his studies and even got a job.

Our family almost never had enough to eat. We had to pay a khand of 50 sacks of paddy to our sowkar, one Prabhu by name. The other big sowkars of Nagzari were Karniks. They lived in Andheri in Mumbai, they did not live in the village. Sometimes the produce from our land was so little that we would not even be able to pay the khand, let alone have anything left for us to eat. When the year was so bad, we had to pay the balance khand in the following year. We would not have anything left even for the seeds. We would have to borrow from the sowkar and return double the amount. If we borrowed grain for consumption, we had to pay back one and a half times. We depended a lot on the forest for food. Our moneylender, Padamji was a Parsi in Dapchari. The other moneylenders required people to stand surety before advancing loans and since we were new and did not know anyone in Nagzari, so we took loans from this Parsi who knew our relatives there. If people were unable to pay back the loans, the sowkar's bhaiyas used to beat them.

Even my father was beaten by the sowkar's 'mukaddam'. At first the sowkar used to stay in Dahanu, but he also had a house in the village. He owned a lot of land which he gave out on khand.

Those days no sowkar cultivated his own land. There was always the fear that he would either beat us or he would not give us the land on khand. Then what would we do? Those were our fears.

My father was a carpenter. He used to make bullock carts. We also had a bullock cart of our own which we used to rent out to others. My father earned some money by renting out the cart. My father was also a bhagat. He used to get fifty paise or a rupee for his bhagtai and chicken and daru. But the bhagat doesn't expect and people don't give anything for minor ailments. Only if there is a major problem, something in the stomach, for example, then daru and chicken are given. I learnt a little about jungle medicine from him. But he did not teach me how to do bhuta. He said I was not meant for it.

I remember a lot of starvation in my childhood. It was horrible. Only two or three families would have grain left over for the transplanting season so that they could concentrate on their field. Others would have to alternate between working on their field and doing mazoori. I am talking about a time when I was a young boy. The others were all like this. They would either go for mazoori to those people who had the grain or bring roots and tubers from the forest and fill their stomach or go to the sowkar for work. But going to the sowkar was not very common. People were required to do veth on the sowkar's land, but we did not have much oppression from our sowkar because he lived in Mumbai. Those sowkars who lived in Dahanu oppressed people in this way. During the monsoons adivasis would be required to take one cart-load of wood free for them and collect a vegetable called kantola from the forest. If our sowkar had been from Dahanu, he would surely have oppressed us.

Sometimes my mother made a watery gruel from rice, but usually we would sleep hungry. Or, since we had good cows those days, we would get some milk from them and the leafy vegetables from the forest were always there. I remember those days very well. I feel bad. But now those days are gone. Now there is not that kind of starvation. Such days were many, but they are gone. This was not just the case with us, it was the story of all the people in the village. Of the 60 odd houses, only three families had grains to last them through the year. The rest would eat for three to four months and then starvation would begin. We would have to go for mazoori here and there. Sometimes those who had grains would say, come with the children and have some 'ambil', some gruel from maize and other coarse grains and my mother would take us. But it is embarrassing to go to other peoples' houses everyday, so we would go only occasionally. Otherwise, mother would feed us leaves from the forest.

Hunger and illness were major problems those days. People used to suffer from fever and stomach aches. There were no wells those days, so we used to drink water from little springs. But the stomach illness is no longer there because we have wells now. The major illness in our village now is fever. If fever creeps into one house, it does not leave you till it has affected every single member of the house.

I experienced and absorbed suffering and starvation and also enjoyed myself when I was young. Diwali was a happy time and those were the days when there was no hunger. The new crop having come in and khand to be paid, only in January, there was enough grain. Those were inexpensive times, fish was available cheap and chicken was always there at home. For one rupee you could buy a shirt like this. People also used to go to cut grass for the sowkar. Those days the mazoori was fifty paise. This is when I was very small. I remember working from the time when the mazoori was seventy-five paise. Then the mazoori increased to three rupees and then to five rupees and now I don't know how much it is. It is about 25 to 30 rupees. Things were cheaper then. If you worked for two or three days it was quite enough. We celebrated Holi. We used to dance to the music of the Tarfa on that day. On the next day we made masks, disguised ourselves, put ash on our faces and went house to house collecting money, killed a goat or a chicken, drank toddy and danced. Those days the whole village would join in the dance. These days only a few young people dance.

Those days everyone used to drink toddy including women and children. Only the old men drank daru. They did not know how to make daru in the village in those days. It had to be bought from far away. People were not permitted to make daru. Parsis and bhandaris had the licence to sell daru. We would buy from them. Not everyone had their own trees. Now there are 'khajuri' trees everywhere and people tap their own toddy trees.

People started making daru in my village only after I grew up. Those days many people did not even know what daru was like. Yes, sometimes they would bring it from far away, add a little water and sell it at a higher rate in the village. That way some people did a little business. They would bring daru from Daman or Nagar Haveli where there was no restriction on daru. But if they got caught, they would have a problem. Usually a bribe worked. But I know people who were sent to jail for four to six months for smuggling daru. The other danger they faced was the thieves along the way, who would beat them and rob the daru. But in spite of these dangers some people used to bring it. Now people make their own and so there is no need to go there. As for toddy everyone, women and children drank it on festivals and weddings. People didn't drink everyday. In our weddings everybody must get a glass of toddy, that is a custom. If you can't go for a wedding your family members bring the toddy home for you in a pot. The custom is that everyone should be given toddy.

Did your mother and sisters work on the field and also do mazoori? What work did you do?

Yes, my mother did both. We had nothing to eat so it was not possible for her to work on the family land alone. She used to do mazoori for the better-off adivasis in the village. She did not go to work for the sowkar. Once there was a famine. I was small. It must have been around the year 1942. I don't remember the year well. Then my mother and sister went to work for the sowkar. And my father went to Jawhar-Mokhada to transport large timber in bullock carts. He did this work for the forest department.

I remember my mother and sister would bring two glasses of nagli as their mazoori and we would grind it into flour and make ambil. Our paddy had been destroyed. There was no question about money. Those days the only mazoori for the entire day was a glass of nagli, as I said. As a young boy I did not feel the suffering much. I would drink the ambil and go around eating wild figs and pass my days. Children don't experience suffering the way adults do. How bad the older people must have felt in those days, my parents, my older sisters.

There may have been other problems, but the main problems were starvation and illness. Food simply did not last us. We were faced with the dilemma of whether to eat the grain kept for seed or save it for the next season. As I told you, people used to get food on credit from the sowkar and pay one and a half times in return. For seed, they had to pay back double. As a carpenter my father would sometimes get one rupee for making a plough or a bullock cart. And because he was a bhagat, he also got a little rice occasionally for doing 'diva', divination.

As a young boy, I used to go to graze cattle in the forest. The tiger does not attack the cattle in a flock especially when they are tended. The tiger is afraid of human beings. They go for the stray cattle. Only very rarely, is an animal from the flock killed. Children would hunt birds, squirrels and roast and eat them. There were also a lot of berries in the forest.

I remember the forest. It was not very dense, but the trees were huge. The sag and the ain trees were cut for wood and taken away. The rest of the trees were burnt and taken away for charcoal. Now there are small trees and bushes. Nothing is left. There is no wood in the forest. Earlier there were rabbits, deer and other animals. Now there aren't many animals, may be an occasional rabbit. As for the tigers one doesn't know where they have gone.

Men used to go for hunting, from the early days. Women don't hunt, but they do kill by stoning an animal or trapping it. Women go for fishing in the river and streams. I know for a fact that women in my village don't hunt. I don't know what tradition that prevents them from hunting.

Why did your father convert to Christianity?

The Christian fathers had appointed teachers in my village to run a night school. My father learnt to read and write there and also became a Christian. But since he was also a bhagat, he was a Christian only in name. He performed all the adivasi rituals. I don't know the reason why people became Christians. The missionaries gave some aid, but that was much later, when I grew up. I don't know if they gave any help in the beginning. Very few people became Christians. Conversions took place in Dapchari, Gangangaon and Talasari. There were only three houses in our village and even the Christians continued to be Warlis and follow Warli customs and practices. Even now the only difference is that the Christians are married by the fathers and the others are married by the 'dhavleri', marriage priestess. Otherwise everything else like eating, drinking, propitiating the gods is the same for all. Other customs like the giving and taking of bride price is the same. I was married by the Christian father. My wife is also a Christian but there is no hard and fast rule that the spouse has to be a Christian. Of us four brothers, the wives of two are Christians and two are not.

Did you and your family also do veth?

Veth was prevalent those days. My family did not have to do veth but we had another form of oppression. We had planted a lot of mango trees on our field. The sowkar said these are my trees, but we have planted them, we said. He got the better of us and cut and took away the mango and tamarind and sag trees. The mukaddam of the sowkar was an uncle of mine. The sowkar merely gave him orders to cut the trees and went away to Mumbai. We gave the mukaddam daru and chicken and pleaded with him to spare two mango and three tamarind trees, saying that the sowkar would never know. The mukaddam agreed and those trees were saved. They are still there. The rest of the trees were burnt in his charcoal kiln and the coal taken away. The 'katkaris' worked in the kilns. I do not know whether they worked for wages or did veth.

We had to do veth in the forest. I have done veth in the forest. It was compulsory. If you did not go for veth, you were told, don't come to the forest, don't collect the leaves and twigs for rab, don't take firewood. So people were forced to go and work. Of course, there was no mazoori, work you do for free is called veth. In my memory the foresters were not British. They were local people, not adivasis, but from our country, mostly Maharashtrians.

Did you have much to do with the foresters?

Some foresters were strict, some were nice, but they also oppressed us. For example, they would catch our cattle and take it to the 'kondwada', where impounded cattle are kept. Then we would have to borrow money from the sowkar and release our cattle. We would have to repay these debts later. There is a village next to mine called Dhanivary. The forest department had planted young saplings there. All the cattle, even ours, used to stray into the plantation, because the grass had grown there. Once the foresters came and impounded our cattle and took them far. With great difficulty I managed to raise some money and release our cattle.

Of course, the forest did not belong to us. Whatever we needed from the forest had to be stolen. Usually we managed by giving bribes. Once we had cut a huge log of wood and placed it in our field as a bund, because our bund was washed away in the flood. The forester caught us. He came to our house, he ate food in our house and then went out and began to measure the wood. My father asked him, what are you doing? He said, Thakre, we have to file some cases so we are going to file this one. My father had to pay a fine of 12 rupees. He sold a goat and paid the fine. Otherwise from where would we have got the money? This was before I got married.

We paid the fine, besides giving chicken and liquor. When you committed a minor crime, then the foresters would tell you, why do you go through the legal procedure? Give me a chicken and I will manage. Those days the idea was to escape the forester and take what you needed from the forest. Now there are some adivasi foresters. They give a lot of trouble. Some of them are more humane, they scold you and if you give them a chicken they are happy. Others are not so considerate. But whatever it is – with fear in our hearts – we have to go to the forest for our needs. What can we do?

How old were you at the time of the adivasis' revolt? What do you remember about it?

I was in school then. Activities used to take place in Talasari, but we were not allowed to leave the school. Once when there was a firing, all children climbed a tree to see what was going on. We were herded back to the school. I don't remember what Godutai spoke. But later I heard about the issues she took up. In those days the Parsis used to harass us a lot. They would take huge khands and make people do veth. They would take everything that grew on our fields. If we did not give them the vegetables they would ask, does not dudhi, bhopla, suran, etc, grow on my land? Over and above the khand we had to give these things. The oppression of the adivasis was in the extreme. The Parsis were dominant in Dahanu and Talasari talukas. These were the issues Godavari took up. She worked for the adivasis and the struggle was good for the poor.

I have also heard that the woman of the lagnagadi suffered a lot. She was kept in the house and harassed. None of my family was a lagnagadi. In fact, no one from my village was a lagnagadi. But we did veth. All that stopped. Now there is no oppression from the sowkar. Now people say, why should we work free for him? Ever since the 'Kul Kayda', tenancy law, the land is in our possession and we have paid for it. Those days we worked for him because we needed the land. Now there is no relationship with the sowkar. Had there been the khand system, the oppression would have continued.

The land was transferred to us about 40 or 50 years ago. We had to pay five times the land revenue. Now we only pay the land tax. We have to pay it according to the law. We got the land we were cultivating. My father had a total of eight acres. But only about two and a half to three acres were sold to us. We made applications for the rest of the land to be transferred to us. But the sowkar only makes promises. Let us see what happens. The land on which we do rab is not in our names but it is in our possession. We keep telling the sowkar, we will pay you the money for it, transfer it on our name. But he doesn't do it. Because we have been cultivating it since many years, it is as good as ours.

What about your marriage?

My eldest sister had a wedding with a lot of pomp. Those who don't have the money, they just apply halad and put gathi around the wife's neck and it is recognised as a marriage. The rest of us were married that way. Only those who have the means have a proper marriage. There is no compulsion to have a proper marriage. The two sister's husbands came to live with us. They were gharoryas. The eldest sister's husband had some land, but the youngest sister's husband had no land. I gave him a little land. They have an encroachment plot. When the gharoryas came we continued to live together, work together, eat together. Those days we had a large house in which we made small rooms. Sometimes people build separate huts but work and eat together. My other sister who was married in another village also had some land, but they were not well to do. They were poor like us.

My wife's family was poor like us, in fact, poorer. Their land was rocky, so they did mazoori. Even in my house she worked on the field and did mazoori. I didn't spend much on my wedding. We had musicians. I got her two sarees, one red and one green, costing 10 rupees each, for which I paid cash down. And I had to give a sack of rice to my father-in-law for the food. That is compulsory. I don't think we spent more than 300 rupees for the wedding. We did not need to take a loan. But others who gave a lot of daru spent as much as 800 rupees to 1000 rupees in those days. Only for one brother we had to get clothes on credit. I had to work for two years to pay back the loan. He is a school teacher. He is my youngest brother, I felt like doing something good for him.

How many children did you have? What are they doing at present?

Seven girls and one boy. All of them went to school in the village, but dropped out at different stages. They failed and dropped out. Only one completed her twelfth class and is now working as an auxiliary nurse midwife (ANM). The others do mazoori.

The last two are engaged, the others are all married. Most of them were married with halad-gathi, simple marriages. For my eldest daughter Meena's wedding we called musicians and all. Another one also had a similar marriage. For the others it was simple. If they want a grand marriage then the children should also be prepared to spend. I alone cannot afford it, and how much credit can I take?

When my children were small we were a joint family. We used to cultivate together. Farming needs a lot of people and we could work well in those days. If the rains were good, we could get as much as 60 to 70 sacks of rice from our lands. This was sufficient for the whole year. My children did not experience hunger as much as we did when we were young. We also get vegetables and other things from the forest. We still bring things to eat from the forest, not so much to ward off starvation but because we like to eat things from the forest. Moreover, we have eaten so much of the forest food that it has become a habit. I long for the taste of it. And even now it is not as though there is plenty so it is a good supplement to food.

Meena doesn't have land. Her husband is a driver. The second daughter's husband has some land and he works as a mason. The third daughter is an ANM, I told you. She is educated. Her husband is like that only. I don't know what he does. The next one does a little mazoori and the one after her is married in a slightly better-off house. They have a little more land. Their food lasts throughout the year. The husband goes far away for sand digging for short periods to earn cash for clothes and other things. My son has studied up to the fourth standard. He works on our field and goes out for mazoori on construction site. He goes wherever he finds work. Sometimes for 10 or 15 days he stays at home. They also get fed up with the work because the contractors give them a lot of trouble, make them do extra work. When the contractor comes to the house, then they go for work.

The majority of the people from my village go to the brick kilns. One of my daughters goes to work on one. I had once gone and stayed with them for 15 days. That is when I observed the work in the brick kiln. They wake up at midnight and work till 10 or 11 in the morning. After that they have lunch and rest for two or three hours. When they wake up they have to start carting the mud and mixing the sand, ash and husk and slowly kneading it with water to prepare the clay to make bricks. By then it is evening and so they wash, go to the shop, buy something and catch some sleep for about three hours. The daily wage rate works out to 50-60 rupees. Now my daughter doesn't do this work because she has a baby to look after, but my brother's children go to the brick kiln. It is a difficult work. Though you get enough money to survive, you have to work for nearly 20 hours. Only the young and the very strong can do this work, not everyone. Someone like me cannot manage it. The kumbhars and the agris who do this business make a lot of money within one or two years.

My son went to work on the salt pans for two years, but last year he did not go. Few people from my village go to the salt pans. They work from Diwali, November to June, approximately seven months. Once or twice they take leave and come home. Now I don't know what the wages are, but when my son used to go, it was 40 rupees and food. Compared to the work on the brick kiln, it is less difficult. My children don't get work from the forest department. They go to forest to get wood, vegetables and crabs. Lot of young boys go for crabs and fruits in the monsoons.

It is not as though there is no shortage. There is shortage, but not starvation. For example, my brother has leased his land for a year because he needed money. But it is not as if he will starve. He will find the means to buy some food. In fact, he will use part of the lease money to buy food. When I was young 75 per cent of the people were starving, now at the most 5 or 10 per cent of the people are starving. People whose crop does not last throughout the year, have some access to consumption loan. It is available from the government or from the sowkar, which you pay back in the form of labour in the orchards or brick kilns or salt pans.

Now our people go out much more for work and those who are dependent on farming alone also get better production because they use high-yielding varieties. Earlier the yield from the traditional varieties was not as much as from the high-yield varieties.

Do you feel a special bond with the forest?

Yes, of course, everyone feels that way, close to the forest. Without the forest there is no beauty. Now there are no big forests, but whatever trees are there on the forest give beauty. Just imagine a head without hair. That's the function of trees on the hill.

People believe that gods dwell on trees. For example, there were two huge ain trees in our forest and people believed that there were gods in those trees. When the sowkar wanted to cut the trees and take it, people didn't allow them to be felled. But today both the trees are no more. I guess they must have aged and fallen. People believe that there is beauty because the forest is there and the gods dwell in the forest and if the forest goes, it will auger very badly for us.

I love the forest so much that no matter how much work I have on the field, every two or three days I need to go and roam in the forest. Even if I have to go alone. My dog also comes with me. I go and sit under a tree and lean against it and that makes me feel good. My mind feels calm. Most people like to go to the forest.

Sometimes we go in groups of six or eight for hunting. We hunt for small games like rabbit. There are no wild boars or deer in our forest. Even the small barking deer and rabbits have reduced in number, because the forests are depleted and destroyed. I feel very bad about the forest being destroyed. The destruction of forests started with the days of the British. They sold the forest to the contractors and did new plantations. The contractors flattened it out. We live in wooden houses, how many years can a wooden house last? Our people also needed wood for the houses so they also took. You don't expect them to live under a tree in the rains. Our hill is not that big and there are villages on all sides who take wood from the forest. If everyone takes from the forest, how can it be saved?

The new plantations are about 20-30 years old. By the time the trees were a little big, people took them and built houses. And they were stolen by outsiders by the truckloads. Only last year our people had caught a truck of the timber trader who was stealing good khair trees. But he gave them some 8000 rupees and they let him go. Now he doesn't come. Another time some adivasis were caught and beaten by the villagers. First the forest department sold the forest to the forest contractors, and now there is illegal felling. How will the forest regenerate. It is still going on. Until last year it was brisk, but this year we haven't heard anything. Actually there are no trees of commercial value any more. So long as teak and khair were there, they were sold.

I have a few teak trees of my own. I have cut seven or eight of them to build a house on the field. I have a house in the village and I want one on the field. They are my own. I have a few ain and some teak trees. I have fruit trees like jackfruit, mangoes, papaya, but they are only three to four years old. They don't give fruit yet. I don't even know if I will live to eat the fruit of these trees, the children will eat them. But I have planted them because I love planting trees. I have satisfied my inner urge to plant trees.

What do you think can be done about this?

Kashtakari Sanghatana has tried very hard to protect the forest, but I don't think the Jungle Bachao will be successful. I have been thinking about this for a long time, even before the Jungle Bachao programme started. But I haven't been able to find a solution.

Because without wood people cannot build houses. Some may decide not to cut the forest but will all the people agree to obey the rule? People are bound to steal. Our people felt that the forest belonged to the sarkar and they had to steal from it to survive, they don't seem to have had a feeling that it was theirs. But now that the Sanghatana has awakened the people at least they say that the forest is ours. This consciousness has come to them through the meetings of the Sanghatana. I am not sure that they nurture and protect the forest but at least they say the forest belongs to the adivasis. People like me know that it is true. I feel that our people have planted the forest, have burnt the undergrowth and planted the saplings doing bonded labour. Therefore it is ours. But I really don't know what should be done to improve the situation. Now that I have grown old, my mind doesn't work.

It is, of course, useful to protect the forest. It should be protected. It must be protected. I feel that way. But others don't feel that way. What can one do? In our village we have not adopted the Jungle Bachao programme because there is a lot of opposition to it. But I know the programme is doing well in other villages. There is plenty of bitter tuber still available in the forest, although over all forest food has reduced. Even forest medicine is reduced considerably. As for firewood there is sufficient now for our village, but I foresee a shortage in the next 10 years the way the forests are being cut down. For rab we do not cut down trees. We simply collect dry leaves and twigs. Until the forest is destroyed, people won't come to their senses.

There are no big trees, no valuable timber left in the forest. There are only creepers and bushes. That's why the foresters don't come to the forest. What is there to protect? What will they protect? Year before last they had done plantations of bamboo, teak and other species and employed some people from the village. Not this year. They gave a wage of 35-40 rupees. The work is not hard, so the young people like it. These plantations are not directly useful for the people. But if there are trees in the forest there is a possibility of stealing them for your needs. If there is nothing in the forest, from where do you get anything? As for the people, they don't think it is a crime. If you get caught you give a chicken and your work is done. Recently some people who were cutting wood in the forest were caught. Somehow they managed to escape. But the foresters confiscated their axe, saw and even their drinking water pots.

What about your children, are you happy with them?

Yes, they are all right. They work hard on their fields. Each of them harvests five to seven quintals of rice, and they also do mazoori. None of them is facing starvation. But my son doesn't pay as much attention to work, as he should. He is not downright lazy but he could give more concentration on work. He doesn't listen to me. It is not that he has any major problem. Just that he likes to go around with young boys, they bring films and watch them till late in the night. They wake up at nine in the morning. Then what work can you do? Most of them are like that. They are often enjoying themselves. I often console myself saying that they are still young, once they have a family, the burden of bringing up a family will make them more serious. I don't see the point in beating or abusing, so I calm myself with these thoughts.

My son is not married. He stays with me. I can't say when I will get him married. It will need money. Among the adivasis, it is the responsibility of the parents to get children married. The children may help by contributing some money. The wedding can cost 25,000-30,000 rupees and if you buy very expensive clothes, it can go up to 50,000 rupees. But then you can also marry within a small budget of 8,000 to 10,000 rupees. My brother spent only 10,000 rupees on his son's marriage.

My son is like me, but he does not enjoy reading as much as I do, though he is quite literate. I always have some reading material next to my pillow. But my son prefers movies. He sings. Has a good voice and sings well. People must read to increase their knowledge. Of the girls, Meena likes to keep alive her interest in reading and writing. The daughter who has completed her twelfth is now doing a job so she does not have the time to read. My daughters are all intelligent but they couldn't complete their studies.

Are you glad that they have had a little education? Do you see any value in education?

The adivasi community does not really see the benefits of education. For one, it is not really possible to complete education.

They don't have the time and the money. Those who have the means or find someone to help them, go ahead and even secure jobs. But what is the use of education only up to seventh class? My girls went to school, only one got a job as an ANM, as I told you before. The others dropped out in fifth, seventh and eighth classes, and of course, with that education they can't get jobs. People are disappointed. In fact, the people in our hamlet look towards us and say, his daughters are educated but it has not been of much use. Children lose the determination to work hard. The girls remain in school till they are in their teens and do not learn about cultivation. Also at that age they don't feel like working in the mud or collecting dung for rab. Those who don't go to school are more inclined to work in the field. That is what I have personally observed in my village. Those who have dropped out of school don't like to do cultivation. Most of them prefer to work in the factory for 20-25 rupees. They don't have the inner urge to cultivate. Some people believed that those who were educated would do better farming, but in our place it is just the opposite. The educated youth do tasks related to farming, but they are not interested in farming as an occupation.

The children are not able to study well and so they get fed up and drop out. There are many children like that in my family as well, my son, my brother's son and others. Their education is no use in getting a job. Of course, they read the newspaper and get to know what is happening, they are able to go places because they can read directions and sign boards but parents feel, why should we send our children to school when it is of no use. Secondly, children have to be provided money, and often parents are unable to do so. This is the main problem. Now if you send your child for education to Mumbai or to Dahanu even the travel costs are so high, you can't afford it. The Christian fathers help in education. A few young boys have got jobs, not big jobs but simple ones. A couple of boys have even become doctors.

But I feel very fortunate and good even though I have studied only up to the fifth class. Others do not have any idea of education. It is as if they are living in darkness. I can read, write, I feel very good. I can come to know what is going on in the world by reading about it. Every night I read a little. That is why I was keen on my daughters' studying, but unfortunately they were lazy and didn't complete their education. But at least all of them have studied up to the fifth class.

What work do you do at present?

I do farming. I like it. I can't give it up because it is our traditional occupation. Before people used to work very hard on their fields. They would build bunds, do rab and other things. But nowadays nobody does any work. They just buy fertiliser and plant and then move out for work. Farming is a very hard work. And what is more, you must plant and transplant on time, your bunding and levelling should be good. Now last year what happened was that we should have got 25 sacks of rice from our field, but the crop got diseased and we got only 15 sacks. If we had had a good harvest, the crop would have lasted us through the year. The young people feel that after working so hard you don't get anything from the fields, so they don't like it. In my village people are neglecting their fields. Very few families do good farming. The bunding system is very poor. If there is a heavy downpour, it can break your bunds and carry away the mud.

Young people like the idea of ready cash from time to time, in farming you get your crop once a year. Therefore, they do not pay much attention to farming. They are more focused on other work. This is the situation in my hamlet.

It is true, the landholdings have decreased, but even those who have land neglect it. In fact, those who do not have land keep petitioning to the government for land, they encroach in the forest and do good farming there. There are only two families in my hamlet who have decent-sized holdings, but even they are not bothered about it.

Personally, I feel agriculture should be improved, land development, bunding, fencing, so that we can take a second crop. At present this is not possible because people leave their cattle free after harvest. If people take collective responsibility for the cattle, it is possible to grow urid, tuar, val in summer but if the cattle are going to destroy it what is the use of growing it?

In my father's time we grew these pulses, we even sold some. In the past, people worked harder and managed their cattle well. Now they grow only rice. They buy their pulses from the shops. It is a matter of shame. What can you do? People don't understand. I myself had 10-12 heads of cattle but I couldn't find a cowherd. So I gave away my bullocks on rent, gave away my cattle here and there. If I had attended to the cattle, then the work on my field would have suffered. So I had no choice. This year I will not get dung for manure. Of course, there are no grazing grounds left. What makes me feel very bad is that despite having land, one is not able to get a good harvest. Now there are new kinds of rice seeds with which you can get a better and higher yield so people concentrate on rice. They have stopped growing pulses, which takes more time. This is especially a problem in my hamlet because we are very close to the forest. Other hamlets are not so close to the forest and the hill so there the cattle are kept tied and stall fed.

We get some help from the government. You can get fertiliser and pesticide from the block development officer. But last year nobody applied for it. This year the fathers provided us seeds through their organisation, Shantivan Shetkari Seva Mandal. I took 60 kgs. They also provided fertiliser, pesticide and vegetable seeds. I have to repay 1000 rupees for the seeds and fertiliser. I have paid some of it. The rest will be repaid over time.

The fathers used to help a lot before, about 20 years ago. Those days they got PL480 grains from America which they used to give as wages. They improved people's fields, did bunding, made small bridges and even built a small dam. They did a lot of work at that time. The programme lasted for two or three years. It stopped long ago. Some improvement did take place. People give them respect because they do some work for them. But now, the father who used to do this work has been transferred and the grains that came from America have also stopped.

What else do you do now? Do you use your knowledge of herbal medicine?

Yes, I know about herbal medicine and I practise it. For example, we eat certain leaves and roots, or tie them to the wrist or foot or ear for certain ailments. If you tie a certain kind of root to your ears, it can cure headaches. There are many such medicines in the forest but not all people know about them. And, not everyone who has knowledge about them tells the others. This knowledge is given to someone special like one's son. Even I don't know what the medicines are, I only know they cure. In fact, this knowledge has reduced because people don't pass it on freely and the herbs are less because the forests are depleted.

As for myself, I first try the forest medicine, if it does not cure, then one has to go to the doctor. But I have never gone to the bhagat. Ever since I became conscious about the reality behind the phenomenon of bhutali, I never went to one. Only once, when my younger brother's ear was paining very much, my father sent me to a bhagat. That was the first and the last time. I don't have any faith in the bhagat, so what is the point of going to them?

My father had become a Christian but he did not know too much about the Christian religion. He used to tell me, adivasis have 33 crore gods and Jesu (Jesus) is one of them. We must show respect to Jesu, but we must respect the others as well. And when I was about 18, one day my father fell very ill, so we called a bhagat. The bhagat did the diva and said well, he is affected by a bhutali and the culprit is from your own family. Who could it be, I thought, my mother or my sister, and was very disturbed that our people should hunt our own womenfolk as witches. That is when I got more attracted to Christianity because there is no witch-hunting in the Christian religion. If there is some substance in the bhutali phenomenon, then there should be a way of identifying bhutalis in all religions – Hindu, Muslim and Christian. Nobody could explain this to me, so now I don't believe in bhutalis. Just think why should my father's wife or daughter want to harm him and why are there no bhutalis in other communities. They are considered cleverer than we are, therefore, there should be more bhutalis among them. Since then I began to reject part of the adivasi religion. I read the bible in Marathi and it appealed to me.

After some time the accusation died down and we took my father to the hospital. He had typhoid. He got cured. I don't have any faith in the bhutali and I don't even care whether they are there or not. As long as I don't see one, I don't believe in it.

Bhutali is a source of much suffering. Now the fear is considerably less because the people are educated and don't rely much on the bhagat and the bhutali. In the past they would make women stand on a hot 'tava', frying pan, beat them brutally and sometimes even kill them. Once two bhagats from my village had gone to a village close to Dapchari, and identified a woman as a bhutali and she was killed. The police patil reported the incident and seven or eight persons were arrested, but the woman was gone. The two bhagats managed to escape. The government and the laws have helped to control bhutali and in my opinion people don't believe in it as they did before, though some people continue to have faith in it.

How do you feel at present? Do you have major problems?

Different people have different problems. The sorrow of the person is in the mind of the person. If someone's son doesn't work properly and is lazy, that is sorrow, if someone's daughter is footloose and wayward, that is sorrow, if you haven't been able to cultivate properly and get a good harvest, that is sorrow, illness is sorrow. It is difficult to enumerate.

Illness, fever is a major problem. The government health facilities are not functional, the multipurpose health worker distributes malaria tablets, but these don't have any effect and the illness persists. So we are forced to go to the private doctor. People have no faith in the government services and private doctors are very expensive. The Kashtakari Sanghatana has taken up this issue, there have been 'morchas', demonstrations and other actions, and there has been some improvement in the government health centres. They take more care now. They have created a lot of awareness on this issue. Earlier you got the same tablet for all illnesses, how could you expect to get cured? So people would take loans and spend heavily on private doctors. This is really a very big problem.

It is not as though the problem of hunger is solved. It is not like before. There is no starvation but there is hunger. Some people's grains last through out the year. Others who go out to work buy grains from the shop, as much as two or three quintals and tide over the difficult period. Still others borrow grains from those who have and pay back when they get the crop. It is not like before when people had to eat roots and tubers for days on end. But grain is expensive. Imagine rice costs eight to ten rupees a kilo. Money is never sufficient. Everything is expensive now. You need money for medicines, salt, chillies, clothes, for everything. If you don't have money, you put a little salt in your vegetables and that's it and if you are ill, you just don't go to the dispensary, you just go to the bhagat or get some jungle medicine yourself because the doctor is expensive. What can you do?

Earlier there was the oppression of the sowkar, now there is none of that, but now there are internal fights among people. Our village is controlled by the CPM, which means that they have a majority in the gram panchayat. They take out morchas, people from other hamlets go, but they don't come to mobilise in our hamlet. For the last two years they haven't had any activity in our hamlet. But before, that there was a lot of tension in our hamlet. The CPM activists used to come to the village, throw stones and try to terrorise people, so that they didn't go to the Kashtakari Sanghatana or the Congress. On one occasion, a woman and some others were badly injured. But there wasn't much destruction because there were men in the village who chased them away. In other places they have caused a lot of destruction. The message is the same, don't go to the Sanghatana or to the Congress. People show them respect out of fear, if we speak against them, they will not let us survive.

Are you an activist of the Sanghatana?

They don't take up any programmes in our village. Yes, there was activity regarding the encroachment of forest plots. They have done work on that. Many people have got forest plots. Only I don't have a plot because I own land, what is the use of appropriating for the sake of appropriating. We did not take up the 'Jungle Bachao', save the forest, programme because we have a lot of opposition to it in our village.

Many people in the village feel that the Sanghatana is doing good work. They are being opposed by the CPM and the Congress. All the fighting and the stone throwing incidents are because of that. I think they do the best work out of the three, but then I am a member of the Sanghatana so I will say so. I feel it is ours and if other people had listened to us and cooperated, we would have done very good work. But I am bound to feel that way. I don't know what is in the minds of others. When I talk to the non-Sanghatana people near by, they get angry and say, we don't care whether you are doing good work or not. They don't want to listen and just walk off.

I was never a full time activist, but I do Sanghatana work in my village. I talk to people, explain issues, but I have never gone out of my village to work, to attend morchas. My son is active in the Sanghatana. He takes part in meetings and demonstrations regularly, but he doesn't take major responsibilities. My brother is not an active member, but his children are. Meena was an activist. She worked for some time. My sister's son was an activist, but he has also dropped out. The Sanghatana does good work, but nowadays there are not too many people who take responsibility for work. Some of the older activists have dropped out, may be they feel that instead of working for the Sanghatana, they can go out and earn money. I don't know what the reason is.

I did not become an activist because I have a well and I am more interested in doing my agriculture. I don't know if it will ever happen. Sometimes I feel that I have done neither this nor that. I have started making a fence for my field. I don't know if it will be completed this year.

I have heard that you have written very nice poems, what are they?

I don't know if they are nice, depends on what people think. I can't sing. I have composed two songs. One of them is "The flight of the eagle". The other one is titled, "Wake up oh poor", it goes like this:

> Wake up oh poor, why are you sleeping?
> the exploiter has looted the adivasi
> the thief has robbed the original owner.

> The adivasi has fallen into scarcity times
> for a sack of grains taken from the sowkar
> the sowkar takes all his grains and the field
> that is how the sowkar has looted the adivasi.

> The adivasi is caught in the noose of daru
> he pays no attention to work
> spending ten days earnings in one
> the adivasi is drowned in the vice of daru.

Boys and girls marry for love and joy
where we need spend twenty-five rupees
caught in false pretenses we spend two thousand
the adivasi is oppressed by such traditions.

Come, oh youth, let us go from village to village
let us enlighten our brothers
let us come together and destroy this enemy
the only way there is to save the adivasi.

I started composing some other songs but they are incomplete so I gave up. It is difficult to write songs while you are involved in your daily chores. These I composed during a Sanghatana camp, some 20 years ago. I am not really a poet. I like to write but where is the time to write poetry when you are faced with the problems of how to feed your family and yourself. I have thought that I would write, but these thoughts are continuously replaced by thoughts like, I can't do my farming well or the children don't listen, and all the thoughts of the things you want to write about just go away. It is like this, for example, this is transplantation time, if you don't work well, and transplant in time you will not get a good crop. When one is under this kind of pressure, where is the possibility to think about other things?

If you were granted a boon what would you ask for?

I cannot say. Well, I love farming, so I would ask for help to do better farming. I will make a fence, plant good trees, like jackfruit and mango and get a bountiful crop. This has been my dream for a very long time. I don't think my dream will be fulfilled, because I am already very old, but this was and is my wish. Whether it will materialise I cannot say. I wish for nothing else.

To achieve this you need money, but from where can I get it? Even with the little money I have I try to do what I can. Of course, if I had more money, I would have done better. I love to plant trees and I look after them as if they are my children. You have to work hard to tend trees, water them, if they have been infected with pests you must bring pesticide and cure them and if by chance the fence is broken, then the cattle eat it up. Imagine how bad one feels.

All this is for my children. They will eat the fruits.

If you were given a lot of money, a nice house, a good job, would you leave the village and go?

I would only go if I was given some land for cultivation. If I was given a nice house and told, live in it and enjoy yourself, I wouldn't go. I would want a little land to farm. I love to do something on land, to plant and grow. I love farming. I have planted two jackfruit trees and papaya trees. I carry water in a pot and water them. Would I get it elsewhere? I would not live in Mumbai even if I was given a house and money. Because I love the forest and I love the trees. I even dream of the forest sometimes. Where are the forests and trees in Mumbai? There may be trees, but they are not mine, the land is not mine. Here the trees are mine, the land is mine. I would not go anywhere no matter how much money I get.

Babubhau's contact with the Christian priests has obviously been an important influence in his life, shaping his personality in a significant way. He is aware of the fact that he is educated and is happy that he can read. He believes that it has broadened his horizon. He sees the value of education although he is aware that it has not improved the condition of the adivasis on the whole.

Although keenly conscious of the problems of the adivasis, he, unlike Radkibai, is not a fighter. He has got a different personality. He is a poet. He can talk to people and try to convince them of the need to resist injustice and to change their ways which are detrimental to their progress. He is very critical of his own people for drinking, destroying the forest and for bad social practices. He expresses himself through poetry. He is not a political activist because he doesn't have the temperament of an activist. Besides, he says, he loves his land, his trees and finds satisfaction in tending to the same. His greatest disappointment is when he can't do it well. Working on the land and growing trees is more than an occupation or a source of livelihood. It is a passion through which he fulfills himself.

He is a sensitive man, unlike most men of his generation, especially with respect to women. He does not like or believe in the practice of bhutali. In a society where wife beating is as normal as getting married is, he does not beat his wife. When I asked him about it, he said he had never beaten her, and then added, visibly embarrassed, "except once when I hit her because I had guests and I asked her to bring some daru from the neighbour's house. She took long to return and when I went to find out what had happened, I found her chatting with the women. I got angry and gave her one".

What bothers him so much that he is unable to even talk about it is the fact that, one of his sons-in-law makes money by illegally selling medicines. His daughter has an access to in the hospital where she works. He disapproves of it strongly and dismisses the son-in-law "he is like that only".

With all the "sorrows", that his son does not take interest in cultivation, that his favourite daughter Meena has a rough time with a domineering husband, he is satisfied. He has his land, he is educated, his children have had a little education and are all settled. There is no starvation. There is enough to eat. He seems to be largely at peace with his past and his present. The memory of the past is painful, but he is able to talk about it and he obviously draws satisfaction from the fact that it is no longer so. At one point in the narration, he did express doubt about his choice of not becoming an activist when he said, "sometimes I think I have done neither this nor that". He also expresses his helplessness to intervene and change the condition of the adivasis in statements like, "I am too old now, I cannot think". He is conscious of the fact that he is advanced in years and the end may not be far off. But he can face it. Although life could be better, easier, he is not willing to change it for money or a big house anywhere else without his land and the forest.

Like many men and women of his generation, he has a strong bond with the forest. He retreats into the forest to find medicines, food, but also beauty, peace and quietude. He likes to think, dream, rest in the forest, escape from the troubles of the world and to find solace. Land and forest are an extension of his habitat, of himself, outside of which he cannot exist.

V

Ramabai: "They called me a bhutali"

I met Ramabai for the first time in the Sanghatana office where she had come to enquire about the compensation due to her from the owner of the boat, which capsized about 10 years ago. Her husband worked on the same fishing boat and was believed to have drowned and died.

She is about 45-50-years old. Dressed neatly in threadbare clothes, she looked absolutely distraught. Her whole being communicated an overwhelming sense of despair and sadness over the enormity of the tragedy that had struck her and disrupted her life. When I met her, she was so distressed and preoccupied with the present that the past and the future did not seem to exist. Everything else seemed irrelevant and I could not bring myself to burden her with the task of going through her life and making sense of it.

After a gap of a couple of months, I met her again and asked her if she would tell me about her life. She readily agreed. She spoke clearly and with a lot of emotions. She wept twice in the course of the narration, shedding tears which seemed to come from the depth of some deep despair.

Insecurity, anxiety, fears and loneliness seemed to fill her life. There is nothing to dispel the hopelessness that engulfs her, no escape from the past and the present, not even a fantasy or a dream of a better future.

Tell me about your childhood.

I was the first born in my family. When I was a month or a month and a half old, my mother started leaving me behind in the house and going out to work in people's houses: If I cried a lot, a little girl from the neighbourhood would carry me to mother who would feed me and then she would bring me back and put me in the cradle. In this way with great difficulty my mother brought me up. Then when I was one and a half year old, mother got pregnant again. She had a second daughter. Since I was still small, mother would feed me from one breast and feed the baby from the other. My father's friends used to ridicule my father for not having a son. One day in a fit of anger, he picked me up and dumped me near the sea. The sea is very close to the house, you see. Fortunately, my mother's father came to the seashore and found me there. He picked me up and took me to my grandmother and asked her to look after me. It was my luck that I survived. Had a stone hit me on the beach, when my father dumped me there, where would I be. He had gone and thrown me on the rocks, and my grandfather ran and picked me up. He also beat my mother saying you have only daughters. Till I grew up my father didn't look at me.

When I was five or six years old my grandmother died. So my father wanted to take me back, but my 'mama', mother's brother, said that they would not give me back now that I was grown up, and that they would take the responsibility of getting me married. But my father had a fight with them and brought me back. And when I was nine years old he sent me to work in a vadi.

Mother kept on having children every year. My father refused to go for an operation although those days they used to visit houses in a vehicle and take people for operations. She had 12 children in all, two died when I was very young. So we were six sisters and four brothers in all. Now we are eight living, four brothers and four sisters.

My father used to work at removing sand from the beach when I was young. He never gave any money at home. He used to beat my mother and ask her to provide food for him. My mother used to work as a domestic servant in people's homes. They would give her the leftover food, and with that she used to feed us.

As a small girl I was sent to work on the vadi of an Irani, here in Dahanu, close to the station. It was a very large vadi. I had to carry two troughs of 'chickoos', one on top of the other. I was small so I could not finish the work fast. I used to work as late as six in the evening. Then even if I had not finished, I would be let off from work. I worked in this vadi till I got married. At first my wage was 50 paise. Then it went up to 75 paise and then it was two rupees 50 paise. I would work the whole day. They didn't give us anything to eat. Sometimes I took my lunch with me, but most of the time I worked on a hungry stomach. I used to feel like eating fruits, which I did. They did not object to our eating some things there. But it is a sweet food so you cannot eat more than two or three chikoos. We were not allowed to take anything home. Sometimes we used to hide chikoos and 'perus' in our lunch boxes, but if we were caught money was cut from our wages. We would be longing to eat something but it was never given to us. Besides, the supervisor was always watching us. One day one of the older girls cut a beetroot into four pieces and we divided it among the four of us. One of the girls got caught and all of us were fined. Only when I went home I would get something to eat at night. Usually it was rice gruel, because if we ate rice it would not last. There were small children at home so the wages were always insufficient. There was a lot of hunger at that time. We would get to eat once a day and that too only rice gruel. We used to go to the forest and come back with bags full of kand. That was our breakfast before going to work. I used to go with my mother and my brothers to catch fish in the creek.

We also had to do domestic work in people's houses. There were compounds along this road, and we would pick sticks from people's compounds to use as fuelwood at home. I used to fetch water, wash vessels and spread cowdung on the floor for which I was given kaneri. In those days children were paid very little. We were asked to assist the older people, for example, to throw away the litter that they would have collected in the farm. Now they don't even employ children.

My brothers and sisters also did mazoori. The older ones went to work and the younger ones were given to families to graze their cattle and goats, and they were fed by the family for which they worked. Some collected fuelwood for cooking and some fetched fodder for our goats. We were in such a bad state that if there was a little bit of 'kanni', broken rice, we would add a lot of drumstick leaves to it and cook 'pala' rice, leaf rice, and make portions of it for each one of us. That's how we were raised by our mother. Now everyone is grown up and standing on their own feet. I remember when I was about 10 or 12 years old, there was a big storm in which we lost all our cattle and our house was destroyed.

At that time there were no 'balvadis', nursery schools. There were only schools for the older children. No one went to school. Bal vadis came to our village only after I was married. None of us went to school, not even my brothers. None of us had a chance to play. Now there are schools, but none of my children have studied. I had sent my son to school, he studied up to the third class, but then he fell ill and dropped out. My daughters also didn't study. They didn't want to go. They used to hide somewhere instead of going to school. I had to work on the field and also do mazoori. If I spent my time getting after them to go to school, then how would I support my family? Now my daughter's children have started going to the balvadi, but soon enough we will be forced to take them to the vadi because there will be no one to give them food when they return.

Did your father have any land?

He had a small plot of land on which we didn't cultivate anything. We only grew grass on it, and sold about two to three cartloads every year.

My grand father was from Asawali. He came as a labourer to Narpad. The landlords must have given him some place to build a house and he continued to work as a labourer and settled here. So the land in Asawali came under the care of my grand father's brothers. Now everyone is dead and gone so why should anybody give us the land? When my grand father's parents were alive, we were not even born. So now who is there even to show us which land is ours?

My father got the plot I told you about. We had to pay a fixed amount to the government for which we got receipts. Then my father fell ill for two or three years and didn't pay the annual instalment and then he died. Two or three years later my mother also died. All of us sisters were married off in different places, except one of my sisters who continued to live with my parents. She was the one who had the receipts in her possession. We don't know what she did with the receipts, now she is also dead. And so the land is without an heir to own it. If you don't have any documentary evidence, how can you claim the ownership rights? It has gone back to the government. We have no land at all. My father died when I had three children and my mother died soon after. It is about 15 years since my mother died, and 10 since my husband died.

Who got you married? Where did you live after marriage?

My father got me married. My mama said he would get me married, but my father didn't allow it. My husband came with some other boys to my village, and the neighbours told him that this poor girl works very hard. So after a couple of days his parents came and did my 'sakhar puda', engagement ceremony. Then after a few days the boy came to my house and found some work near by and he began to live with us. So my father said, work well and I will get you married. My father got us married. We had a proper marriage, clothes and everything. We stayed there till I had two children. He worked as a ploughman on other people's fields during the rains and also on vadis. He lived like a gharorya. His parents gave us nothing for marriage. They were upset that he stayed at my father's place so they took away whatever gifts we got and gave us nothing. My husband began to cry because he didn't have even a paisa in his pocket. They took away about 800 rupees, given mainly by my father's non-adivasi contacts whom he knew from his work at sand digging. For the marriage expenses father had collected a little money and we also took a loan from the vadi owner, which we returned over the next few years.

Those days it was cheaper to get married. We used to make rice and brinjal with dried prawns. But now you have to make peas, dal, potatoes, those days we ate on teak leaves, now people want plates. It is more expensive now. It was better before. Now people want better and more expensive clothes. Earlier, clothes were cheaper and simpler, only the two sarees, red and green, were expensive.

We continued to live in my mother's house and visited my in-laws once a month or so. My husband was the youngest in his house. His brothers were all married and lived separately. Because my mother-in-law was old and father-in-law was a bhagat, busy with other things, my husband was the only one to work on the land. They never gave him any money. That is why my husband had gone away. Then the family decided that each son would feed the old folks for a month, that's how they looked after them for some time. Then my father-in-law fell ill and they came and requested us to move to Kosbad and cultivate the land, which they promised to give us. If you don't come now, you will not get any land, they said. So we went with our children to Kosbad. By that time I had two children. After a few years my father-in-law died, and my mother-in-law decided to divide the land in each one's name. By this time my son and daughter were old enough to be married, so we decided to have one marriage for both of them. My husband used to migrate to Gujarat on the fishing boat. When he returned from the trip, the family of the girl whom my son was to get married with asked for a loan of 2000 rupees before the marriage, and put a condition that the girl would live with them for five years. We felt that this was unfair, so the agreement broke up and only my daughter was married. We planned to look for another girl for my son in the following year. My husband said, I will go on the boat one more time to raise some money for our son's marriage, then I won't migrate any more and he went away. On Ramnavami day, on which the Sai Baba fair is held, I got the news that my husband was missing. It was nearly four or five days after the accident. At that time people said that all the 14 men on the boat were killed. Others said that they had run away. But how can that be? Someone would have returned. How can 14 of them disappear? People tell all kinds of lies.

Either the boat crashed against a rock or another boat, or they were carrying smuggled goods and were pursued and they jumped into the sea for fear of being caught. Only later, did we come to know that the boat had crashed. I don't know the name of the boat owner. I don't even know the name of the village in which he lives. Three of the men who were with him on the boat survived. They say that the others died because they jumped off the boat. I have also heard a story that my husband swam to the shore on the back of one of these men, and they killed him subsequently. Some say that my husband's body was swept ashore and that my son saw his dead body. But, of course, my son did not even see his face. If the body was found, my son should have at least been shown the body. He was buried immediately. If my son had seen it, he would have felt convinced that his father was dead. He would have felt better.

My son was married after we came back to Narpad. He himself raised the money for his marriage. He earned some money from working on the boat and I supplemented it with a loan from the vadi owner. I also got my second daughter married along with him. Our relatives helped, knowing that I was very poor, especially my husband's sister who provided for the toddy and food. My youngest daughter who has these small children, has not had a proper marriage. I could not afford to get her married. My son did not stay with me even for 15 days after his marriage. He lives with his in-laws. His wife is a dangerous one, she has beaten me several times. My son does not give me any money. Sometimes he takes five or ten rupees from me. When I look at his face, I feel pity for him. I think of him as a small child, and for the sake of the child I keep on giving money. He does not give me anything, not even a blouse. That's why I prefer to live with my daughter and work and survive. If I fall ill, my daughter takes the babies and tries to find work. If she earns something, she feeds me. If my son was more understanding, he would have supported me.

How long were you there in your in-law's house?

It must have been a long time, because my children grew up there. We had little land, which was divided among four brothers. Now I have no land, they have divided up my land also among themselves. My father-in-law's land was tenancy land. I don't know much about his landlord. This land belonged to my father-in-law's father-in-law. The work on the land was not much. On the days when I worked on the field, I would also collect fuel in the morning for several days at a time, so that I could go out to work on other days. I had no cattle, so there was not much work at home. I had to find other works to support my family. I worked on a vadi, it was a big vadi with chikoo, papaya, peru, banana, growing in it. It belonged to a wealthy Muslim, who lived in the city and came only once a week. He was also a salt pan owner.

I got 12 rupees there. This was my wage, to begin with, it increased over the years. At that time my husband didn't migrate on the fishing boat, he also worked on the vadi. He worked for several years on the fishing boat. Initially he went to the nearby places, then he began to go far. Other people from our village, the neighbouring hamlets, also went on the boat. I do not know how much my husband earned. They were not paid per month. He would come and give me a fixed sum of 5000 to 10,000 rupees. Men don't say how much they earn because they are afraid that we may ask them for all the money. He would come with 1000 or 2000 rupees on festivals, and buy clothes for the family, and food for the festival. When he came back in the rains, he used to get provisions and salt, chillies and other things for those months. He used to come for Sankrant festival in January and then for three or four months during the rains, when the season was over. Occasionally he came for Holi in March.

Sometimes there was more, but sometimes we would even be in debt. But whatever the payment, he would complete the season because of the respect he felt for the owner. Those who had land, worked on their it, but those who didn't, worked for others. Only those who had extra money could sit and eat throughout the transplanting season, otherwise after having worked on the boat you had to work again. If you didn't, there wouldn't be money even for a cup of tea. Sometimes we didn't even have seeds, so we used to invite other people who had extra shoots to come and plant in our field, and tell them to at least give us the straw. When we planted the shoots in our field with our own labour, then we had to give them the straw. That way we did share cropping. Sometimes we would borrow seed and plant our own rice. Our field was very small, you see. If we kept aside for seed then the produce would barely last for the transplantation season. We would have to work elsewhere and eat for the rest of the year. Even this was true only if we had a good crop. Our land is not of a good quality, the better plots have gone to other brothers.

My husband was also a bhagat. He used to brand for treatment of ailments and also gave medicines for snake bites and scorpion bites. He knew a lot about jungle medicine. He used to go as far as Vajreshwari and on the Barad hill to collect herbs. He had cured a lot of people. He did not teach me much. He would sometimes make the medicine and tell me this is for this ailment and you take it like this. But I did not know which plant or tree it came from. One needs to see the plant to identify where the medicine comes from. He did not identify bhutalis. Even if he suspected someone, he did not say it because it would lead to a fight. I have never seen a bhutali all in my life. I have heard this one or that one being called a bhutali. I have been accused of being one.

Why did you come back to Narpad after your husband's death?

My husband's nephews would drink till late at night and then come to my house. I would be sleeping with my children. One night my husband's nephew opened the door and tried to molest me. I got frightened. It was my husband who had had the operation, not me. How would it have looked if a widow had got pregnant? I tried to tell them to spare me. Then they called me a bhutali. That is how they tried to chase me out of the village. So I decided to come away. If I had directly confronted them, I would have lost my honour. After all, my land and my house was there, I would have had to go up and down. If they did something on the way, what would I have done? So, I left.

There was a big fight, and I decided to take my children and come to my father's house. At that time I decided that I will eat the little I get, but I don't want this harassment. That is when they accused me of being a bhutali and took over my land. Now they come to my house and eat and drink. My husband's niece, this boy's sister is married to one of my brothers, so when they come to my brother's house they come to my house also. Even their mother comes to me when she comes to see her daughter. Now they also invite me over, but I never go. I never want to eat in their house. I will never go. Once I have decided no, it means no. After all I made this major decision of coming to my mother's house. When my children were young, they grazed other people's cattle and survived. We can still somehow survive.

Both my parents were dead at that time. I made a little makeshift hut like a toddy shack in my brother's yard. My brother and his wife used to drink and fight regularly. One day my brother's wife came and hid in my hut. My brother asked me if she was there, I lied to him that she wasn't. Then his wife ran away but he continued to fight with me, and threatened to burn my hut.

I huddled in the corner with my children and wept all night. The next morning my mama's son came. He took me to his mother-in-law's house and gave me a tiny patch in the backyard of her house where people usually wash vessels, and asked me to build a hut there. Since then that is where I cook and eat. Those days we didn't have many utensils, only mud pots. I bought the mud pots after coming here. Whatever I have, I have worked here and bought. My son doesn't help at all. His wife is a terrible woman. She doesn't allow her husband to keep money even for tobacco. She takes it all away the moment he returns from the boat. Even if my son wants to give me, he has nothing to give. One of my daughters gives me 10 or 20 rupees almost every week, that is if she goes to work. My other daughter also gives me four-five rupees for snuff. My youngest daughter and I share everything, we live together.

The day before my husband left for the boat he was a little drunk and he began abusing my sister-in-law. I told my husband to keep quiet. But she had heard it and called out, who are you abusing and cursed him, you are here today but you will not come back to see the village again. The next day my husband left. I had gone to the bus stop to see him off. My sister-in-law had gone to fetch water. She passed us with water pots on her head. My husband called out I am going, and she said, go.

They have taken away my land. Even my house has collapsed. Village people took away the wood from inside the house, that's why it collapsed. There were 5000 tiles on it. Some of them broke when the house collapsed. Many were taken away by people and put on their roofs. I don't want anything from them, I will eat what I get, otherwise, I will starve.

Will you never try to get back your land from your brother-in-law?

No, I am too scared. If I go to the village and they are standing at the door of their house, I speak to them, but I never go inside the house. I don't and I won't even drink water in their house. It is because of this land that I have been reduced to this state. My husband's nephews have the land. They told me, send your son he can also cultivate one field. As if he can stay alone and hold on to the land. He is also sad, but he will not go. These nephews are tough guys. They fight amongst themselves. Last year they fought over our land, and the older brother broke the younger brother's leg with a crowbar. He had to be taken to Mumbai for treatment. He was convicted of murdering his wife and has just finished his sentence and came back. He was in jail for six years. He killed his wife one year after I came back to Narpad. How will my only son survive there? I am not going to send him because he is not going to be able to hold on to the land.

I feel I took the right decision to come away. If I had stayed there, I don't know what condition I would have been in. I will even beg, but I don't want to face that again. The fact that I survived and my children survived is enough for me. If I go back, I may not survive for even the few days that are left of my life. For land they created other problems with me. So it is better to let the land go. After all, my husband was like a father to these boys. Isn't it a shame for them to molest me? If they had allowed me to live in peace and cultivate my small patch, wouldn't I have stayed there with my children?

But then even my son began to beat me, because he would spend all day drinking with his cousins who would fill his head with all kinds of stories. So after having worked all day I would have to come and suffer beatings from my son. One day I had bought some rice, onions and gram flour and was going home to cook. I was carrying it in the pallu of my saree. My son came from behind and pushed me, and all the rice fell on the road. He had come out of their house. I felt bad when they called me a bhutali. I told them as long as your 'kaka', father's brother, was alive you took food from my kitchen, and now I am a bhutali. I insisted them to take me to a village close by, where there is a 'dargah', shrine, to prove if I am a bhutali. They said, let us go, but each one pays for their travel. I said, why should I pay for my travel? You are the ones calling me a bhutali, so you spend on it. I am a widow, where will I bring so much money from? You need about 200 rupees to go and come. You take me and my relatives also. But they didn't do it. There they chain the bhutali and if she is really a bhutali, she jumps into a well. I haven't seen these things, but I have heard people talk. A lot of people who are ill go there to get cured. It is alright to spend money if one is going out of one's free will, but here they were accusing me, so why should I spend money? We didn't go.

Some people say that my sister-in-law, their mother, is a bhutali. She had told my husband in a fit of anger that he would not return and that is what happened. So my doubts were confirmed. But I prefer not to talk about it. I have not even told my son about the molestation, because it will lead to a fight and my son is weaker than them. These fellows stop at nothing, they would not hesitate to kill. That is why I have decided to keep quiet. All my husband's brothers are dead. Even if one of them were alive, I would have had some support.

What was life with your husband like? Do you think of it sometimes?

Before, there was not a care. We had a little land so even if one wanted to go out somewhere, one could pound the rice and leave it for the children. And they would have enough to eat. If there is a man in the house, there is really nothing to worry. Even if there is nothing, he can get a loan. Children need not starve. From where can we women get money? Only if we get work, can we buy food and eat. At the most, the vadi owner may give a loan of 50 or 100 rupees. If he gives a loan today, he begins to cut five or 10 rupees from the wages from the very next day.

My husband was a bhagat, so when he was at home, people would come and ask him to do the ritual to find the cause of illness or bad luck. He would sit on the 'verandah' and spend time with them. I used to look after the house and cook. Sometimes I would go to the market and bring fresh vegetables and fish. Then I would prepare the meal and he would say, feed the children first. I would feed them quickly and we would relax together and eat. The children also remember the good times and the good food they had.

Ever since he died there has been nothing, even on a festival we don't eat well. It costs money. He used to make puris and buy mutton for us. There were new clothes for festivals, for children and for me too. After his death, nothing. Not a single festival, not a single bit of clothing, not even for Diwali. The Sai Baba temple is close to where I live. I go there sometimes. But as luck would have it, I never have a paisa on a festival day. On any other day I may have four or five rupees, but on a festival, I don't have a paisa. I have not celebrated a festival, no clothes, no sweets, no vegetables, no mutton, no chicken. If we are lucky, we have 'dal', lentils. When my husband was alive, we used to really celebrate. I often dream of my husband and my home. We had money then, if he didn't, I had, and if I didn't, he had. We would bring daru, toddy and eat and drink together and enjoy ourselves.

Now there is nothing, absolutely nothing. No joy like before. On festivals I do not even dare come out of the house. Others eat and drink and wear new clothes, we have no clothes, no food, no fun. So I stay quietly at home. It is not right and no fun to go to other people's houses on festival days when you have nothing. They might think, these people also work like us, how come they don't have anything. But all my money goes because the children have to eat.

We need tea powder and sugar and kerosene. There is no electricity and we need two or three lamps. On the vadi where my daughter and I work we tend the vegetables, fill the sacks, attend to the whole farm and yet we have to buy vegetables from outside. The owner doesn't even provide that regularly. We have to buy everything, dal, rice, fish, salt, tamarind. Only water is free. So all the money gets over, and who will give us more money? If someone feels bad for us, they send us sweet bhakris on festivals.

I feel bad that my daughter cannot apply haldi-kumkum on a wedding because she herself has not gone through the marriage ritual. Other young women wear flowers, my daughter doesn't. She remembers her father and says, if my father was alive, we would not be like dogs living outside someone's house.

Even if he was just around and slept in the house, it would have been a source of support to me. He never beat me, we lived like brother and sister. He never raised his hand even once. Those days all one thought about was how to work hard and live well. There were no fears and worries. After his death I have to worry, how will we eat, how will we live? Actually, I am not so worried about food, but I have lost all hopes about having a place to stay. I cannot rely on my son or my sons-in-law. There is a lot of tension in my head. They think about themselves and their families. No one thinks of giving me five kilos of grain in a year. In all these years since my husband died, no new clothes have touched my body. My daughter also buys cheap, second-hand clothes. In fact, I wear clothes discarded by my daughters. Even if the three sons-in-law contributed 50 rupees each, I could buy a saree. Is that a great burden?

I dream of my husband and my home. I had really improved my home and my family. I had plastered all the walls, right to the top. I had climbed on a ladder and plastered the reed walls with mud and cow dung. Only god knows why this happened to me. And, now I don't want that house or anything. When life has gone out of my life, why should I stay there and allow anyone to come at nights?

Now my fate is to work and survive. I don't even have a house. I have built a small hut with dry coconut and toddy leaves in the backyard of my mama's son. It is completely broken down but there is no way I can make a house.

I have never got any help from anyone. I have four brothers but none of them have helped me in any way. If only one of them had given me a little space, only as much as to accommodate a string cot, I would have been happy. I have a sister. She has a lot of problems of her own. Another sister lives in Narpad, but they are very poor. They have no land. Another sister was married in Chinchani, her husband got a second wife, so she was also in a bad state like me. Only last year I got her married to someone. We negotiated the alliance over two bottles of daru, no proper marriage. How could I have supported her? It is better that they have their own life.

My daughters are settled. One son-in-law works on the fishing boat and they have enough to eat. The other is here in Narpad and her husband works as a construction worker. My daughters work occasionally on the vadi. One of them has no children, so they have enough to eat because there are only two mouths to feed. They had a child, but it died.

Are you in this condition because of your husband's death?

No, that is not the reason. The real reason is that I was dispossessed from my land and house. I lost my security and support. My brothers haven't supported me, my son hasn't supported me and now my cousin's wife is also creating problems. Where will I go? When my husband was alive, my life was much better. After he died, I was forced to leave the house and wander from place to place. I have my daughter to worry about. As long as I am alive she will stay with me. But after me what will happen to her? Her husband cannot think straight.

What is wrong with her husband?

He is a good-for-nothing fellow. Every time my daughter gets pregnant, he goes away. I suppose he is afraid that he has to work and earn and support her during pregnancy and after delivery. He has done this on three occasions. Each time I had to look after her. Last time also he left when she was three months pregnant and came after the child was born. He stayed for five days and went away again. I just can't stand him because he doesn't work or provide anything. If he stays in the house with us, I have bad fights with him. He tells people, my children are looked after by my mother-in-law. He goes around borrowing from people, sometimes even from the owner of the vadi where my daughter works. Sometimes he asks me money. My cousin's wife fixed the alliance with him, saying he does not have a father and nor does she. They will earn and live. My daughter did not have a marriage ceremony. He was supposed to be a gharorya. But who could see what he was really like.

We never know where he is. He lives in make-shift huts in the vadi. Surely there are people coming and going from wherever he is, but he never bothers to find out how his children are. This is the kind of man he is. This daughter has three children, two sons and one daughter and all of them are good looking. My daughter is dark, but the children are fair. They have their father's face. I feel sorry that my other daughter has no children although she has taken so much medicine. And this daughter has three children from this useless man. Now we have decided not to keep him in the house because he doesn't give any money. The villagers also tell me, don't keep this man even if he comes back. My daughter doesn't want him.

Both of us take the children and go to the balvadi. The youngest one is so tiny that we wrap him up and put him in a cradle in the vadi. We earn 30 rupees each. Earlier, only one of us was employed there, we could not manage with only 30 rupees. Now both of us are employed. We want to put aside a little from our wages for the children.

Did you not consider living with a man after your husband died?

No, I have never had anyone and I do not want anyone. If I had wanted a man, I could have had a man in Kosbad itself. But my children felt embarrassed about me getting another man. I do not want any man in my life. It was not even a year after my husband had died and somebody from a village close by came with a proposal that could have lived with a man. So I told them the fire in my mind is not yet extinguished and you want me to think of another alliance. I had still to do the last rituals for my husband.

I dream of my husband sitting next to me and holding me and I wake up with a start. I have this dream regularly, once a month or a month and a half. I keep remembering him. Sometimes I think that after having suffered in childhood, I started my family with my husband and I experienced some happiness. But hardly had I begun experiencing happiness that it changed into sorrow. Now I am once again in a state of sorrow.

Are the other adivasis, Warlis, in the same state?

No, it is only my condition that is so precarious. Some Warlis are better-off, most are poor, but only I am in this state because I have no land, no house. I have no extra food to tide us over. Some have land, some don't, but they have husbands or sons or educated children with jobs. Some have brothers who are better-off or parents who are better-off and good to them. Only I have nothing.

There are other women also who lost their husbands in the boat accident, but they are not in such a bad situation. Only one woman is in a state like mine, she has no land. Some have their fathers-in-law and mothers-in-law. Others have grown up sons who look after them. I have no parents-in-law, no parents, no land, no support. The villagers also say about us, poor women, their condition is so bad. In this cold, even before sun rise, when it is still dark, we have to take the little children and trudge to the vadi. But what can we do? If we don't work what will we eat? My uncle's son also pities us. Sometimes they give us tea when we come from work. I hope he would give us food, if we didn't have anything to eat. But who can say it? We feel bad to ask for food. In my husband's house, there was no scarcity of food. And now, let alone food, in summer we don't even get water. We fetch water from the Sai Baba temple in our village.

In fact, the condition of other people in Narpad has improved. I often think what will happen if I fall ill, how will my young daughter manage? Will someone enter our hut at night? There is no man in the house. Even when I am around people are fighting with us, threatening her. When I die what will happen to her and the children. She will also live in the backyard of someone's house. Her situation will be the same as mine. If someone asks to marry her, I will give her in marriage.

Because of this anxiety, my health has gone bad. I cannot eat. I eat well in other people's houses, like I ate today, but in my own house I cannot eat. Nowadays I don't feel happy at all. I forget the problems when I am outside, but when I get back home, I feel bad. It is hard to go through the night. I keep thinking of my children, my house, my situation.

Do you think your life will be better in future?

No, definitely worse. In fact, the worst has already begun. I have my daughter's children to bring up. We often wonder whether to buy wood and kerosene or food. These days each one lives for himself, no one helps another. Enough work is not available. If it rains we get work, if not, all is lost, and there is no food. No one offers us even rice water.

One can get domestic work in the house of the Vadwals, but it is too much work, washing clothes, cleaning vessels, fetching water. Even if one works the whole day, it does not seem to get done, and all you earn is 150 rupees a month. How can one manage with that. Sometimes when work is not available, I collect edible leaves and try to catch fish, small ones along the shore. We take a saree and catch a little fish, if you take a net you get a lot. Some women make daru in my village. I don't know how to make it. One needs plenty of fuel to make daru. Where will I get so much wood?

I have to work even when I am not well. These days my body hurts so much that I can't even bend. But I have to go to work for the sake of my daughter's children.

Do you think if you were educated it might have been better?

No, I don't feel anything like that.

Have you received any compensation or help?

No, nothing. Nobody got me anything. I don't know what to do. I can't think. In Narpad, the Congress and the Shiv Sena are influential. We came to the Sanghatana for help, they gave us hope. I will ask them what is happening about our compensation. In the beginning I used to participate in the demonstrations, once I went to Jawhar and twice to Dahanu. But now for some years I have been too preoccupied with my work. When I was living in Kosbad I used to come to know about meetings and programmes, when and where they were, and I would participate in them along with the others. Now I live alone, there is no one to inform me. I have become isolated in my mother's village. If I was a part of the community, I would have thought of doing this or that with other people. Had I been in Kosbad, I would have felt strong. There, they have a sense of collective strength. I am a lonely being. I don't think there is any hope for improvement.

I tell God to keep my body fit so that I can work and eat. We can only be happy if we can work, or someone gives us a little money, or if we have a proper house. Then we can feel good. Surely I ask God to give me a little happiness. I have a lot of worries in my life. If I got a little happiness, it would have been good. I worry for myself and my daughter. Only if my husband was alive, only if my daughter's husband was a decent man.

I have lost all courage. I can't think of any other option. I will work and eat as long as I can. When I am too old I will go from one daughter to another. They will surely give me some kaneri. If there are babies in their house then I will rock the cradle and get something to eat. And if I don't get anything, I will eat nothing.

Ramabai's life is full of painful experiences of extreme deprivation, insecurity and moreover, loss of faith in human relationships. She has no close relations, she and her daughter being alone in their struggle for survival. No one helps, she feels, the sons, sons-in-law, brothers, sisters, in-laws, neighbours, no one. She has no feelings for the community. She does not identify with the other Warlis or adivasis because in her perception others have improved their situation. No one is in such a bad condition as she is. Her use of the distinct "I" in her narration rather than the general "we" which most narrators predominantly do, is probably a reflection of this alienation. She does not even have the forest to turn to. There are no forests near where she lives. Even that support base, which gives some security, joy, relief to the adivasis from the tyranny of everyday life, is missing from her life.

Her situation is typically that of a landless adivasi without any resources whatsoever, only made harsher by the fact of her being a woman, and worse, a widow. Land, as pointed out earlier, is a major cause of women, especially older women who are widows, for being identified as bhutalis. She is certain that not only her husband's death but the molestation by her husband's nephew which forced her to leave her home and land, is responsible for her present condition. Leaving her husband's home is clearly a major decision and also a turning point in her life. This recurs again and again in her narration. But in an otherwise overwhelming state of helplessness and vulnerability and although life seems to be extremely burdensome for her, she is certain about one thing, that she does not want to return to her in-laws home. This humiliation of having been molested she has not forgotten nor does she want to forget. Although she did not say so clearly in her narration, in all probability, her husband's nephew had raped her. Her conviction seems to give her courage to cope with the extremely difficult condition of life. She does not want to compromise on that.

She feels isolated and alienated from everyone. In fact, she feels abandoned by all her near ones. One wonders if this feeling is a recurrence of her earlier experience of being rejected and abandoned by her father in her infancy. The fact that she survived the sea but lost her husband, a part of her, ultimately to the sea is one of those strange twists of fate which beg an explanation. Given her personal circumstances of alienation from the family, the community, there is little hope of a better future. In the meanwhile, Ramabai continues to make rounds of the different government offices, the court, the Sanghatana office, in the hope of getting some compensation.

VI

Dasma:
"I am proud to be a Warli-adivasi"

Dasma is around 45-50 years old. He is a lean man with a neat appearance. When I met him he was dressed well in shirt and trousers, his hair oiled and combed and his overall bearing one of ease and confidence. He seemed extremely clear in his ideas, opinions, explanations, with little confusion and few doubts. He spoke with conviction and emotions, and at one point during the narration, I was surprised to see tears rolling down his face, when he spoke in a choked voice about his illness which brought him close to death.

His was a systematic narration. He was more specific than the others about dates and places and there were not many unnecessary diversions. Dasma had a good sense of humour and seemed to enjoy laughing at himself. Like Babubhau he laughed often during the interview, when he talked about getting drunk, about gambling and winning and about going to see Hindi films with his friend, Albert.

From where would you like to begin your life story?

You ask me questions.

You can begin from wherever you want

When I was very young, I did not like to go to school. With great difficulty my parents made me go to school. We were very poor. I had no pants, no bush shirt, no slate, no pencil, but Augustin master persisted and got me admitted into school. Those days masters used to come house to house in the villages for motivating the parents. But once I was in school, they used to beat me very badly, beat all of us. They would hit us either with stone slates or with foot rulers. So I began to lose interest in school. I would run away for the whole day, often even without food, just to escape school. One day I hid in a water pipe, pipes were made of wood to carry water to the field. In the afternoon when other students came for a bath, they saw me sitting in the pipe. They went and told the master. So I was pulled out, taken to the school, and so badly beaten that I fell down and my ear was bleeding. My father used to go for coupe cutting in forest those days. He happened to be passing by and he heard my cries. He came with his axe and told the master that this is my only son, if he doesn't study it is all right, but don't beat him. After that the beating stopped. Even though the teachers were adivasis they used to beat us and if we made a mistake, the father, priest, also beat us. We could not complain to the father because he came to the school only once a month, and anyway, who had the courage to do it?

All my teachers were adivasis. We had one teacher, Augustin master, for first to fourth class, who was from village Varkhande. In Talasari, there were two adivasi teachers from Varkhande, and one from another village, Sambarpada. In Talasari we had one teacher for one class. I studied in Shisne school till the fourth standard, after which I went to school in Talasari. I left school after the first term exam of the sixth standard, although I got a second rank. Seventh was matric in those days. I could not finish school because of poverty. This much I can tell you, after I went to Talasari, not a single master beat me. In standard five, I got 100 per cent marks in maths, not a single mistake. I was good in maths. We had English, which I found difficult and we had Hindi, Marathi, geography and history.

In Shisne, we got maize to eat in the afternoon, and in Talasari, we would have maize in the morning, rice in the afternoon and two chapatis at night. None of us liked maize, so we used to be really hungry. Often we ate one chapati at night and saved up one for the breakfast in the next morning. If some one caught us with a chapati, we were punished. We had to really hide it. We used to drink a lot of dal, no mutton, no vegetables, only dal.

We had fun playing games together, football, kho kho, and kabaddi. But no singing, no competitions, no drama, no adivasi dance. In Shisne we once went for a hike to Karanjivira fort. We didn't have a library, I saw one later in St. Mary's School. I remember, father Miranda had kept a monkey in Talasari school, just for fun. Once all the fathers had gone out for a picnic. I had gone to the Talasari market and bought myself a catapult. As I was returning, the monkey saw me and got angry. So with my catapult I threw a stone, it damaged his eye. I was with a friend, one Shingda from Sutrakar, he had seen the whole thing. In the evening father Miranda came to the hostel, and asked what had happened. I said it was my fault, I did not mean to injure the monkey. Those days the punishment for such mistakes was 25 canes, and caning was done in public – your relatives, father, brother, sister, boys and girls of the school, teachers, fathers and sisters (nuns) would come for it. At that time there was one father Rego, he has now become a bishop. I went to him crying, if I have committed a mistake, please forgive me. He explained to me that the monkey is kept for our amusement, and then I said, I will never do it again. The father said, ok take this cake and go give it to the sisters. I went to the convent with the cake and escaped the caning. If I got caning, I would have left the school.

In the village there were about 40 students upto the fourth standard, in Talasari in the fifth, about 35 to 40, but every year there were dropouts, and by the seventh standard there were only about 20. After the seventh, some students went to Papdi in Vasai to another Christian institution, but most did not go because it was too expensive. And one always got a job after the seventh standard. Some people from Warkande went for further studies. Somu Dhangda and one Rinjad from our village also went to Papdi. Those who went for higher studies were all Christians.

In the village school, there were two girls, Nirmala and another girl, and we were 40 boys. They studied only upto the fourth. In Talasari high school, there were two or three from other villages. But none of them finished the seventh, they just got husbands and went away. The girls stayed in the convent. They were Christians. There were few Hindu boys also, about 5 per cent. We also had to go to the church, it was compulsory, but what they spoke, we did not understand.

The fathers used to take 32 'pailis' (approximately 130 kilograms) of rice per year as food expenses. Even that my father could not afford. The student's father had to do free labour if he could not afford to pay the fee, this was compulsory. My father neither worked nor paid the fee, so I had to leave. All my brothers went to school, not my sisters. My father's thinking was that there is no use of giving education to the daughters because it would only benefit their husbands, so why educate them?

What did you do after school?

I got married in 1972. After school, I did a course in carpentry for one and a half years, after which I went to Saint Mary's Cambridge High School in Mazgaon, Mumbai. I worked on the telephone, I used to receive calls when the operator was not there, give messages, call people. Before this I was in the tailor room, I used to sort out fathers clothes, give the dirty clothes for washing, and when the clean clothes come, sort them out and give them to the fathers. I was there for five years.

I did my carpentry course for one and a half years, after which I had no money to buy the tools that I needed. Father Banyon was in Talasari. I told him, father, I am very poor, please give me some work if there is any. Then he said, there is work, but you need a partner. So I said, I will tell Albert Dhangda. Father said, come to Talasari on Thursday. The next day someone from Varkhande, had to be taken to a hospital in Andheri. Because we had no money for travel, we travelled with him to Andheri and from there, one brother took us to St. Mary's.

There was a father Pordo, a Spanish priest, there, who was in charge of all the workers. He asked me to read some numbers written on the steps, 1955 or 1957. When he found that I could read numbers in English, he put me in the tailoring room, because there everything was in English. Albert was given the job of a 'mali', gardner.

At first they gave us a weekly wage of 30 rupees for six days, with free food and place to stay. After one and a half to two years, we became permanent, and our salary was 199 rupees. See, I got married in 1972. I had taken leave for 20 days for my marriage. And you know how adivasi marriages are, they spread over several days. On the day of my wedding, my wife got her menses for the first time and during menses we adivasis cannot receive the halad. They told us, you will have to wait for seven days. Seven stretched to 10 and I returned to work only after one month. When I went to the school, the father was very angry and asked me to at least produce a medical certificate. I thought that since I had gone for my wedding they would condone it. He said I should have telephoned, I agree I could have, but I thought they would understand. After all it was my wedding. Someone advised me to beg for forgiveness, but I did not. The accountant told me, you may go home there is no more work for you. I got very angry. The other people from Goa and Mangalore working there were good friends with me. They advised me to go to the rector and ask for forgiveness, after all I had worked for five years. But I was very angry. I thought, I have land, why should I beg them for work? So I came home.

When I came back, I began working as a mukaddam for one Bhuyal from Manor. It was a road construction work. I decided things like how to route a kuccha road, dig gutters, etc. He, too, paid me five rupees a day. I worked for him for five years. Those days I was in the habit of drinking and that is how I fell seriously ill. I had TB (tuberculosis). I was cured in the mission hospital in Vadoli. The moment I came home from work, I would be after drinks. Even food did not matter. I spent nearly four and a half months in the hospital. Since then I have stopped drinking.

I was drinking long before I got married. I know every lane in Mumbai where you get liquor. I once went to Worli with a friend to buy liquor, it was cheap there. We bought two bottles. But then my friend was accosted by some men and robbed of his watch. Nothing happened to me. We ran for our lives. I never get into this kind of trouble.

I got into heavy drinking when I was working for the contractor. I was doing road work in a village called Vankas. Often people would come to me pleading, save my mango tree, my jackfruit tree. It was in my hands to save the trees. If I saved their tree, they would invite me for a meal and a drink. I would bring my lunch box back home. My wife used to plead with me to eat, but I would continue to drink even at home. I felt that I was getting it for free, so why not drink. After all I was not spending my own money. Of course, my wife objected. She used to tell me, but I was not willing to listen to her at all. There are women who nag their husbands, especially those who drink, but my wife has not spoken one harsh word to me to this day. At that time I thought it was fun. Now when I look back, I think I could have died. My wife had left home with our two sons. I had only two children then. I spent a lot of money for my treatment. My situation became desperate. Had I died, what would have happened to my children.

I was working in Zari and I got high fever. I fell under a tree. Father D'Cruz had come to the village for mass. My father was still alive. He went to father D'Cruz and asked him to bring a vehicle and then I was taken to the hospital and got admitted there. I had taken my son to the hospital the previous week, and everyone had seen me. So they were surprised to see me. The doctor said I had TB. I was very scared. After the illness I quit the job with the contractor around 1978, now I work in my field, and if I get good carpentry work, I do that. I don't go for mazoori. There is enough work at home.

I spent two years in misery. My wife is very, very intelligent. After that we have a happy life. We have sufficient land and we cultivate all of it. We collect cow dung together, we prepare our rab together, and she would tell me, come on we have to do this and that. When I got married, my father's land was already with me. Both my parents were alive. My mother died first soon after my marriage and my father died five years later. Both died on August 14, and on a Friday. Two years after my father died we divided the land among three brothers, because although the brothers might have wanted to stay together, the wives did not get on well. Each brother got two and a quarter acres. Our sisters did not get any, but their husbands have land. None of us are in extreme poverty.

Do you remember everything about your illness and the time of recovery?

My wife and I often talk about those days, about what would have happened to her and our children if I died. My wife had a quarrel with my younger brother's wife when I was in the hospital and she had left home and gone away. My brother informed me, so I asked the doctor's permission to go home and sort out the problems. I went to my in-law's house and told my wife, as long as I am alive, you stay with me, after my death, you are free to go. My wife came back with me. Whenever I think of this incident, tears come to my eyes. She was a good woman, so she came with me. Had she not been good, she would have made excuses, put my children through misery, and I would have died. Her father also advised her to go. I told her, I haven't said anything to you. If you have a problem with anyone in my family, come and tell me in the hospital. As long as I don't say anything to you, don't leave.

From where does your wife come?

My wife is from Dapcheri. Her father had land, which was lost to the Dapcheri dairy. Actually he had got the land from his sister, he was a sub-tenant on his sister's husband's land, so he only had the right to cultivate that land. This is how relationships were in those days. My father-in-law was the son of a second wife, and those days the children of the second wife did not get any land. It is only now that there is a law whereby they also have a right to the father's property. My mother-in-law is from Ganjad but her father died early so her mother remarried. My wife came from a better-off family, my father-in-law's father was rich enough to marry two wives. They were not happy to give their daughter into our family, but the fact that we owned land was in our favour. A cousin of mine from Haladpada was the one who chose my wife for me. I was in Mumbai at that time.

Tell me about your parents, about your childhood.

Both my father and mother were from Shisne, my mother was from the Vavre family. I think my ancestors came from Zari in Talasari. I don't know why they came to Shisne, whether they married in Shisne or what. Navshya Dhangda came first and then my ancestors followed. But Shisne village was established by the Gowaris. Then came Vasawlas, Parhads, then Dhangdas, and after them came Vavryas, Bodles, Vangads, Rabads. At present there are no Vasawlas and Parhads in the village.

We were six children, three brothers and three sisters. I was the eldest of the sons, my sisters were older than me. Since we are of the same father, all the three brothers have a little land. The sisters were married off outside, one in Dhamangaon and two in Vadoli. Although I was the eldest, the land was divided equally.

My parents were very poor. They had land but those days no work was available. We had four acres and ten and a half gunthas of land. We also had a three-acre plot in the common grazing lands. Each brothers has about two and a quarter acres of ancestral land I have also cleared a forest plot of about three and a half acres. I have approximately five acres of land. I grow mainly rice, some varai, nagli, udid and tur.

Last year because it did not rain, the crop was not sufficient. It was a drought year for everyone, but otherwise the crop lasts us for the whole year. We never have surplus. Somehow we stretch it till the new crop comes. No matter how frugally we eat, we have to buy at least one sack of rice. After all, we are 13 members in the family, Rajesh has a wife and Sunil has a wife and three children.

My father bought the land from Bafna, the Marwadi landlord who lived in Naresh vadi. It was a tenancy land. My father and mother worked on the land together. My mother's father had a lot of land, but he had two wives and many sons. They didn't give any land to my mother.

There was enough food cultivated, but no work was available those days. So my parents had to sell their rice to the Marwadi for money. He gave only 12 rupees for four 'pharas' of rice. Whatever we grew was taken away by the Marwadi. Then we had to take loans. Despite having land we were starving. I remember those days of hunger. Had there been enough, I would have studied comfortably up to the seventh standard, and then taken up a job. Others who were with me became school masters, but because of my father's poor condition, I couldn't.

The sowkar was very oppressive. My father used to say, "I have urinated blood because of this man. Many people left their land because they couldn't bear the harassment, but I have earned this land for you with my blood."

As soon as my father was married, he was taken away by the sowkar to Dahanu and my mother stayed behind. He must have been beaten, I don't know. My mother was not sexually oppressed, many women were.

The sowkar took a khand of five manns. Whether you had food or not was immaterial. Whatever was harvested was taken by him. Those who are landless today lost their land because they could not bear the oppression. They took the position, we don't want land, we don't want oppression. So their sons don't have land. Bodles were the village patils, so they got land without paying khand, because these were government lands. The sowkar lived in Dahanu, but his mukaddam, by the name of Rabad, lived in the village. Although he was an adivasi, he used to oppress us on orders from the sowkar.

My father did veth and so did I for the forest department. I must have been 12-14 years old then, soon after I left school. The patil or the 'kotwal', village revenue functionary, used to call us to work. They must have been paid by the forest department, and they must have eaten it up, I don't know. But we got nothing. Sometimes we got firewood in exchange for labour.

We were extremely poor. What joy can I speak of, there is not a single day which I can remember when I had three square meals. I cannot remember any joyful moment about my life, I can tell you about sorrow. My parents were kind and they worked hard, particularly my mother, she was very caring of me, of us, but they simply had nothing, so what could they give us.

My father spoke of a famine of 1856, when people ate honey and the inner kernel of the jowar stalks. And if they had to dance, they would hold the reed walls of the house to keep their balance, they were so weak. And to sit, they would make a cushion of cloth and sit on it, because their buttocks had become skin and bones.

I did not experience anything quite like this, but I have memories of a drought. You see the mud check dam above Somu Vavrya's field, it was built by the Marwadi during the drought. It is still there. In the afternoon all the labourers were given kaneri. We have also faced hunger, but there was more hunger before. We have eaten red jowar, the only thing that was available in the ration shops, and a porridge made of 'jhou', a cereal given in jails. From the forest we got roots, leaves and tubers. I used to go regularly to the forest to bring some leaves, plain dal doesn't taste good, so we added leaves to the dal.

Who trained you to do jungle medicine?

My grandfather and father were 'bhut bhagats', and also practised a little jungle medicine. My father had two brothers, Kakdya and

Lahni, but neither were bhagats. Kakdya was not married and Lahni died young. My 'khaki', father's brother's wife, remarried in Palghar and took her children away with her.

My father didn't get any money from bhagtai. When you do bhuta and the patient is cured, they give you coconut, chicken and daru, but not money. When you do jungle medicine then whatever medicine you bring from the forest, you bring it in the name of the person who is ill. For that people pay. Earlier they paid five rupees, but now they give 50 or 60 rupees because you have to roam in the forest searching for the medicine. There is also danger in the forest. When you move in the forest, you have to keep a witness, and pray that I am moving around in the forest in order to heal so no harm should come to me and after the person gets cured, I will repay you. The witness is in your mind.

For certain medicines, like, for example, for cough, one has to go to the forest early morning before sunrise, go to the river, put some vermilion into the river, then find the root, crush it and make the medicine. My father taught me about different medicines for different illnesses. My father also did diva and 'bhuta', propitiated the spirits and identified the witch and also gave jungle medicine. He learnt it from a big bhagat called Dalvi in our village. I voluntarily decided not to do diva and bhuta. Bhagats get a lot of respect, for giving medicine he gets a little money. The money is used to fulfil the promise made to the spirit of the forest for protecting the bhagat and healing the patient. The spirits ask for coconut, chicken, toddy and in their name we take it. We call this 'usgal'.

I learnt about jungle medicine after my marriage. For a long time my father just told me about medicines and their value and asked me to bring this or that from the forest. I began to take interest. When I had learnt enough, on two or three occasions he asked me to bring the medicine with my own hands. After that in my name he sacrificed a chicken, did a ritual, and said, from now on you will effectively treat people. My father had only told me about the various taboos and rituals, but then I began to practise them on my own. It is not enforced, but it is a self-imposed discipline for the treatment to be effective, the bhagat has to do it.

The taboos are related to everyday life, food, sex, etc. For example, no one should see you bringing the medicine, preparing the medicine and administering the medicine. No one should even talk to you till the medicine is brought, pounded, prepared, administered. The patient is also instructed not to speak a single word. Only after the patient has eaten the medicine and washed his mouth, I would be free.

Also, rituals must precede collection of the medicine. You must utter names of gods before collecting the herbs. The herbs and trees are themselves gods. We say, for example, I am giving this medicine in your name, not from my hands, heal the person. Give me your protection, I have surrendered myself to you. Whatever happens to me, I am in your hands.

Young men who want to learn about diva and bhuta are trained by a senior bhagat in a remote place in the forest near a water source. Their training starts in June. They work during the day and at night they go in a group to this spot to worship this 'vidya'. They are there until the month of October. Till then they can't eat food cooked by a woman, they have to cook their own food. After they have acquired this vidya, they have to sacrifice a chicken, offer daru, etc, only then can they practise. Even 10 or 12 year olds can be a part of this vidya. I did not go through this, but my father did. If I had not gone to school, I would definitely have gone for this. Because I went to school, I lost my faith. Every year there is a group that goes for this training. Now there are very few old bhagats left, most of them are like me.

My father was willing to teach me, but I did not have the desire to learn it. I know how to drive away the evil spirit, but I don't do it. I feel there is something wrong in it. I don't have faith. Often people who are ailing are desperate and the bhagat, rightly or wrongly, points to some poor woman who is hunted by the sick man and his relatives. But she may not be a witch. I feel it is better to heal a person with your own hands, rather than by blaming another person.

Do you believe in bhutali?

Yes, I do. My father could distinguish between the work of the bhutali from an ordinary illness, but this is a highly advanced vidya and few bhagats have it. For example, my son used to hiccup and whine. I took him to the hospital a couple of times, but the medicine had no effect. My father told me that this was the work of a bhutali. But he asked me to take the diva to another bhagat called Kom. He confirmed what my father had said, and asked me to do some rituals. I performed the ritual and my son was cured. This knowledge is acquired from god. They take the name of Mahadev and do their work.

Since the bhagat identifies the bhutali, women are naturally their enemies. They can do bhuta to kill even a bhagat. Bhutali is more powerful. If the bhagat is good, and there are such bhagats, then he can overpower a bhutali. For example, my father-in-law, who was a good bhagat, was once afflicted by a bhutali. He couldn't get up for two days. He knew that a bhutali had done it, he even knew who had done it, but he could not reveal the name. In some cases the bhutali threatens the bhagat, if you reveal my name, I will kill you. So after having identified the cause, the bhagat goes ahead with the cure without naming the bhutali. In the past, bhutalis were named, but now the bhagats don't reveal the names because it leads to fights.

I was also pursued by a bhutali once, but not harmed. My mother had gone to the shop near the highway, and did not return till very late. So my father asked me to look for her. I went to Amboli and started drinking. As I was returning home at night, I heard footsteps. Suddenly I found myself face to face with this old woman. We looked at each other but I couldn't bring myself to say anything. Then I moved on and after a few steps a cold breeze swept over me.

I had an experience with a cat once. I was sleeping and a cat came into my house. I recognised it as a bhut cat, so I thrashed it and pulled its hind legs apart. The next day I saw an old woman walking with her legs apart. It was she that had come in the form of a cat at night. I asked her what had happened, she said she had fallen down. After that my son Rajesh fell ill. The old woman lives near my house.

Why would she want to harm you?

For example, if you are eating good food, and she doesn't have it, she will cast an evil eye. There are clear indicators whereby a bhutali can be identified. For example, a woman who is learning 'bhutali vidya', training for a witch, does not even touch her husband till her education is over. You just can't call any woman a bhutali. There are examples of old and helpless women being hunted as bhutali, but those bhagats are crazy. There is a lot of madness in our society, but that goes on.

Many bhagats are very powerful. I will tell you an incident, When Rajya's child fell very ill, he was admitted to Swastik hospital. The child was operated, they must have spent nearly 20,000 rupees. Then someone told Rajya about this bhagat in Randha, and Rajya immediately took the diva and went to him. The moment the bhagats saw the grains of rice, he immediately told him your son is dead, what are you doing here? Then he told him someone had harmed his son. He asked him, had two women come to grind flour on your grinding stone, Rajya said, yes, had you bought fish that day, yes, did you share it with them, no. The bhagat told him now your son is dead, had you come earlier I would have done something.

If you don't believe in it, it is all right. I have nothing to say to those who don't believe in it. But I believe in it because I have seen it.

What kind of treatment do you do?

I have full faith in forest medicine. I cure all ailments, A to Z. Mostly women come with women's problems. Last year a lot of men came to me. I even cure people from far off places. People come in carts and rickshaws. That spectacled Dhodya, his wife was about to die and I cured her. He told me, brother, I have no money, I will go out to work and pay the 'usgal'. But it is two years now and he has not shown his face. Now I will have to spend that money, because I have made a promise to the spirit of the forest.

I give medicines for stomach ache, teeth problem, fever, anything and everything. I know what illnesses I can cure and what I cannot. I ask the patient for the symptoms, and I have no problem of sending them to the doctor. We don't have the cure for TB. I knew I had TB, so I did not go to another bhagat. People go to the bhagat and they go to the doctor. I also opt for the doctor when my family members are ill. I have never done bhuta on any of my six children. Only once I took Sunil to Kom bhagat and he did bhuta. Nobody had harmed him, but there are things in nature that can cause affliction, then there is a need to do bhuta.

Most bhagats only practise what they are taught, but I do a lot of experimentation. The bhagat has to eat a lot of herbs to see their effect. The coupe felling and the clearing of the under growth in the forest, have reduced the availability of herbs. It is strange that some herbs, which have disappeared from the forest, you can find only near towns, in the creeks near cities. Sometimes we have to walk for the entire day to search for the medicine. That is why we take mazoori for giving the medicine. You cannot travel by train or bus, you have to go by foot, because some rituals have to be observed. I know a medicine, which is available only in Nala Sopara, but I don't give it, who will walk for days to bring it. Some people do travel by trains and buses, but then it is not so effective.

There are some herbs, the important ones, which I collect during Dassera, others during Sankrant and store them. Herbs collected at that time have special properties. I go to the forest near my village. I enjoy roaming in the hills. Sometimes I go with others, sometimes alone.

But I am certain this knowledge will not die, nor will this medicine. It will be found. Man will find it from somewhere or the other. What you need, you need, what you really want, you get. Those that are important, have to be planted. What is available far away has to be planted or stored, otherwise how can we practise?

Somehow people want to be cured. If they don't get cured by the doctor, they go to the bhagat, and if they don't get cured by the bhagat, they go to the doctor. I don't consider a doctor as my competitor or my enemy. They are different, the bhagat relies on 'mantra', chants, the doctor does not. The diagnosis may be the same. For example, my 'mami', mother's brother's wife, had a swelling in her intestine. I told her so. Then she went to the doctor and he said the same thing. Then my mami told me, Dasma, you were right. I examine with my hands, I learnt the skill of examination from my father. I also learnt to brand and to give injection. I have given injections to many TB patients and cured them. One multi-purpose worker taught me to give injection. I am so good at it that people come to me. Once a child was given an injection by a doctor and it turned into an abscess. They finally brought the child to me. I cut it with an injection needle, and cleaned it, and it got all right. I have done many small operations. My wife fights with me, why do you do this dirty business, I will not eat food touched by you, she says. People come to me because it doesn't hurt them when I do it. They get all right, they are still alive and well. I swear this is true. I cannot make a long list of persons I have cured. Many serious patients have been brought to me in my house and I have cured them. That's why I have 100 per cent faith in my medicine. It is against illness. It is my duty to give to whoever comes.

I don't pray to your gods, will it work on me?

100 per cent it will work on you. But if the medicine is to be effective, you have to observe all the food restrictions. You can take the medicines wherever you want, in a motor car, in a train, in a plane, it will work. I pray to the gods to make it effective for you, so the question of your belief doesn't come.

Would you have liked to be a doctor?

Personally I would have preferred to be a doctor, because the work I am doing is that of a doctor. I would have had more information, money is not that important, but yes, more recognition. I had an opportunity to study Ayurveda, but then I don't have much education, I don't know English, it would have been difficult.

How many children do you have, what are they doing?

I live with my wife and six children, three sons and three daughters. Sunil, Rajesh, Gita, Babita, Vandana and Dilip. The eldest son studied upto the sixth standard, then he dropped out. I tried very hard to make him study, I even beat him, but then he fell ill and I got very frightened, so I let him be. The second son dropped out after the eighth standard, the third daughter appeared for the tenth last year, but failed in two subjects. She has filled the form to appear again. The younger three are studying, one in the ninth, and the other two are in the eighth. My thinking is that I have nothing to give them, so let me give my daughters good education, it may come of use to them.

Two of my sons are married, we live together. The elder one has been working as an electrician for a contractor for the last 15 years in Dapcheri. He doesn't get much of a salary, the contractor gives him advances of 500 or 600 rupees. He gets 80 rupees a day and food. He doesn't get work everyday, and when he does, he has to spend at least 10 rupees on travelling. Besides, he has a wife and three children, how can this be sufficient? There is no security with the contractor. My son doesn't have the necessary certificate to work independently, which he can get only after appearing for an examination, but to do that he needs a certificate from his employer. Every year his employer promises to give it to him, but when the time comes, he makes one excuse or the other. My son is very clever. My second son is also an electrician but refuses to work for the contractor seeing how he has exploited his elder brother. So he goes here and there.

My sons-in-laws are very well-off, they are the 'khandanis', people with a little surplus. They have plenty of land, they were the village 'karbharis', traditional village administrators. My daughter-in-law does agricultural work and son goes out to work. I don't need to employ outside labour, we have five persons to work on our land. The children have their vacations during the harvesting season, so they also help. My son has three children, but they are small, they don't go to school yet.

My sons go for sand excavation sometimes, the rate is 100 rupees for two truck loads. Lots of young people migrate for this work. My sons work in the brick kilns, there the work is very hard. They don't want to do it, so they just don't go. Women go to harvest rice or to work in the vadis around Vasai and Saphala. We have no big vadis, no big sowkars in our village. Some adivasis now have small vegetable vadis and grow tomato, onion and vangi. There are a few Warlis who are rich, they have grains and money. There are also those who don't have enough for the next meal.

I have been teaching Rajesh about forest medicine. I did not teach Sunil, because he is not meant for it. You ask the boy to bring medicine and then see if it is effective, whether he has the quality in his hands. For example, my bullock was ill, so I first asked Sunil to bring some medicine and tie it around the bullock's neck, The ritual involves standing stark naked while tying the medicine. When Sunil did it, the bullock didn't get well, but when Rajesh did it, it worked immediately.

I will teach my sons. I don't mind sharing my knowledge with others, but the medicine is not effective unless you observe all the dos and don'ts. As long as I am alive, my sons will not practise.

My children have been good. I am concerned that they should study and do well. I often worry whether my daughters will get good husbands. My one daughter has failed in two subjects, of course, I am disappointed. She didn't study hard enough. Otherwise, they are all right. They respect me, obey me, listen to me. I am really worried about my children's future. I tell them, study well, today we have some land, tomorrow it will not be enough, I will not be there.

I feel things will only get worse. How much land will my three sons get when it is divided and what will their children get? Even if they study there are no jobs. Our situation will only get worse.

You are a practical man, you seem to have managed your life sensibly, what do you think is responsible for this?

Just like I tell my children do this and that, and guide them in life, my father and mother used to tell me, dadu do this, do that. My father would tell me, don't follow your wife, she may put wrong ideas in your head. They would nag me about work, about agricultural work. That's how one is guided in life. Lots of people say that Dasma was sensible, that is why his family could come out of poverty and misery.

Actually, it is a long story. When I finished the carpentry course, there were three or four girls who were after me. One of them was even married, but she was willing to live with me. Around the same time the instalment for our land was due for payment. A lot of people eyed our land because it is very fertile. They thought we had nothing to eat so how would we pay for the land. Our relatives offered to pay for the land, and give us another piece of land in return. My father was seriously considering that offer, but I told him, don't do anything like that. I was engaged to many girls during that time, each family offered to pay for the land, keep the land for themselves and give me their daughter. I said, I will not marry till I get my land. Then I went to father Banyon and told him, if I stay here, I will go mad. Please give me work outside, I have to earn to pay for the land. I told my father, arrange for the money, take a loan, do whatever you like, I will earn and pay it back.

I went to work in St. Mary's. It was Christmas time, and 15 boys had taken leave to return to the village. I had not taken leave. I went to brother and told him, I also want to go. He did not give me leave, but gave me 50 rupees. I had 15 rupees of my own. I bought toddy and drank with my two friends. In the end I was left with only 15 rupees. I was just lying down, thinking. I didn't even have my clothes on. I couldn't sleep. Those days I was into playing matka (gambling) and cards. I took the money and went to play matka. I played 12 and a half rupees on number 55 and I won 1000 rupees. I went back and told my friends, I will give you a treat but this is not my money, someone has given it to me. The next day was my weekly off. So I took the money home. I gave my father money to pay for the land and bought a saree and a blouse for my mother, she didn't have clothes. I bought things we needed for the house and then went back.

All the fellows there were saying, we have been playing all these years but we have never got 1000 rupees. I am lucky in gambling, I always win. Once I had a torn five rupee note. My friends were playing. When you are gambling torn notes are allowed. So I put my money and in the beginning I lost and lost and lost and came down to 20 paise. Then I won nine rupees, and I really played, and I won and won and won till I had 350 rupees. I took a taxi, and took my friends with me and went to see the film 'Mother India'.

My parents did not know these stories. Till they died they did not know where the money came from. I told my parents, I am working, I have earned the money. I told my wife and my children also. But no one in the village knows.

I would definitely have lost my land if I hadn't won the money. But my destiny worked in my favour, and I had the blessings of the gods. I often think, how could I have saved 700 rupees and paid for the land. My illness and this money from matka changed my life. I don't think matka is bad, it is a game of luck, a sheer chance. My life improved because of it. Just imagine that day when I earned the money, I would have slept hungry and because my leave was cancelled I would have been depressed. I had had toddy and most of the money was finished, so I thought, let me see, if I lose everything I won't go home.

I don't ever lose. Even in cards I don't lose. I have kept a rule for myself, if I lose 10 rupees I stop playing, because it means that my luck is not good that day. If I win today, I don't play tomorrow. Once during Diwali, I gambled with five of my friends from the village. We played till five in the morning and I cleared every one out. Next morning I went to Talasari and bought steel vessels, clothes for the children and came back. I also gave Radki's son money because he didn't have any money for toddy. They came on their own to play, I didn't ask them, so I didn't feel bad. In fact, I asked them to stop but they wanted to go on. Now I don't play much because I don't want my sons to get into the habit of gambling. It can destroy everything.

Do you have happy memories of your stay in St. Mary's?

Yes. The Goan and the Mangalorean workers were very good to me. The cook was from Ratnagiri, we called him Mama. He used to call me last to eat and give me mutton and chicken. I really enjoyed myself there. The fathers used to drink wine, made from small grapes, during mass. I used to be in-charge of that. Once during Easter I drank a lot of it at one go, it is so sweet, that it went to my head. I was knocked out. I slept till nine in the morning, I didn't know that it was so intoxicating. I thought I am used to drinking daru, this won't affect me.

But I am still angry with the fathers because they did not sanction my 10 days leave. And they call themselves father, serving the poor. Is this their service? I am not afraid of the fathers, are they tigers? If a Marwadi had behaved badly with me, I would understand. But fathers who preach love for all beings treated me so badly, that I cannot accept. I have never been to St. Mary's since I returned to the village. I have no reason to go. Even those fathers must have died.

The priests have helped your family, didn't your father or you think of converting to Christianity?

They may have expected us to get converted, but my father was a bhagat, and he was clear that if he converted he would lose his bhagtai. Those days we also had our clan gods, Naran dev and others in our house, so there was no question of conversion.

Naran dev is now in Zari and Hirva is in Nagar Haveli. These clan gods are not stationary, they must move to different members of the clan. Everyone has a share of the gods, and whoever wants to, takes the god home. But it is expensive to bring them home.

There are people who practise both religions, but my father and I feel that we must stick to one religion. If you are a Hindu, then be a Hindu. In our Dhangda clan only one family converted to Christianity, and in the village, one Pagi family did. But besides them no one. I don't know why they converted, but my father told me this story. Navshya Dhangda was a big bhagat, he had killed a woman suspecting her to be a witch and then he converted to Christianity. The other story is that there was a cholera epidemic, and the priests cured someone from Navshya Dhangda's family and that's why he accepted their faith. I don't consider their faith superior to ours. After all, god is one. We believe in Naran, Hirva and Himaya.

When I was in Talasari I participated in all the activities. I know all the Christian songs. I often led the choir.

Do you like to live in your village?

No, if I could get a good price for my land, I would leave my village and go elsewhere. My relatives from the village are very bad. When I had just returned from Mumbai, and hadn't yet fallen ill, my family was eating and drinking well. One of my relatives got jealous and filed a false case of theft against us. He himself brought his radio and left it in our yard, and put his trunk of clothes on the road and began to scream that he had been robbed.

Next day, the villagers were gathered and the matter was brought up. I told them when we were in extreme poverty we never stole, what is the need for us to steal now, when we have enough of everything. These relatives of mine are 'khandanis', and they are the ones who wanted our land. So they were just jealous that we had enough food and clothes, and there was no way they could get our land. Since they couldn't get the villagers against us, they went to the police station. I told the police the same thing, you can come and check my house, there is still enough grains, and everything is in order, what is the need for me to steal. These people are after our land.

Then they tried another way. They went to a bhagat, paid him 500 rupees, and told him to say that he had done diva and found us guilty. But this bhagat came and told us. So, I went to the police station, the police called the bhagat and those people and finally the matter was closed. They are very bad people. Useless people.

They harass me because they are khandani people and want to dominate, but they can't ride roughshod over me because I answer them back. They can't take it from someone as poor as me. In the past when we had nothing to eat, my parents would borrow from them and repay with labour, transplanting for them, grazing their cattle. I stopped this. My father would say, we will have to remain hungry and I would say, it is better to be hungry than labour for them for free. They are angry because they have lost their control over us. They say that I am responsible for not allowing them to usurp our land. Also because I didn't accept their daughter in marriage. Had I done that they would surely have claimed the land. I have continuous problems with them. They have even beaten a lot of people, but people don't stand up to them. I am not afraid of them. After all, what can they do? At the worst, they will kill me. One day we have to die anyway.

They have been bullies from the time of their father and grandfather. Terrible people. A lot of my family members say if we could only get some land elsewhere, we would leave this village and go.

With the family, brothers and sisters, when we are not drunk our relations are very good. We visit each other. If someone is in trouble and we get a message, we immediately help.

Relationship with the neighbours is not good. Some are with the Bharatiya Janata Party (BJP), some with the Congress, some with Nationalist Congress Party (NCP) and some with Kashtakari Sanghatana. There is a distance between people belonging to different groups. At first it was good in our village, everyone was with the Sanghatana. Then the Sanghatana broke. My children are not active, but we have no political differences.

Anyone who tries to bring awareness in the village, anyone who speaks of good things, gives good advice, is opposed. People go to those who are after money. Since last year the BJP has started Ganpati puja in our village. They collect 15 rupees from each household and 30 rupees from each young man. I have two sons, so I have to contribute 75 rupees in all. From where am I going to get so much money? Do you think things will improve this way? After sometime, they will think of something else and collect money for that. Instead, if they collect money to help some poor person who is ill, to go to the hospital and so on, things would improve. Spending money on gods does not improve things, often it creates problems where there are none.

Has there been some improvement since your father's time?

Of course, there has been much improvement since my father's days. Now children are better educated, there is more food to eat, there is a variety of food. In my father's days there was a situation of extreme poverty. We did not even have chilly powder. It is better now.

Me and my wife are responsible for all the improvement in my house. We built a house and got everything. My children have contributed nothing, nor my parents. So far we have neither received nor sought help from anyone. I have never taken any government schemes, it has too much paper work. We developed with our own resources. My wife often says, when we started life we lived in such poverty, now we are much better-off.

Would you go to the city, if you got an employment there?

No, I don't like the city. In the city one gets some illness or the other. When I was there, I had some problem with my ears, pus used to come out continuously. The doctors wanted to operate, they had even given me the date of the operation. But I got scared. I took seven days leave and came home. I put some herbal medicine and the problem has not occurred since 1972.

Even if I got a big house, money, I wouldn't go to the city. By one big illness, all your money would be wiped out. I like agriculture, I like open spaces that are not crowded, clean air, fresh leaves from the forest. What do you do in the city – from one building to another, one lane to another, with all the filth, not to speak of the mosquitoes. In the forest you can move around, there are no lanes. You are like a king. You can go anywhere you want.

People do go to the city, but they go for work. They have to do something to fill their stomach. If they got what they needed here, they would not migrate. I also went to the city for work.

But the good thing is, you have films in the city. I learnt a lot from movies, from films like 'Samaj Ko Badal Dalo' and 'Mother India'. I saw 300-400 movies in five years. I have written the names of all the movies I had seen, I have the list with me. Really, I learnt a lot from films, I decided for my life which line I wanted to take, where it would take me. They have influenced me. From 'Parivar', for example, I learnt about family planning. I saw 'Do Kaliyan' also. It has had a good influence on me. In the end, the bad man suffers and repents. That is important. It teaches what is important in life. I also saw 'Mera Naam Joker', made by Raj Kapoor in the R K Studio. Someone gave us 17 tickets free for that film.

The new films are rubbish, the old films were very good. I have named my children after film stars. There was not a single Sunil in my village. People did not know how to say it, they used to say Shinal, which means an adulterer. One day a woman called my son Shinal, so I told her, has my son seduced your daughter that you are calling him this dirty name. My second son is named after Rajesh Khanna, Vandana's name I saw on a poster on a truck, Babita was named after I saw a film with Babita and Jeetendra, Geeta I did not name and Dilip was named by Sunil. I gave my wife the name Anita after I saw a film called Anita. Her real name is Rami.

How do you manage at present?

I do agriculture and a little carpentry at home. I don't go out to work. It is difficult, often we have to buy rice to supplement the produce from the land. I don't have money. I keep telling my children, you study well, I will arrange for the money somehow.

In the village, except some fights and quarrels, there are no problems. There is enough water except in the month of May. We have facilities like a road, we can move about freely even at night. Some people have lost a little land because of the road, they are unhappy. For example, two of my brothers have lost a little land.

We have lights, but ever since metres came into the village, we have never got a proper bill. Once I got a bill for 2,700 rupees.

Of course, I didn't pay it. Then Maharashtra State Electricity Board (MSEB) people came to confiscate our metre because we hadn't paid the bill. Fortunately, they saw my son, who is an electrician and a friend of theirs, so they didn't take it away.

Factional fights are a problem. Earlier people who were with the Sanghatana supported it till they got the plots and other things, then they got sold out to other parties, groups and sought political protection for their criminal activities. They went in different ways.

Only after the Sanghatana came, did people learn to speak up, to stand up against injustice. Before, every petty official demanded a bribe, even for a head load of wood, you had to pay with chicken, daru, tur, udid. But now there are robberies and thefts and crimes and the adivasis are involved in it. There are boys from our village who are involved in these things. Sometime ago a case was reported in the newspaper of computers and tyres being stolen. Those boys were from our village. They brought the stolen goods to the village and buried them. My own mama's son was involved in it. They were caught and very badly beaten by the police. One Varkhande boy from our village had stolen the computer. This was done in a car robbery near Udhwa. They had blocked the road with a log of wood. The car belonged to a manager of a company. They also took the gold chain from the woman in the car and molested her.

There are adivasis who are big thieves. You beat them but they do not utter a word. Presently, these boys are out on bail, they are very happy, but they don't know what awaits them. The tyres were found on top of one fellow's house, the computer was found in another person's house and the chain in someone else's. With such evidence do you think they can get away, never. But they don't have any thinking power. I don't let my sons go anywhere close to these boys. I often think if they get on to that line, they will ruin everything that I have built. I have explained to my sons, don't climb the steps of the sarkar, which means no going to the police station or courts. Once you are made to climb those steps, you are ruined for life. But these boys are not going to be released and I also think they should not be released. Only when they are inside, will there be peace in Shisne. It is a habit. They have got into the habit of getting easy money. Their parents did not bring them up properly. One day my mama's son almost took me, saying, dada, let us go and bring something. I realised what he meant. I said, I don't want to come with you and I don't want to get anything. You can go and steal and murder and do what you like, because you are not going to listen to anybody. He went. Earlier this didn't happen. It is only in the last five or six years. When I was young I had not even heard of a murder.

Do you think if they got work and money, they would do this?

None of the boys are educated so how will they get jobs? They are from the families that migrate to brick kilns. They are into a lot of vices from a very young age. They drink and make the plans, and then they carry them out. I realise that where there is no work, no land, no employment, people are left with few options but as long as there is a capacity to work, one can always ask for work.

But it is also true that once the habit forms, even if they have the option, they will do it. For example, my mama has a lot of land. Had I done a case on him, I would have got my mother's share of the land. But I didn't. In fact, I was the one who got the land transferred to my mama's name, they didn't know how to do these things.

Yet his son does these things. The real poor, the landless are not into these things. It is those who have a little land and money that get into criminal activities. If the father and the mother share in the loot, if they are happy because the son brings good things to eat, meat, fruit, then the children feel encouraged.

All the hamlets in our village, except ours, are very bad. One boy was working in a place close to Virar, there he stole the seth's motor cycle and came to the village. You hear of people robbing cycles and other things. What do you think the women do in the vadis in Vasai? Even if the husband and the wife migrate together, the husband is in one place and the wife is in the vadi. That is why I don't like to send anyone of my family members with other villagers to work in the city.

I feel very bad that it has happened in my village. Most people migrate to Gorai, Sopara, Vasai. The women, too, come back with the habit of drinking. Even by mistake I wouldn't like to eat or drink in their house. There are a few who are not into these things.

The adivasis are all finished. I don't see any hope for improvement, I only see that such crimes will increase. Let us take government schemes, there is the 'gharkul' scheme to provide houses for the widows and the landless. There are widows and landless in the village, but all the money for the houses has been taken by the khandani people. How can you expect any improvement? The ration shop owner took 10 gharkuls and built a bungalow. If the better-off and the respectable people indulge in such activities, how can the village improve?

Look at the bhaiyas. When they came to our village, they sold cashew fruits. Two brothers would share an egg, they were so poor. Now the same bhaiyas have bought bunglows and vadis and cars and trucks and land. It is not as though they had any support, no father, no brother to support them. How did they improve? Where there was one bhaiya, now there are ten, because they support each other, they teach each other. But among our people, if one person does business, he doesn't teach others, if one person goes up, others pull him down.

In my father's generation, there was a lot of cooperation. Even if someone is dying, others do not share with him. The next generation will probably be worse.

The destruction of the forest is still going on and it is being carried out by our own people. The other day a large quantity of wood, one inch wide and seven feet long, was carried off to Khatalwad. Even women were involved. Forest department is useless. It is our work to save the forest and their work to destroy the forest. I feel confident that we will save the forest so that our children will have the wood to build their houses. We have struggled so much to protect the forest so that we don't even let the sarkar come. I feel good about it.

Of course, in every village there are people who go against the common decision. Just a couple of days ago somebody stole bamboos from my land. I feel very bad. I didn't even allow my wife to take the bamboo shoots for cooking and now they are gone.

What do you consider yourself, an adivasi or a Warli? How do you feel about it?

If someone asked me who you are, I would say, I am a Warli. I am an adivasi-Warli. Koknas and Kathkaris and we are a little different. But our gods are the same, our festivals are the same. We are one, but we are Warlis, Koknas, Kathkaris. It has been the same from the beginning. They believe in bhagat, there are Kokna and Kathkari bhagats. If they come to me for medicine, I give it to them.

In our village there are only us Warlis, no Koknas, no Kathkaris. In other villages they are there. Warli and Kathkari don't marry each other, nor do they eat with each other. A few young Warli men have married Kokna girls, but Koknas don't marry Kathkaris. Koknas are better-off than Warlis and Warlis are better-off than Kathkaris. But now even these taboos have weakened.

Kathkaris have a few women bhagats. They do diva and bhuta. They also identify bhutalis. I knew a Kathkari woman bhagat, but she is dead now. There was a Warli woman bhagat also, but it is rare. There was another big bhagat, but she died young because of excessive drinking. Bhagats sometimes teach their daughters, but it is a thing of the past. A lot of women know about the jungle medicine, but they don't do diva.

The Dhangda's clan god is in Gujarat. My father must have gone there, but I have never gone. They have a big pooja of 'Saonri', the spirit of the forest, on the Bhanwarkada mountain. Nowadays, other gods like Ganpati and Sai Baba are also accepted. But I don't believe in them. They are gods of the Brahmins. These days people collect money to celebrate Ganpati in the village. Last year I didn't give any contribution, and this year too, I won't give any. They can do what they want. I am happy with my god, it is my choice. The BJP has brought Ganpati, tomorrow another party will bring another god. I would tell them, let us keep the culture of our forefathers. The younger generation is giving up the old culture and bringing in new things. Slowly they will forget their own culture.

The BJP has made inroads in our village. I have heard of two persons in another 'pada', hamlet, who follow the Malkaris, but there are none in our village. I don't know much about them except that they don't take meat and daru. They don't eat and drink in other people's houses. My mother's sister's daughter in another village has become a Malkari. Once her mother had gone to her house but she did not allow her inside the house, because it was a festival day and her mother had a little drink. She was sent back home. Since then I have been very turned off by the Malkaris. The other sects are also spreading. People go to Mumbai for their annual meetings. Even my sister's daughter has got into one of these sects. She doesn't drink daru or toddy. But when I go to her house, I ask her for chicken and toddy. I am not afraid of her. After all, I am her mama. When I asked her about it, she said it had done her good.

I would never become one. Many people tried to convince me to become a Christian, but I did not. They expect you to give up your gods, Naran, Hirva, Himaya. You have to worship the gods they want you to worship, that is not possible for me. I was very clear that this was not my line. I learnt some good values from the Christians, you should not kill, you should not steal. I have integrated these in my life, they are good for me. I was very clear that I didn't want Christianity, so I was not affected. I never for a moment forgot my language, my culture. How can you?

I am proud to be a Warli-adivasi. I don't feel bad when I am called an adivasi. Those that know who the adivasis are, don't feel bad, those who don't know feel bad. Adivasi means the original inhabitants. Before the outsiders came, we were self-sufficient. We had a lot of knowledge. Whatever is of the forest, will endure. Your food is chemical, your medicine is chemical. Just like your rice doesn't grow without the chemical fertiliser, so also a person does not feel well without the chemical medicine.

I like our dance, our art, our music, Tarfa, kamdi, gauri, all. The oppression of women by men in our society is not good. Sometimes the women are bad, but sometimes when the women are good, the men are bad. Even I have beaten my wife. I would come home drunk and ask for this or that. From where could she get it. Now when I look back I feel very bad. If something is there and she doesn't give it, it is her mistake. But if something is not there and I ask for it, it is my mistake.

But the adivasi culture is in the process of being finished. So many ceremonies and pujas are not being done. We are the last generation that knows of these rites and rituals. People don't do the rites on the threshing floor. Instead of doing the adivasi pujas, people are doing Ganpati. They don't do the traditional dances, the collective dances. They just see the television and copy. It is certainly bad. They go to Mumbai and other towns to work and pick up things there, even gods and bring them to the village.

Have you ever been active in politics?

Never. It is an itch. It is fine as it is. In the beginning I was active in the Sanghatana, I didn't drop out but nobody told me about any thing. They have appointed new leaders and Albert and I had been completely sidelined. We were 100 per cent loyal to the Sanghatana, and if we were given any responsibility, we would 100 per cent do it. But we can't impose ourselves. So far I haven't gone to any party and I don't think I will go to one.

Albert and you seem to be very good friends.

Albert is my partner. But as long as transplanting is on, there is no getting together. After transplanting if we find toddy we will drink together. I am about a month older than Albert. We were together in the same class. Albert drinks daru so I am not his partner for all that. We used to go for movies together, but nowadays who has the money for movies?

Movies I was very fond of. I don't think I have left out any cinema house in Mumbai except Metro and Regal, because English films used to come there. To be exact I have seen 351 films. Along with movies, I liked matka, but I never got lost in it.

I remember it was a Sunday and we were absolutely broke. This Kathkari friend from Khandala asked me, Dasma, what shall we do? I said, we have no money, what can we do? I have a torn one rupee note. So I said, let us take it and try our luck at gambling. We went to the Cambridge Hall of the school where the Goan and the Mangalorean fellows were gambling, and I sat down to play. I put down one rupee, and won 15 rupees in the first round. Then I played more and more till I won 300 rupees. Then we took a taxi and went to Maratha Mandir to see a film. We saw three shows that day, going from one theatre to another in a taxi. After all, it was easy money. Before marriage, I used to play at home also. Now I don't. Those were good times. Now all that is not there.

Many friends of my age are dead. I became a friend of Dama Kode, a CPM leader, in the hospital. He also had TB. Now he is not good to me. Another man from Jawhar, he died, and Dombrya from Saswan, he was a dacoit also became my friend in hospital. Dama Kode was good to me then. He used to share his mutton with me. I also shared the bhakri, my wife used to bring for me. There was food in the house, but no money because I was not there.

One day Dama Kode got toddy in the hospital and he said, dada, let us drink. I said, if the sisters see us we will be in deep trouble. We will not drink here, we will go to the side and drink, he said. And we drank.

I have heard that many people from your village had gone on a treasure hunt. Did you also go?

Yes, yes, I had also gone. The first one was a man from Kazli, who informed us that under an Apta tree somewhere in Umbergaon there is a treasure, but you need a good bhagat to locate it. Two or three bhagats had tried earlier but had not succeeded. So we took some bhagats and left. Kalu Ram, Albert, Janu's son-in-law and some Koknas went. People from other villages also came. We dug and dug and nothing happened. It was just a rumour. Another time I went to a village near Virar, 50 of us were there. One bhaiya had taken us. There also we dug and dug but did not find even 10 paise. Money was spent, but it was not ours, because the bhaiya who took us spent the money. Many people have lost a lot of money on treasure hunts. I have also spent about 1000 rupees. I have gone up to Gujarat. I made friends wherever I went. But whoever took us for the treasure hunt, fed us well.

If I had found gold, I would have made at least one bangle for my wife, and sold the rest. I would have kept the money for my children in the bank. But I have enough, I don't need anything. Sometimes when Albert's and Kalu Ram's wives and my wife get together, they really ridicule us. But this is just amongst us, no one in the village knows.

I have never gone around with those who multiply money. They are tricksters, they just run away. Good I didn't have money otherwise I would have got cheated there. Now I don't go in for all these tricks.

Do you have any regrets in life?

No, I have no such thoughts because since childhood I have neither committed theft nor have I had fights. Even when I was starving I did not steal. Had I done something wrong, I would have regretted.

When I look back, I do feel that had I not been drinking I would not have suffered so much in the hospital. But since that major illness, I have not been to the hospital. I have peace of mind. Now occasionally my wife, my elder son and I drink in the evenings. Sometimes when we have a guest, we even drink in the afternoon, but not much. I hope my life goes on like this, but I don't know what will happen tomorrow.

Who and what has been a good influence in your life?

Really none. Sometimes I feel the fathers did a good thing by starting a school in our village. Those days there were no zilla parishad schools. At least I got some education. My father remains the most important influence. He brought me up, educated me and taught me bhagtai. Had he taken his knowledge with him when he died, I would have been nothing. Then I learnt a lot from the interactions I have had with other people on forest medicine. I went to Kasheli and Nagpur conferences where doctors and other medical practitioners from different places exchanged knowledge. These were good experiences, but not everyone revealed everything. In Kasheli, one person even gave false information. He suggested a poisonous herb which could even kill. But I learnt a lot.

You have told me about your life, how does it feel?

I have told you the truth. I have never spoken at such length to any one, but I feel good about having spoken to you. After all, I have narrated things as they were, I have not hidden anything. Albert knows everything, so what is the use of telling him. My family and relatives know about my life.

I often tease my sons, you are not as smart as I am, you are dumb. Had I not used my brains, you would not have got the land.

If someone asked me to tell my life story, I would say the samething. I have not forgotten anything.

Dasma appeared to be a practical man, very much in control of his life. Within constraints, he has managed his economic situation well, having succeeded, thanks to a fortuitous chance, in retaining the land. His earnings from carpentry and bhagtai ensure enough food for the family. His family life is stable, he seems to be close to his wife. She features significantly in his narration. Unlike most men in his community, Dasma appreciates his wife. In his eyes, she is intelligent, she is hard working and she is a good woman. It was obvious from his narration, and Dasma articulated it clearly that he is grateful to his wife for having stood by him during the most vulnerable period of his life, his illness. She returned to him when he asked her to do so. That seems to have been a crucial factor in laying the foundation of a good relationship. They share a lot, they work together, they communicate with each other and they go for films together.

In general, too, notwithstanding his belief in bhutali, he is sympathetic to women of his community, who, he feels, are beaten and harassed by their men for no good reason. He seems to have no major problems with his children, although he would have liked the elder ones to study more. He wants to and does impart "right" values to his children, as his father had done, and he is happy that they are on the right path at least at present.

His association with the Christian fathers seems to have influenced his life, which he does not acknowledge sufficiently. His anger against them for penalising him for taking extra leave at the time of his wedding prevents him from appreciating the positive influence of the fathers. After all these years, he still sees no justification for their action, after all he had taken a few extra days off because of the special circumstances of his marriage.

Bhagtai is not only a source of income, it is also his passion. It is a source of satisfaction and pride. Collecting herbs from the forest and administering them gives him pleasure and a heightened sense of self-worth. He spoke animatedly and in details of the large number of persons who come to his house to consult him and of those who have been cured by him. He feels confident that this knowledge system would never die. He acknowledges the importance of allopathic doctors, who are effective for certain ailments and is comfortable with both systems. In his practical way, he can accept both the bhagat and the doctor and the systems they practise, without seeing any contradiction, just as he can combine his belief in the practice of bhutali with his criticism of men's oppression of women in his community.

Dasma has a strong Warli/adivasi identity, which he communicates forcefully in his narration. It is a source of strength and pride to him. In spite of all the madness that goes on in his society, he is a Warli and would like to remain a Warli. Under no circumstances does he want to give it up. The adivasi gods cannot be replaced by Jesus or Ganpati or Sai Baba, he is clear. And although he perceives and acknowledges threats to the adivasi culture by insiders as well as outsiders, he holds on tenaciously to his culture.

Dasma does not see any hope for the improvement of the adivasis, or the Warlis. He is clear that the better-off and more powerful non-adivasis as well as adivasis corner all the benefits from government schemes and programmes. The poor are completely marginalised, and even tyrannised by them. There is no cooperation among the adivasis, and Dasma sadly recognises that the adivasi, Warli culture and society is rapidly declining.

Dasma does not have happy memories of the past, of his childhood and youth, because it reminds him of hunger, scarcity, deprivation and difficult times. He is anxious about the future, he is certain that with further fragmentation of land and in the absence of alternative sources of livelihood, it will be harder for the next generation. But his present is happy. Although he does not have enough money, he needs a well, his eldest son has not been made permanent after so many years of service, his second son does not have a job, his kins create problems for him all the time, but in spite of it all, he is happy. He is alive after a major illness, there is enough to eat, there is land, there are herbs in the forest and his world is still intact. One could see that for all the bad times, there has also been a lot of fun and joy in his life. Like Babubhau, in spite of problems, he is at peace with himself and his situation and does not want to change it for anything else.

VII

Suman:
"I only know to work"

Suman is an attractive young woman, approximately 24-years old. When I met her she had come to the Sanghatana office to ask for help to recover her wages from the brick kiln owners. She was so anxious and preoccupied with the fact that she and her mama's family had not received the payments due to them for the last two years, that initially it was difficult to get her to talk about anything else. However, as the interview progressed she opened up and was willing to talk about important experiences of her life. Right through the interview she kept talking about work, repeating that she has worked since childhood, the need to migrate for work, the hard work at the brick kiln and not being paid for their work, and so on. The theme occurs through the narration.

She expressed sadness over the untimely death of her husband, but did not display any great emotion. She did not laugh or cry during the interview. She sat upright and still with her hand on her lap, almost like a dutiful student, right through the sessions, answering all my questions in a somewhat matter of fact manner. She often spoke fast and without pauses, so that sometimes it was difficult to keep pace with the narration. Although concerned about her own and her son's future, there was no despair in her voice. Dressed in a bright saree and a blouse, her hair prettily done with ribbons and flowers, there was an almost childlike simplicity about her.

Tell me about yourself, your childhood, your family.

From childhood I have lived with my mama and his wife, my mami. I like it there. My parents lived in Dhanori. We are seven sisters and two brothers, I am the eldest. I don't know how old I am. Had I been educated I would have known. I have never been to school. I did not study because I was not sent to school. If I had stayed with my parents, I might have gone to school. Sometimes I feel bad that I was not educated. Had I had some education, I would not have had to work so hard. I have been working since I was a child. Those who don't study have to go for work. My sisters haven't studied at all. My brother went to the village school. He studied till the second or third standard in the village school. They didn't put him in another school after that.

I have been with my mama ever since he had his first son. I was his babysitter. When my mama and his family migrated for work, I used to look after the children. Then when I was a little older, I was needed to cook and fetch water, and now that I am grown up, I work along with them. I went to the brick kilns with my mama and his family. He made an agreement with my mother. My parents had land. My father had got land from Kul Kayda. I don't know how much. I was too young to know, but I do know that both my parents worked on the land. My mother is old now but she still works.

My parent's house is close to my mama's house, there is only a river in between. I go to my parent's house and they come to my mama's house. It is only natural because I have lived there since my childhood. When my mama's children were small, he used to take me around here and there with him. My mama and mami, maternal aunt, tell my mother, we took her to work and brought her up, she is our daughter, not yours. I like to stay with them.

I used to go to the forest to fetch wood or graze cattle. That was our work when we were young – look after the children, graze cattle and fetch wood. I used to go to the forest with my friends almost every day. Take our sickles, chop wood and gather leaves. If we saw a particular creeper, we would dig around it and we were sure to find kand. We would take it home, boil it, peel it, rub ash on it, boil it again and keep it overnight, then boil it again and eat it in the morning. Occasionally we would collect mangoes and berries. And if we saw an animal we would run. We were scared that it would chase and bite us. We didn't kill even small animals, we were too scared. We used to go to the river to bathe and also play in the water.

One was afraid to enter the forest, it was dense. But now it has all been cleared. Now people cultivate the forest. You can't find anything in the forest. In the old days we used to tell each other, don't go to the forest, it is not safe, but now it is open, bare. Those who do not have land, cultivate in the forest. I don't know much about the contractors and traders. We just stay here during the rains. Once the harvest is over, we pack our bundles and move to the brick kilns.

You get vegetables in the forest. In the rains all the leafy vegetables are got from the forest. Even now you are sure to get some leafy vegetables. There are no big trees, they are rare. The trees are gone. It is true that even the leafy vegetables are reduced, and so is firewood. Sometimes we don't get even firewood. Sometimes when we chop wood, the foresters confront us. But we tell them, this is for cooking, how should we eat? Do you expect us to eat raw rice? If we are many of us, we tell each other, don't be afraid, don't run, let us confront him. I have never had any bad experience with the forester. Women tell each other, don't go today, the forester is coming or we went in that direction yesterday and met him and things like this. I am very afraid of the foresters.

Since when have you been working?

I have been working since I was too small to carry a regular pot of water, I could only fetch water in a small pitcher. Sometimes I was so wet from carrying water that I would have to change my clothes and start on other chores. I would have to cook. My parents would return from the field and ask for rice. If I hadn't cooked any, it sure meant a thrashing. And then I would have to run. I used to go here and there for work. But since I was 12-years old I have been going to the brick kilns, sometimes here, sometimes to Gujarat. You have to go to work for the seth from whom you have taken an advance. Upto now there has not been a single year when I could sit and eat.

One can go to the seth anytime one wants an advance, whenever you need money you can ask for it, for 2000 rupees or even 3000 and 5000 rupees. He needs people to work for him so he gives it. Once you finish transplanting there is nothing to eat, so you go to the seth, get an advance, buy rations and eat. After gathering the harvest we leave for work in December or January.

The entire pada migrates. If you come to my village in December-January you won't find anyone, only the old people. Only two or three persons stay back in the village to mind the cattle. You may find the better-off there, but the poor have all gone to work, along with the children. There is one Warli family, the Gimbal family, they have land and they also have a television. Those who don't have any old people, they close the door and go away. In our house there is an old woman she looks after the house and the cattle. Those who don't have any cattle, just go. Several families from the village go to the same brick kiln. We take others from the village to our seth to get an advance and tell the seth, he is from our village, give him an advance. There we build our huts close to each other. We wake each other up in the morning, help each other with work, and chat with each other while working. We feel good that there are a lot of people from our village working together. If there are strangers then we feel lonely. When we work and chat together we feel at home.

I don't remember where we went when I was young, but it was mostly to Gujarat. We couldn't go by bus, they wouldn't take us with our big bundles. So we would have to wait a long time to get a ride on a truck. We would sit at the back, exposed to the hot sun. It would take us a whole day to reach. We carried rice, some pots and pans and all our clothes with us, since we had to stay there for six months. We also took our work implements.

We came back home for Holi for seven or eight days and then returned to work. When it rains we have to come back to cultivate our field. The first thing we do is to fetch firewood, because once it rains you don't get firewood.

What kind of work do you do at the brick kiln?

On the first day we cook and sleep in the open field. The next day if there is a forest we fetch material to build our huts. In Gujarat the seth gives us bamboos to build our huts. Then we clean the land and make our huts, this takes four to five days. Usually there is a well or a stream nearby. The seth does not give us any wages or advance during this period. We have to eat the rice that we carry with us. Our mazoori begins when work begins, we tell the seth, we begin work from today, give us money to buy our rations. Then the seth gives us an advance. We buy kanni for a week. After some days we get a second advance. Right through the period of work, we are only given advances. Only when the work gets over, are our wages settled.

In the very beginning we don't start making the bricks. We wake up at five in the morning, fetch water, cook and begin work at seven. First we have to strain the coal and the ash from the kiln through metal nets. Sometimes we work for the entire day and get paid a daily wage of 30 rupees. Sometimes we are asked to carry the bricks, which are already made, from one place to another. The payment for this is on a piece rate. 500 bricks make a 'maap'. We are paid according to the maaps we carry. We do not get any breaks while working. When we plead a lot for time to rest and to eat, then we are granted a short break at about 10 o'clock. The men work on the lorries, unloading the mud for brick-making. They get a daily wage of 50-60 rupees. Earlier it was much less, 40-45 rupees and women got 20 rupees. Only since last year do we get 30 rupees. At one o'clock we get another short break to eat and bathe. There is hardly any time to rest. The moment we relax a bit, the mukaddam calls out us to return to work. Our next break is in the evening. We have to rush to fetch water, since all the women go to the well at the same time. Even if our children ask for our attention we have to brush them aside saying, let me fetch water otherwise how will I cook for us? In Gujarat the seth provides us with firewood, but in Talasari we have to go to the forest to get our firewood. Often the foresters chase us, so we have to run with the firewood bundles on our head. After fetching firewood we take a bath and go to the seth for an advance. Then we go to the market to buy our rations for the week. Then we cook.

For brick-making, we have to knead the mud with our feet. We wake up at midnight and make bricks. We must finish all the kneaded mud by about seven in the morning. Then we eat and sleep for barely two hours and go back to remove the mud, and knead more mud, which has been put in the pit. Between the three of us, my mama, mami and myself we make about 1500 bricks per day. We carry the mud with our hands and collect it in one place. My mama moulds the bricks that we put in a straight line. About 150 bricks are kept in a line called 'kadi'. Then we have to arrange them in stacks of 25 called 'ghodas'. Other people then carry the bricks from the ghoda to the kiln. We have to be careful and count our ghodas otherwise we get cheated.

Once we start making bricks we don't get any rest as this is not on a daily wage basis but on piece rate. My mama and I work continuously. My mami goes to cook and fetch water. We don't get much sleep. The quantity of mud to be kneaded is enormous, approximately one truckload of mud. Water is provided by the seth through a pipe. Our clothes get completely messed up. The men wear only the loincloth. It is very hard work. It takes so long to tell you about it, just imagine what it must be like to do it. Even if our children cry, we ignore them and work. If we spend time with our children our work will suffer. The younger children cry a lot but if we sit with them, our work will remain incomplete. So we don't even look at them when they cry. Sometimes we bring them to the place where we knead the mud and make them sit there. Often I give my child a coin and ask him to go and eat a sweet, and continue working. And after working so hard, this rascal hasn't paid us. We haven't got our wages.

What happened? Why didn't you get your wages?

Last year we did not take an advance. We went to work for cash. We came home for Holi and returned to the brick kiln. Hardly had we worked for two weeks, the seth gave us 500 rupees for travel expenses and asked us to go home. He told my mama, take your women and children home and come back on such and such date to settle the accounts. So my mama went, but the seth said, I have no money to give you now, come back another day. My mama told him that we have work at home, with great difficulty I have borrowed money to come here. How can I come again and again? The seth gave him 100 rupees and asked him to come back another day. This happened many times, four or five men would go on the fixed date, and come back without money and go again. He would give them 500 rupees or so, which would be spending on travelling since it is so far, and the men would bring back some vegetables and so on. They made five to six trips like this. Our rightfully earned money hasn't been paid to us. For two consecutive years now, two Diwalis have gone by and our money has not been paid to us.

This year I could not even buy bangles for Diwali. Even after working so hard we have no bangles, no spices, no clothes. The seth must have gone to his native place. My seth is from Gujarat. Last year his kiln was in Gujarat, this year we don't even know where he is. He has run away to another place, because he has duped us of our wages, and knows that we will try to find him. This seth had, in fact, promised us that he would help us locate the previous year's seth and recover our wages. He took my mama to our old seth, who began to threaten both of them. But he did exactly what the other seths had done – did not pay us our wages. Two days back another man from our village had gone to the seth, he was given 1000 rupees. When my mama asked for the money, he said, come back on a such and such date. Now my mama will go on that date. I wonder whether he will bring back any money. Imagine we take our little babies to work and in the end we don't even get paid. None of the other labourers from our pada have got their money.

It costs about 200 rupees to go and come. It depends on the driver, if he is good, he takes less money. After spending all that money the seth does not give anything and when we protest he gives a 100 or 200 rupees and asks us to leave. After working for six months for him, he tells us he has no money. How does he expect us to leave without any money? How can we live – we need money to buy rice for the monsoon, some vegetables, spices, we need clothes. How are we supposed to live without money we have earned? When we work on our fields we don't get any money for the other things we need. We have to use the money we have earned from our work for the period of transplantation.

What did you do about it?

What can we do? We managed with the old clothes. When my mama sold some rice straw we brought somethings, sarees and so on. We feel angry but what can you do in another village. If we try to beat the seth, we will get beaten up. What are we poor people going to do in a village where we don't belong? If we were in our own village, we would definitely have beaten him up. I came to know about the Kashtakari Sanghatana this year when we lost our wages. So we came to them and asked them to help recover our wages. But we haven't got anything yet.

In our own village we don't find any work. If we work on our land what will we eat? When we migrate for work, we can buy kanni. There is no wage work available in the village. We have to migrate. But now even if we migrate we don't get paid. There is no food, no clothes, and the seth keeps calling us every 10-15 days, and barely pays us for our travel. We have made at least 10 trips. If there is a good seth, he settles our dues and offers us an advance for the next season. We poor people often get cheated.

I don't know if they keep our accounts properly. I can't tell. I am not educated. There is no way to understand if we are cheated. Even if my mama had studied upto the fourth standard, he could have figured out if the accounts are proper or not. But since we are illiterate, there is no way we can find out. We have to rely on the seth's word, so much money is due to us.

Once I went to work at a construction site, but I was very confused because I was not used to the work. The mason would ask me to get this or that and I tried to follow his instructions. I know the work on the brick kiln although it is very hard. You have to kill sleep. One has to work at night even if it is very cold.

With some seths there isn't too much harassment but with some it can be very difficult. Sometimes the mukaddams are from our village, sometimes they are not. If the mukaddam is nice, he doesn't harass us, but if he is not good, he really makes us work, hurry up, do this, do that. I have worked since I was a child, no mukaddam has ever touched me, but there are some women who may have had this experience. If the woman is also like that then she doesn't talk about it.

Tell me about your marriage?

I have only one child. He is now eight years old. I was 15 or 16 years old when I got married. My husband died when my child was two years old. My mama got me married. My husband was from Dhanori. He had land, a large house and a small mango orchard. There is plenty there, but since my husband is dead, and my father-in-law and mother-in-law are also no more, how can I stay there?

My mama spent money on my marriage. He didn't take a loan, it was our money. My mama used to take me to work ever since I was a child, so slowly some money had been saved which was used for my marriage. I got new saris, blouses and bangles, whatever I needed I got for my marriage. There was a plenty of food. My parents didn't give me anything, I asked them for a piece of jewellery, but they didn't give it.

My husband was a very nice man. He did not beat me or drink daru or toddy. I would not have had to work like this, if my husband had lived. I was married in a well-to-do house. I have worked on brick kilns since my childhood, when I got married I did not have to migrate out for work. Now that I am back at my mama's place, I have to work hard again. At my husband's house I had to work on our land and eat, there was no need to go to the brick kilns. Many women suffer because their husbands oppress them. There are quarrels if the woman is lazy and doesn't work enough. He may beat her because she doesn't serve him on demand. No, No, my husband didn't oppress me. Till he died he didn't beat me or trouble me. If a husband oppresses a woman too much she goes away from him. She says, I will not stay with you.

My mama chose him. He said, it is a good home, let us give our girl there. They have plenty of land, a big house with plenty of things and cattle. When we migrate to the kilns there are people from other hamlets also. If there are young girls they are quietly observed. So that's how someone from my husband's hamlet saw that I was a nice girl. When we returned there was an engagement.

I must have stayed in my husband's house for three or four years. It was a time for happiness. I used to think, I have worked hard since childhood, now I have a good home, so I will not have to work.

After my husband's death, I left my husband's house because my child was very young. I told his brothers, once he grows up, I will come back, but while he is small I will take him to my mama's house. I said this and came away. Because if I only worked on our land, who would buy clothes and things for me and my child. If I stay with my mama, I can earn some cash income.

My husband had five brothers and 10 sisters. No one harassed me. But even if my brothers-in-laws are good, their wives would have resented me for migrating out for work in summer and not working on the family land along with them. The men would migrate out to earn cash income for short periods and bring money for their wives and children. Who would give me and my child money? The wives would not like their husbands to give us money. I felt that if I go away, I would be free to earn money, to buy clothes or to go to the doctor.

Both my father-in-law and mother-in-law were very nice but they are dead. Had even one of them been alive, I would have stayed there. Now all three are dead, only my eight year-old son is left. It has been six years since my husband died.

How did he die?

He had gone mad. There was a problem in his head. One day he told me I want to migrate out to work. I want to meet your mama and work with him. I told him, there is no need for you to go out and work. But he insisted. He said he wanted to see my mama, so he left the house and walked to a dry well in the village and jumped into it. The village children came and told me that he had fallen into the well. He was badly injured. We rescued him and took him to the hospital in Kasa but they did not give him proper treatment. They told me that he would have to be taken to a bigger hospital in Bombay. I was alone and I had no money. My husband's brothers had also migrated out to work. It was impossible for me to bring him to Bombay by myself without any money. So they discharged him from the hospital and I brought him home. Then I got a bhagat. His bones were dislocated. The bhagat tried to set the bones, he said that someone has cast a spell so even after fixing the joints they keep slipping. For nearly a year he couldn't move, so everything had to be done for him. He couldn't even go to the toilet. I could not lift him so I had to take someone's help. His legs wouldn't move, his hands were fine. I used to bathe him and clean him. After a year he died. My father-in-law had died a year before and my mother-in-law died soon after.

At that time only my husband's elder brother was married. The younger brothers were not married. My younger brother-in-law didn't trouble me. In such situation, other people marry their bothers-in-law but we should not do such things.

I came to stay with my mama because I had grown up in his house. I didn't feel like going to my parent's house. But before I left, I told my brother-in-law, I will return and you will have to give me a share of the land, a share of the house and you have cattle so you have to give me at least one bullock and you have goats so you will have to give me at least one goat. They assured me, your son will surely get his share. So what if the father is dead, the son is just like his father. They told me to stay but I insisted, I will go because no one will give me any money and if my son falls ill, how can I take him to the doctor without money. I could not leave my child there, he was only two-years old. And now that he has grown up with me, he doesn't want to stay with them. He is used to stay with me. Sometimes I tell my son, why don't I take you and leave you in our house and I stay with my mama. The child says, I will stay there, only if you stay there. I will not stay alone with my uncles.

The first years of my marriage were happy. I did not have to migrate out for work, there was enough to eat. My mami used to tell me, now you have a nice, well-settled husband, now you don't have to go out for work. And I used to say, well, I have worked hard since childhood, now I can take it easy. But now again since I have come to my mama's house I have to work. I told my mama, I will also help you with work in the brick kilns. If there was enough to eat, there would be no need for us to suffer in the cold and work from midnight on. We could quietly sleep through the night. There we only work and earn, no singing or dancing or anything. When one is working on one's own land, if there are days when one doesn't work one can still eat. After one finishes transplantation one can relax. But on the brick kiln one has to work continuously. There is no question of sitting and eating. Even if we are unwell, the seth tells us to work slowly. Sometimes he gives us money to go to the doctor, but when you come back you have to work.

The grain from my mama's land lasts us only till Diwali. After all we need to eat three times in a day. So once the new crop is harvested we store it and go to work. We keep some rice for the old woman who stays in our house, and take some with us to the brick kiln. Once that rice gets over we have to take an advance to buy kanni. At the end of the season, if the seth is good he gives us our balance wages, otherwise he keeps calling us back for our wages every 10-15 days till we get fed up. But this has happened to us only since last year. I have been working since childhood, I don't remember not being paid.

Did you suspect anyone of harming your husband?

No bhagat ever identified a bhutali but I have a feeling that someone must have done some magic, fed him something during the ceremony of the threshing floor. After the harvest the god of threshing has to be propitiated. At the time all the men, women and children of the village drink daru and toddy and eat bhakri together. I feel something must have happened at that time. Soon after that my husband started saying I want to go out to work. That is the time he lost his mind. Earlier he was all right. I told him don't go but he didn't listen to me. He was very nice before. Whenever my relatives came he would chat with them. His other brothers are quiet but he was very sociable. He would never send away a visitor without feeding him. He was very nice and very stable.

Do you believe in bhutali?

Bhutalis are there. When one falls ill or has fever, the bhagat says the bhutali has cast a spell on you. I have never seen a bhutali so I don't know. If a woman is a bhutali, she is not going to tell you that she is a bhutali. No one was hunted in my village, but it happens in other villages.

There was an incident in my husband's village. Actually that woman was related to me. She was my mother-in-laws elder brother's wife. It was transplantation time. Her field was in the forest. Her son and daughter-in-law had come to help her to transplant. She asked them to go ahead to the field and she stayed back to cook for them. A little later she set out for the field with the food on her head. Two men were hiding in the forest. When they saw her they asked her to stop. They made her put the food down and began to beat her. She started screaming and asking, why are you beating? They said, you are a bhutali. She said, if I am a bhutali take me to the bhagat. Only after he proves it, you can kill me. They were in the forest so none could hear her screams. They strangled her to death. They killed her. Her son came that way and found that all the food was strewn around, her bangles and necklace were broken. Her body was thrown behind a tree, so he could not see it. He came to the village and began to inquire, where is my mother? We told him that she had gone to the field. He thought she may have gone for a delivery because she was also a suin (a midwife). He went back to the field but didn't find her there. So he told his sister and brother-in-law, our mother hasn't come to the field, and there is food strewn on the path, broken bangles and broken necklace, it must be our mother who has been killed. Then they began to cry. We were all busy transplanting when we heard the crying and wailing. We were sure one of our relatives had died. They didn't find the body. So all the villagers went to the forest to look for her. We began searching in the afternoon, and found her by late evening. Her body was partially buried under a tree. If we hadn't found her, we would have thought that she may have gone visiting someone and would have waited for two or three days for her to return.

Later the two men were caught. They were from our village. They worked as forest guards. They were brothers. After killing her, they had run away to their father-in-law's place in another village. Her family members immediately went and lodged a complaint. These men had quarrelled with her earlier also, calling her a bhutali. And the fact that they had run away further confirmed the suspicion. When the police came, they were not there. Their father was at home. On previous occasions this woman had challenged them to take her to a bhagat but they were not interested in verifying. They took her by surprise and killed her. Her son knew these things. The police caught hold of their father and took him to the in-laws house where they were caught. For two years they were in jail.

The wife of the older brother used to be very ill. They took her to the doctors and bhagats, nothing helped. So they were convinced that the old woman had cast a spell. There was no connection between the two families. Some bhagat must have told them about her. But after the men were caught, her own father began quarrelling with her saying, you are the one who got these men to kill the old woman for no reason at all. She was not a bhutali and now these men are in jail. The woman became very depressed. She must have thought if my father is quarrelling with me so much for having my husband and his brother put in the jail, it will be much worse at my in-law's place. It was transplantation time and everyone was working in the field. She was at home because she was very ill. She told the children, go out and play, I want to sleep. Then when there was no one in the house, she took a rope and hung herself. She probably thought, my husband is gone, my father is fighting with me, who will look after me?

Tell me about your parental family. What do they do?

I visit them sometimes. During the rains my brothers do cultivation. They have a little land and both my father and my mama also have forest encroachment plots. After the rains, my brother migrates for work. Last year he went as a labourer on a truck along the highway close to Bombay. The truck used to transport mud as well as bricks to the brick kilns. It is a strenuous work. I am the eldest. The sister after me also works in the brick kiln. She is not married. The others are too small, they play and eat. They fill water, graze the cattle, cook, wash dishes. If they don't work my mother beats them. They look after the younger ones. None of my brothers or sisters is married. All of them, mother, father, brothers and sisters migrate to the brick kiln. We go separately. We exchange information on which seth is good or bad. We tell them don't go to that one, he is not good, or go to that one, he is good.

On an average we get 30 rupees per day. We ask the seth to increase our wages. He refuses saying, this is the standard rate. Come next year I will increase it for you. Even kanni, is 10 rupees a kilo, vegetables are expensive. How can we fill our stomach? When we are at home in the village, we can bring at least something, some vegetables from the forest. We grow some vegetables in our yard, which we eat. We have also planted some fruit trees so we can get fruits. Over there we have to work and buy everything – vegetables, grains, pulses, everything.

My parents have suffered a lot. My father's brothers separated them from the family and asked them to manage on their own. They gave them two or three small rice fields. They had no house, no pots and pans. They began going out to work and slowly built a small hut and bought some pots and pans. Now they cultivate their fields, keep just enough grains for seeds and migrate. They buy kanni with the wages they get for their work in summer, and return to their village to cultivate their field. With the money they have to buy clothes and other things. Even now their condition is bad, difficult. My father's brothers are much better off. They were three brothers in all. They separated my father, the other two live and cultivate together. They take other people's land on rent. They have a source of water so they grow tomatoes, chillies and sweet potatoes.

The problem with my father is that he is a carpenter, so earlier he used to go to build houses for people in summer. Often people fed him but did not pay him. So while he worked he got enough to eat, but the family, the younger children were starving at home. If they didn't get food for two or three days, they would come to my mama's house. So I began to tell my father, go and work on the brick kiln, because when you go out to do your carpentary you are fed well, but these children go hungry. Where can they find food in the village in summer? If you go to the brick kiln you can be sure of buying kanni and clothes.

Ever since I gave them this advice, since the last few years they have been migratir.g to the brick kilns. They have had enough food in the rains and have also bought roof tiles. If only they had gone out to work when I came to live in my mama's house, they would have improved their condition. Within a few years they have been able to buy clothes and are not starving. Now they have to start thinking about my brother's marriage. Where will they get the money from if they sit at home. They have to go out to work. How can I help? I have no money. My mother also understands that I help my mama with work.

Are you happy to return to your village?

Yes, very much. When you return people call out and say, oh, when did you come back? I say, just today. It feels very good. Lots of people come to meet us. Even visitors from other villages come and invite us to visit them. We tell them, we still have to gather our firewood, when we finish we will come.

I go to the market with my friends, three or four of us go together. I see nice things in the market, but I have no money to buy things. If I had money, I would buy bangles, earrings, necklace or anything that looks good. We sometimes buy biscuits or other little 'khau', small snack, for one or two rupees and eat it. Sometimes I take my son to the market because he wants to go with me. Sometimes I tell him, don't come today, I will bring you what you want and get a banana or some khau for him.

I like Diwali. I also demand a new saree from my parents because all my friends have new sarees. Then all of us dress up and go to dance on Diwali. Children as well as old people dance for two days. After that if there are weddings in and around the village we go to dance at the weddings. Otherwise, we just migrate to work. If the seth comes to fetch us we have to go.

After Diwali if there is a wedding in the family we come back for it. But this means spending 200 rupees or more. If we stay back and work then we can earn, which comes into use later.

Do you know about the old practices like veth and lagnagadi or about the Warli myths, rituals and so on?

No, I don't know anything about veth and other things. No one told us old stories. Girls are not told these stories, if girls sit down to listen, they are scolded and asked to fetch water, to do this or that. I don't sit in the 'jagrans', night vigil in memory of ancestors. Even my brother doesn't know the stories. During the rains when he is at home, he is working on the field and after the rains he migrates out for work. Sometimes, we sit down to listen, but I don't remember anything. One has to work and eat, that's all. Who is going to give one to eat without working?

My parents say that there used to be storytellers. They are called 'thalawala', storyteller. But I don't know anything. Older women know about a lot of things and they talk about them. They are full of stories about how they would listen to the thalawala or dance to the 'dhumsa', a musical instrument. We only go to watch people dancing to the dhumsa if we hear about it. The 'suvasins', married women who perform rituals, sing songs at weddings, but we forget them immediately. I don't know anything, I only know to work.

.I don't know the gods of the Warlis. The ceremonies are performed by men. They know where to break the coconut or make the offerings. Women only cook and give them. On Diwali, for example, we make the bhakris, with 'valuk', a big cucumber. If one has money, one grinds the flour at the rice mill otherwise you have to grind the flour yourself. If I remember something of what I have heard, I will tell my child, if not, then there will be nothing to teach.

Has any political party or organisation done anything to improve your situation?

The Congress and the Lal Bauta are there. Neither of them do anything for the people. If they did anything, there would be work in the village. We need work. People should get enough to eat. Sarkar should do these things. If the police patil informs the sarkar about our condition, may be we could get work in the village, so that we don't have to migrate to the brick kilns. The sarpanch and the police patil are most inactive. They are only bothered about finding work for themselves. They don't even inform us of any kind of work available in the neighbouring areas.

If the people united, we could demand a road to our village, and also a bus because we have to walk a very long distance from our bus stop. Then we could also demand work in the factories and vadis. There are many factories at Ganjad. Then we would not have to go out. In other villages people find work close to their homes, but there are no such possibilities in our village.

After working so hard there is no happiness in our life. If only we could get work, we could work for a whole week and rest for one or two days. It would be ideal. But there is no work like that. Even if we are dying we have to work to get something to eat. It is not as though adivasis are happy, they have nothing. They have to migrate out for work. Many people face hunger in the rainy season, if they don't have food stored at home. Then along with doing their own farm work they have to work on other people's fields for which they get some grain. When they can't find some work they starve. Those who don't have their own fields they have to work constantly on other people's fields. They don't even have proper houses, they live in huts. I have not faced hunger, because my mama makes sure that there is something for me from their share. My mama is good, so I am all right, otherwise I would definitely have faced starvation. They keep an equal share for me. If they eat less, then of course, I also have a smaller share.

If someone offered you good money, would you leave your village and go to another place?

Where will I leave my village and go? Nobody has told me anything like this. I wouldn't like to be alone in a new place. I have never been to Bombay. I hadn't even been to the police station before I went to lodge a complaint recently. I didn't even know how to go there, I hadn't even climbed the steps of the police station. I didn't know what to do or say there. Where will I go?

Once my mama had gone to the seth to recover our wages. My mami and I were alone with the children. At night we shut the door and went to sleep. A little later someone came knocking at the door. We asked, who is it. He said, me. We recognised his voice as the man was from our village. We told him that there is no man in the house, and we will not open the door. He insisted. We asked him to come in the morning, what work do you have with us? He then climbed the reed wall and jumped into the house. It was the same man, Gimbal. He is one of us from the village. So my mami and I and all the children started screaming. But our house is on the field and isolated so even though we screamed there was no one to hear it. But then he ran away. My mama reached the next morning and we told him what had happened. So we filed a case.

All the villagers gathered and decided to resolve the matter. Gimbal has quarrels with everyone in the village, with other families. He is well-to-do and has influence also. The better-off people say, we have plenty of grains and money, you are poor, what can you do to us? They say, the police station is ours and threaten us. But this time he asked us to settle the matter quickly and we did so.

Such things don't happen, but then it is hard to say because we are out for a good part of the year. For the last five or six years we have moved our house from the hamlet to our field, so now we know less of what goes on.

Why did you not remarry?

I have a son, so why should I remarry? If I had a daughter she would have married and gone to live with someone, but if I get married now who will give my son land? How hard will he work for others to earn a living?

Right now my son's uncles are cultivating the land. They don't give anything to us. There is not a single occasion when they say take this 50 or 100 rupees and buy something for your child. I go there sometimes, sit for a while, chat with them and come back. They are nice to me but just don't give anything. I keep telling them when my son grows up he must get his share of the land. I don't stay there so that I am free to do wage work on the brick kiln and wherever I can get work, to earn some cash for us. But, I tell them, he is your son. Now he is small so he cannot cultivate but when he grows up he will. There is plenty of land, cattle and trees. After all, my mama is not going to give him any land, his sons will get his land.

I think they will give my son his share. At present they are a joint family. Two brothers are not yet married, but once all of them are married they will say, let us divide the land amongst us brothers. At that time they will have to give land to my son. When they divide the land I will have to go there and ask for my son's share. As long as the land is undivided, I will stay here. If I don't take him back when he grows up, his uncles will say, your mother took you away when you were a baby, now how will we provide you with land. If they don't give my son land then he will have to work in the brick kilns and after working hard, if he is lucky he will get his wages. But if they don't give us land I will lodge a complaint. I have a photograph of my husband in my father-in-laws house.

Does your son go to school?

I have been taking him along to work ever since he was a baby. It is important to send the children to school. At least they won't have to work hard, if they have a little education. For those children who migrate with their parents to work, there is no other option except to work like us. They just play there. At meal times they come for food, eat and go back to play. Sometimes the older children mind the younger ones. We have no time for them.

I worry about my son. When he grows up he will need a house and some money to buy clothes and other things. At present he doesn't need anything. I work and provide for him, he plays and eats. Sometimes he complains, you haven't bought me good clothes, but I tell him, if I had the money, I would. If your father was around, he would have bought you good clothes, but your father is dead. You don't even know him. For the last two years I have not been paid so how can I buy good clothes?

If he studies and gets a job, then he will probably be better-off, but so far I haven't sent him to school, and he is eight years old. This year I was determined to put him in a school but we came so late from work that I could not admit him.

If my son is educated he will look after me well. He will get a job and then he will feed me without me having to work. He will say, you have suffered a lot to bring me up, now I will look after you. You don't work, don't go to the brick kiln. But I know boys who have studied upto the 10th and the 12th standard and are now sitting at home, doing cultivation. They haven't got good jobs.

I often think that my son is alone. His life should be better than mine, but when there is no money in my hand, what is the use of thinking of a better future. How can one think of a better future?

The major turning points in Suman's life are her marriage and the subsequent death of her husband. After a life of want and deprivation, she experienced happiness in her husband's home, which in her scheme of things means not having to go out for work, to get enough food, clothes and sleep. It was obviously the best phase of her life, and although there might be some exaggeration in her description, nevertheless, she has very good memories of the time she spent with her husband. The fact that they have land and that they did not migrate out regularly for work, suggests that life was relatively easier and more secure for her.

Quite clearly Suman experiences work differently from the way Babubhau does. He enjoys working on his land, it is a source of satisfaction to him. In fact, if he had the resources he would have expanded his cultivation. In contrast, Suman hates working on the brick kiln, she would stop it if she had a better alternative. For her it is a terrible experience from which she wants to protect her son.

Like Ramabai, the trajectory of her life has been from extreme poverty to relative security and back to poverty because of the death of her husband. But unlike Ramabai, she is still young and energetic, she has her mama's family and her parental family to provide emotional support. She still has hopes of her son providing her with some comfort and security in the old age. Most important, she has not lost faith in her relations, near ones and in human beings. She took an important decision to leave her husband's home after his death, and she does not express any doubt about it. She seems convinced, and justifies it again and again by saying that she needed cash for herself and her son, to buy clothes, to go to the doctor and who would give it to her since her husband was no longer there. Her view of the future hangs on the hope that her son would be given his share of the property and then they can live happily. By repeating this she seems to want to establish the legitimacy of the claim. There is no other hope, and the prospect of him working on the brick kiln, like she has done all her life, is daunting.

Like many of her generation Suman has no clear idea of how the future could improve. Typically, all she can say is, it should get better. Both Suman and Subhash are not politically active. Suman is far too occupied in her work to explore and engage in political activity.

Like many other seasonal migrants of her age, Suman is not very involved or knowledgeable about the Warli rituals and culture. Unlike Subhash there is no special bond with the clan or the family to bind her to her culture. She has no time, or more important, money to celebrate festivals that she would like to. The fact that she could not buy new sarees or bangles last year is a source of dissatisfaction to her and she repeats it often in the narration.

In the absence of her husband she pins her hopes for a secure future on her son who she hopes would get a good job and feed her. While she hopes for a better future for her son, which may be possible if he gets his share of the land, or good education and a good job, she also fears that if none of this happens, he will have to work hard like her in the brick klins. The fact, however, is that the son has not even begun schooling because they migrate every year. It is common among adivasi women to treat their sons as providers when the husband dies. One often hears the expression used by widows, why should I remarry, now my son is my protector, he will provide for me. Suman ends the narration on a note of despair, when there is no money in my hand, what is the use of thinking of a better future?

VIII

Subhash:
"If we had wings, we could fly"

Subhash worked as an assistant for me during my fieldwork. He is 20-years old. He accompanied me to the villages and helped me contact people for the interviews. He was always dressed in shirt and pants, and had a pleasant countenance. Subhash is educated, and this explains the fact that he speaks accurately with regard to time, the year, month, duration, etc. For example, he knows his exact age, the year his grandmother died and so on. He was a good assistant, although not particularly hard working. He did not turn up on many days, and there were days when he came bleary eyed, sleepy and tired, because he had attended a wedding or a religious function and had drunk and danced throughout the night. And these occasions were not infrequent. His eyes would light up when he spoke about celebrations, obviously they brought a lot of joy to him. His friends and his extended family, which, as we shall see, is an important factor in his life. He expressed his feelings freely, his fantasies, desires and wishes were revealed to me easily. Compared to Suman, Subhash seemed far less mature and responsible. He was also very confused about his immediate plans, not quite sure what he wanted to do, whether to pursue studies or look for a job.

What is the earliest memory you have?

I remember from the time when I was four years old. I am 20 now. I was the eldest and for some time the only child. In our house, I was there, my mother was there, my father was there, and my father's two brothers and six sisters were there. We were together in one house. It was very nice. The aunts used to take me to the market. When they got married, only one went away, three continued to live in our hamlet. And two didn't marry at all, they also live in our hamlet with their brother and sister. They are very good to me, but they are good to others also. Only when I went to the seventh standard, the brothers separated and they began to live in three houses. When I was one and a half year old my grandfather died. I don't remember him, but I remember my grandmother. She died in 1996.

One of my aunts worked as a nurse in a mission hospital. She was very fond of me. She used to take me to the hospital with her sometimes. People brought little children to the hospital. Seeing them cry, I also used to cry, but at other times I used to go around happily with the hospital staff.

When I was very young, I didn't speak much. I didn't even play with my cousins. I used to go out alone and sit alone. I used to take a stick and pretend that I was riding a bicycle. Children used to push me and even beat me sometimes. When I was a little older, I used to go to the river with the other children. But I was scared of drowning because I couldn't swim. My father's sisters used to bathe me in the river. I remember all this.

Till I was four years old I went to a balvadi. The food that came for the children in the balvadi used to be kept in our house. Children used to ask me to bring some food for them, which I did on the quiet, and they would give me other eatables in return. It was great fun. Everyone was good to me.

My grandfather had some land. I have heard that he lived in another village, Karajgaon, and from there he came to this village, Haladpada. His son-in-law was a patil in Haladpada, and he had a lot of land. So he called my grandfather to Haladpada and gave him some land and my grandfather began to live here. The condition in Karajgaon must have been bad. The land was given to other people to cultivate. Now we have land in Haladpada. That uncle is dead now. They still have a lot of land. He has two sons, one is a mental case, he was even taken to a mental asylum but he didn't get all right. He is better now and works as a tailor.

I didn't know anything about the system of kul or veth or anything. I came to know about it for the first time since I started working with you. My grandmother used to talk about the old times, about the family relations, but she didn't tell me about kul or khand or lagnagadi and other forms of oppression. No one told me about it. My father and I don't talk. I am scared of my father. We speak only when there is any work, otherwise we don't talk. Even those who have studied up to the 12th or more don't know about these things. If they were written in our textbooks, we would have known about them, but no one talked about them in school or at home.

My father worked on the land, my mother also worked on the land. They never went out to work. We didn't have to buy grains from the market, we got enough from the land for the whole year. We still get enough. My mother has told me that there was scarcity of food earlier, when I was a year or so old there wasn't enough to eat. When my parents separated from the family and began to cultivate their own land, there was enough to eat. But my father faced a lot of difficulties when he was young. My grandmother told me that they used to cook only one meal, and the other meal was just of leafy vegetables.

Did you go to school, did you like it?

There was a school in the village up to the fourth standard. I went there only for one year. I didn't know what a school was all about, so every afternoon I used to run away. Then my father took me to another school, this school was run by the Christian fathers. We are Christians. The school was about three to four kilometres away from home. I studied up to the seventh there. I learnt about the Christian religion and about the Bible. The fathers used to help us when I was in the fourth class, they used to give us meals made out of wheat. We were told that wheat, milk powder and corn flour came from America. Once they gave us clothes also. But when I came to the seventh, I didn't get anything.

Their education was the best in this area. They looked after the students well. I liked it so I studied there. But going to school everyday was troublesome, we had to walk three to four kilometres everyday through the forest. There was a small hill, and I used to get tired of climbing it. So I would stop and sit and climb again. My cousin was also there, in the third or fourth standard, he used to take me on his shoulder. He used to frighten me by making sounds like a tiger's, and I would often cry. We had a lot of fun. When we were young, we didn't have any slippers. So we often got hurt, many times my toe nails came out. We didn't use any medicines, we used to get leaves from a tree and apply it on the cut. My father's sister was a nurse, she used to take me to the hospital and give me an injection. I was very scared of the injection so I would try to walk carefully. It was fun. I have happy memories of those times.

We had heard that there were robbers who came into the forest and took away children. One day when we were returning from the school, we saw a person who looked like a robber. We were so scared that we left our bags and everything and ran. Then a person came along, asked us what had happened, brought our bags and took us to our village. After that the father appointed a person from our village to take us to the school and back.

Those days we used to take rice chapatis for lunch. We didn't have any vegetables. But there was a tamarind tree close by, and ripe tamarind tastes very good with chapatis. So we used to throw stones and bring down the tamarind, and eat it for lunch. The owner used to chase us away but we managed it well.

In our village only our clan became Christian, now the whole hamlet is Christian except for a few families. We were not harassed because we were Christians but because we were with the Congress. The Lal Bauta was also there, and they used to have fights. I was young and I used to be hidden away, so I didn't see what really happened. But I know that fights took place. But all that is over now, we don't have any more trouble with them.

My father used to beat me if I didn't go to school. He would pick up a stick and take me with him. If we children went running to school, it used to take us one hour, but if we had fun on the way then it was one and a half or so. We went through the forest. We have seen a lot of animals like python, rabbits, snakes of all types, birds. We used to carry a catapult with us, and kill birds and other small animals on the way. We used to eat fruits from the forest, mangoes, jamuns and many others. The older ones would climb the tree and shake it, and the younger ones would stay down and collect the fruits. It was a lot of fun.

In fact, I just killed a rabbit. We still go to hunt in the forest. The elders didn't take us children when they went to hunt. Only those who can climb a tree can go for a hunt. My father was very strict, he didn't let me go. I was not allowed to climb a tree, if he saw me doing it, he used to beat me. We go for shikar on Sankrant. Now-a-days if 10 or 12 of us youngsters get together we go for shikar. Every year all of us from the hamlet contribute five rupees each and go for a picnic in the forest. We hunt, play cricket, enjoy ourselves. We don't have many big trees, the forests were finished, but recently we have started protecting our forest and slowly the trees are coming up.

None of my friends studied further. Out of those who completed the seventh standard, only two of us have passed the 10th. Some five boys went to an Ashram Shala, boarding school, but it was close to a cremation ground and the boys used to get scared at night, so they left in the first week itself.

After the seventh, I went to an Ashram Shala in Talasari. It was a government school, but run by the Christian fathers. The children were all adivasis, Christians and Hindus, although there were more Hindus than Christians. Everyone said the same Christian prayer. There was no difference. Girls were also there. But they were not as mischievous as the boys. They were not allowed to go out of the compound, they could eat the fruits of the mango, papaya and tamarind trees that were there. Boys used to go out to the bazaar every day and bring chillies and dry fish, and roast it over a fire and hide and eat it. The school was good, food and everything was good. They gave us books, and we had to buy the note books. Sisters were very good. Only we had to walk about three kilometres every evening to go to the river to bathe, we went at five and had to be back by half past six.

The discipline in the school was good. We had to get up at 5.30 in the morning and have a wash and get ready. The superintendent used to go around at night to see that the boys were sleeping in their places. He took care of us. But sometimes we used to get up at night and go and sleep in an unknown spot so that no one could wake us up in the morning and we could sleep longer.

There were a lot of toddy trees in the compound, and we took out a lot of toddy from the trees. In the morning the toddy was fresh and sweet, but by the evening it would turn sour and strong. We used to go to drink toddy in the evening, but after drinking even two glasses we would be swinging. Once, six of us had gone for a bath. One of the boy's sister was married into that village and they had a huge toddy tree. So we debated whether to drink the toddy there or take it to the boarding. If we drank there itself, it would have been difficult to walk back, so we drank a little and brought about five litres to the boarding. Should we tell the superintendent or not was the question. Anyhow, we started to drink, and since there were no glasses, we drank from saucers. Then we asked the superintendent if he wanted toddy. Good idea, he said, and brought out glasses and all of us drank. There was still some left, so we woke up the small boys, they came running and drank toddy. Then sister D'Souza came and asked us what was going on. We didn't say anything. The next morning we woke up very late. Then sister called us to her office and scolded us. She was a very nice person, everyone liked her. She cared for us, and taught us not to do wrong. She explained things nicely to us, that is why we obeyed her. We didn't repeat it. She was most liked. We were supposed to get mutton once in 15 days, but she gave us mutton once a week, out of her own money.

I studied in this school till the 10th. I was very happy then. I used to go home once a month on Saturday and return on Sunday. If we went back on Monday, we got a scolding from the head master. I remember there was a toy tortoise on his table which could shake its head. We liked it very much, so we used go to the office quietly and move its head. Of course, once in a while we were caught. The teachers were all adivasis, they taught us well. One teacher was dangerous, he used to beat us with a stick. We had fun playing, but we had to study a lot. I learnt a lot there. Our school gets very good results. I liked maths, science and history but English was dangerous. I passed in it but I didn't know anything more than what was asked in the question paper. We started with ABCD...and simple things like ball, bat and so on in the fifth standard. We weren't taught to speak in English. We had difficulties in the 10th class, because we started English only in the fifth class. We still find it difficult. I passed my 10th from there. In the 10th class, each one of us had to teach five boys for an hour in the evening. I liked it.

My mother's brother spent money on me. He still does. My father doesn't work. He works on his own land and is an activist of the Sanghatana. My father has been working for them since I was young. In our village, we had the Congress and the Lal Bauta. The fights were between the Congress and the Lal Bauta because people gave their votes to the Congress. My father was in the Congress, then he joined the Sanghatana. My uncle also supports the Sanghatana. They do good work so people have faith in them, they go to their meetings and listen to them. Now more people are with the Sanghatana.

Then I didn't want to go to college, but my father told me to do so. I listen to everything my father says, so I joined a college in Palghar. I studied commerce, theory and practical, and Marathi, English and maths. I like it. My mama and my cousin – my father's sister's son – paid for my studies. My cousin has rented a room in Ashagad, I stay with him. My college is about seven kilometres away from here. I travel by bus and then walk, it takes about half an hour. I passed the 11th, and then for the 12th, I didn't do the exams, but I am going to do it this year.

Why did your family become Christian?

I have heard that my grandfather used to work for the Christian fathers. He looked after their horses and even lived with the fathers. They must have taught him things, explained things to him and asked him to become a Christian. He became a Christian, then my father was baptised and he became a Christian, and then we were baptised. My grandfather died at their place.

All my father's brothers and sisters are Christians, the sisters are married to Christians. All of them observe the religious practices. My aunt goes to another village to attend mass. Most Christian Warlis marry Christians, sometimes they marry Hindus as well. When men marry Hindu girls, the girls follow the Christian religion. In our family one person has married a Hindu. We haven't given up our gods, our festivals, our religion. We follow our own and also the Christian religion and practices. We say the Christian prayers. We don't eat beef, we don't have to. We do everything on Diwali and Holi that the others do, only we don't do the puja. There is no difference between the Hindu and the Christian Warlis.

I like being a Christian. Among the Hindus the bhagat has to be fed. But the Christians just say the rosary, they don't have to give anything to the father. The father spends and he also teaches us things which are good for our society. I like that. They also help. They give us credit for buying seeds or making a compound and so on. They have started schools in many villages. There is a dispensary also. They do good work. The Christians say good things about them, the Hindus don't.

My one aunt's husband is very ill. He used to drink a lot, he was drunk everyday. Now he can't swallow, he has stopped eating. He is paralysed on one side. Now he tells us not to drink. He was a Christian and was also a bhagat. He used to give medicines, only he didn't get possessed. He had also taught my aunt about medicines. He didn't do bhuta. When he went for the training for bhagatai, people say that he did not observe the rules. One cannot eat raw or dried fish and one cannot hear the sound of a woman's bangles. The woman must tie her bangles with a kerchief. The man has to stay out of the house during the period of the training. But my uncle ate fish and also when he ate in the morning, his wife used to sweep the ground and make a sound with her bangles. She didn't know these things because she was a Christian. Then he had to leave the training, because the bhagat knew he had broken the rules. But he must have learnt about medicines from somebody. He was very good. People had a lot of faith in him, if anyone was bitten by an animal, they used to come to him.

Earlier when people fell ill, they went only to the bhagat. Now they first go to the dispensary and then to the bhagat. It is better now. Jungle medicines are good, but one doesn't get completely cured with that. Besides, the bhagat is very expensive, even for a minor illness the bhagat makes you spend a lot. In our house we don't bring the bhagat much. But in the neighbouring houses he is often called. I sometimes go and watch the bhagat perform. People still have a lot of faith in the bhagat.

Since when have you also been working?

I have always worked during the vacations since I was 10-years old. I once worked in a dairy. I used to help my father on the land, to plough, transplant, everything. Children work on the field. I have been working with the plough since I was in the third standard, eight or nine years-old. I have cut grass, done agricultural work on other people's fields and also worked on a Musalman's vadi. He was dangerous, we were scared of him. He did not live in the village, he lived in Dahanu. Now he is in Mumbai. He always carried a knife with him. Whenever he came to see our work, we worked fast because we were scared.

I worked in the power plant, just to put water on the cement. I must have been 12 or 13-years old. For two years during the May holidays, I worked in a daru factory. It is an ordinary factory. They don't make you permanent. Daru is filled in bottles and bottles are packed in boxes and the boxes are carried to the godowns. I used to carry the boxes. It was easy. The boxes weigh about 10 kgs and we have to carry it over a short distance. I was paid 30 rupees a day and I worked from 8.30 to 12.30 in the morning and then 1.30 to 5.30 in the evening.

Older people worked on making daru. After the bottle is filled with daru, it has to be capped. That is difficult. If you don't put the bottle properly in the machine, the bottle can break in your hand and hurt you. One boy from our village lost his finger. Many people get hurt. Also, when the bottle is being filled, sometimes air gets in to the bottle and it bursts. Anyone close by can get injured from that. Nearly 40 bottles burst in a few hours. One boy stands there just to collect the broken pieces of glass. The labourers are all adivasis.

I went once to work on loading sand on trucks. The sand is removed from the sea, other people do that, and then it is brought to a place where it is loaded on trucks. We did that. Ten or 15 young men like me go together from the village work there. When the truck comes, everyone rushes to the truck, sometimes two or three trucks come together. Five persons have to work to fill one truck. The driver tells us to hurry, there is no time to waste. So we have to run up and down a plank with a basket of sand. Each basket weighs 20 kgs or so. Since there is nothing to hold on to, we often fall, but we fall on sand so we don't get hurt. We get up immediately and continue to work. The truck has to be loaded in half an hour, so one has to work very fast. When the truck is full, one of us goes on the truck to Mumbai. At the check posts we have to run and collect the receipts. Everything has to be done fast.

Sand is sent to Mumbai to Esselworld (a water park), and to the builders in other places, so we also get a chance to see Mumbai. For loading the truck we make about 150 to 200 rupees a day. Most of the time trucks come at night, at 10 pm or even later. Work goes on the whole night. Since there is less traffic at night they can travel faster. You sit for a while and then the truck comes, the driver blows the horn and calls out, come on fast. Young people can get up fast, but older people are slower and we tease them, get up uncle, don't sleep.

At night you either sleep in a small hut with many boys or you sleep on the sand. We take a mat and a sheet with us. The sand irritates the sole, it gets sore. When you first work, the skin on the palms peels off, but after one month of work, it becomes very hard. Then nothing happens. Even if you hit hard, it doesn't hurt. It becomes good. After doing this work you can't have problems with any other kind of work anywhere. You can carry big baskets weighing even 30 kilos. When I went there, seven new persons were there. The older people taught us how to fill the baskets with sand and throw it into the truck. That is how we did it and it worked well. But on the second day we couldn't do it properly. In the first week we couldn't even hold our plates to eat, our hands were so sore. The whole body becomes very stiff. In the first week many fall ill. But after one week it is all right. This work is very strenuous, weak or sick persons can't do it. Only young people can do that work, old people would be finished if they tried. You can't work continuously for a month, in two months you can do work for about 30 days. How can you work like this? Few stay for a whole month, you have to take off for a week or 10 days. Sundays are off days, trucks don't come on that day, and, of course, you don't get paid for that day. We can go out or do other chores. Bathing is a problem, there are thousands of persons there, and no water.

Last time I got 1500 rupees from this work. I bought clothes and gave money to others. If anyone asks me for money, I give. I gave 700 rupees to one person, and 200 to another as a wedding present. I buy Pan Parag for others. I drink toddy. There you really feel like drinking daru, if you drink and work you really don't feel tired or lethargic. If anyone asks you to carry a heavy thing, you can do it fast and easily. Toddy costs 12 rupees a litre, I can drink even two litres. Everyone drinks there. You have to spend on food, because you feel very hungry there. No stinging on that. We buy provisions for a week at a time. Everyone gives money to one person and he keeps all the accounts. Once a week we get mutton. Our money collects over many Sundays, and then we take it and go home to the village, buy clothes, toddy and go to the forest and drink together. We get our money, the seth doesn't cheat us. He gives the money to the driver and the driver pays the labourers. Although this work is much more strenuous than the work in the daru factory, I like it more because you get more money here.

Do you prefer to work on your own land or get a job somewhere?

You see, my grandfather had three sons, he distributed his land amongst them. It has more or less sufficed up to now, but after us it will not be enough. It will get further divided. Father had three brothers, and now we are three brothers, the younger uncle has three sons, and the older uncle has two sons, and one of the sons has two sons. We will get some land but for the next generation it will be impossible. It will not suffice. I don't know exactly how much land my father has. It was distributed only some years ago. On the land records it is still in my grandfather's name. My father must be having 12 acres. He has also bought a field from another person, an adivasi who worked for a Parsi, and probably got the land from the Parsi. My father also works as a night watchman for someone, probably a Gujarati, who trades in grass. His father was a timber trader, he used to manufacture charcoal. This man doesn't harass anyone. When my father cannot go, I go in his place. He buys grass and paddy grass from the adivasis in our village. We also sell our grass to him, every one does. On the rocky land, which cannot be cultivated, grass grows. Those who have cattle keep some paddy straw for themselves and for the roof and sell the rest to him. In our village there are no big non-adivasis, may be there were big sowkars earlier but now there aren't any. He buys all the grass and stores it in one place till he sends it away. We keep watch over it. He told me that he was going to send the grass to Assam.

My father is educated till the seventh class and he has a lot of general knowledge. My mother is not educated but she works as a health worker. She even gives medicines, knows the names of medicines that even I don't know. My two brothers and two sisters are in school. Two sisters and one brother are in boarding and one brother is at home. My father wants us to study, but he has told me, don't study too much, study till the 12th and then get a job in a company.

I don't want to study much now. I would like to work now and do something. In our house only my father works on the land and as a night watchman. I work on the land. I know every thing about cultivation. You have to plant the right thing at the right place and also in the right season. You have to know where to grow jowari, nagli, varai, different types of paddy, and how much water they need. You have to use your brains. It is not difficult. I saw and learnt. No one teaches you, you just see and learn. Outsiders can't manage it. During the rains work has to be done fast so we employ three or four labourers on the big field and pay them paddy and some money. All of us work on the field, except the youngest, he goes to catch fish in the river. We have a river in our village, it has water throughout the year. We used to get a lot of fish, but now the fish have got diseased.

We have two bullocks and one cart. I have driven the cart and carried grass. It is well paying, but it lasts only for a few months of the season. The rest of the year there is nothing. The poor bullocks do a lot of work through out the year. We leave them to graze in the neighbourhood and they come back on their own from wherever they are. Once my uncle had hired a bullock from another village. The bullock was here for a year, but then he probably thought that he got better food at home, so he went away without any one accompanying him. They know everything.

But if I get a job in a company, the salary will be good. On the land I could employ labourers. But till I get into a company, I will have to work on the land. I want to educate my brothers and sisters. If I get a job, I can spend on their education. In the boarding it is all right, but for the 11th and 12th in the college, you have to spend money. There is a problem of money. Food from the land is enough, in fact, we have a little extra. We buy vegetables and other things from the market. Rice we have, but vegetables and dal is not enough. Sometimes we have to eat rice with just chutney. If my father spends on vegetables and other things, there won't be any money left for clothes, for house repairs. I have faced a lot of difficulties. I won't let my brothers face it. There isn't enough money for the bus fare, for books, for the house. All this has to be done. Our land is not enclosed but there is no money for it.

Do you think education has helped you and the adivasis?

It is good that we study, but then we don't get government jobs. Boys can get into companies as labourers, but if you want a government job, then you have to give money. Some adivasi boys had gone to a Dahanu office, they wanted a bus conductor's job, they were told, if you bring 4000 rupees, you will get it immediately. But we don't have so much money. Many boys who have studied up to the fifteenth standard are sitting at home. They don't get jobs. They tell each other, it is all right to study till the 10th or 12th but not more than that. One should take up a job whenever one gets it. Those who work after the 10th, just work as labourers and carry goods. Some work on the machine or fill cards. What is the use of education? There is a capsule company in Ashagad, they take 12th standard passed boys. There was a boy with me in the 10th, he had got 62 per cent marks, he got a job immediately. He didn't even see college. He gets about 2500 rupees per month. But such people are very few. I also want to do that. I want to educate my brothers.

My friends are educated, some of them studied up to the eighth and then left it. Their fathers were not too keen on education. If they didn't go to school, father wouldn't say anything. My father used to get very angry, but now he doesn't say anything. I don't say anything to him, only if there is work we talk to each other. If I need anything, like money, I ask my mother for it. Others are not like this, only we are like this. He is not angry, we just don't talk. I don't drink toddy with him at weddings. I speak about everything to my mother.

Till five years ago, he used to scold me a lot, but now he doesn't. When I was young, sometimes, I used to play with other boys and did not work on the field. Then at night I used to get punishment and not be given any food. He used to get angry, but now he doesn't. My father has been an activist since long, since I was very young. He has a lot of faith in the Sanghatana. He does Sanghatana work in the village. People look up to him, respect him. It is good. Not only we, others say so too.

The Sanghatana doesn't work for itself, it works for the people. Everyone feels that. But other parties put pressure on people not to go to the Sanghatana. In our village, we have the Congress, and the Lal Bauta. Shiv Sena has come since a few years. We must demand our rights from the government. The Sanghatana does this kind of work, and we must tell the Sanghatana that we support the protests and demonstrations against price rise and such things. In our village we give it support, when meetings are called we discuss the programmes and so on.

My father has been working as an activist since long. If he did not, I would have taken more interest in the activities. If I also work for the Sanghatana, then it will create problems for us. Because I am the eldest, I have younger brothers and sisters. My sister is in the ninth, brother in the eighth, another sister in the seventh and the youngest brother in the fourth standard. I am in the 12th, my examinations are in February, and I must look for a job after the exams. I have to get something soon because the sister who is in the ninth will go to the 10th and that means expenses. There are other expenses, gifts have to be given on weddings, people have to be invited, family members have to be looked after and fed when they visit us. I have to earn something for all this. That is why I don't do much for the Sanghatana. My father is working for it, I don't tell him anything.

Do you talk to your friends about things you would like to do?

Sometimes I feel like going away, forgetting everything and improving my life. I haven't tried it out, but I have talked about it to one or two others. We thought of running away for 10 years, without telling anyone. We didn't do it, just thought of it. I thought of it because I was in a bad condition. I needed money and I didn't get it, and so my work was not done. I had to buy some things, clothes, etc. I felt very bad. My friend and I sat together at night. Both of us work as night watchmen. We think of everything, of the past and the future. We talk about why things are like this and not like that. He also works at filling sand in trucks. Sometimes at night when we see a plane flying, we think that if we had wings, we could fly high and capture the plane and loot it. Planes fly everyday. Sometimes, we tell each other this is your truck and this is my car, now my car is coming. If we had all this, how would it be, how would we feel sitting in the car and going around.

We have even thought of becoming dacoits. We could even blow up a train, it wouldn't take us time to do it. We really thought of it, but we cannot do it, because we like to live here. Once we had gone to a wedding and in the adjoining compound there were a lot of raddishes. We jumped over the fence, and although there was a person keeping watch, we stole some and jumped over the fence and ran away. He chased us but he couldn't get us. We thought of how we could go to the city and snatch someone's bag and run away. What we see in the films is after all not real, the running and jumping and all that, but we could actually do it. No one could catch us. Like this we could collect a lot of money. We feel like doing it and we could do it, but what to do?, it is better to work hard and earn money. We even think that we could loot a bank, steal a lot of money and distribute it among everyone and then die. But we can't do anything. Both of us really think of all this.

Two of us can drink up to five litres of toddy. On 31st December, we had 10 litres for the four of us, and in the end only two litres were left over. Someone had given us toddy, chicken and vegetables, because we had once brought some wood for him from the forest. We drank and ate so much that we couldn't even stand up. My cousin had also drunk a lot, so he had fallen asleep. When we went to wake him up, he hit me, but that was all in fun.

We think about many things. We see films and dance like they do in films. I don't go to the cinema hall. We have a television in one shop in the hamlet. Sometimes we collect money and bring a film, and then we all see it out in the open. Many people come. I like films with a lot of fighting. It would be nice to have a TV at home. My father has a radio, but he only listens to the news. I don't even have a tape recorder, my cousin has one, so I listen to music sometimes. All of us young boys sleep in the church in our hamlet. We go together for a bath in the river every morning, and have a lot of fun pushing each other in the water.

There are boys from our village who have become robbers. They rob cars and trucks that pass our village. There are many such boys in the other villages. Their fathers and brothers haven't brought them up well, that's why they become like this. They really loot. Some years ago boys from our village stole a computer from a car, they mistook it for a television. About 25 boys were involved. The police used to come every day, and finally they arrested two boys.

Earlier boys used to steal things from the houses, like a chicken or something, but now since the last seven or eight years, they steal not only from the adivasi houses, but also go out to steal. Many boys do this. They are generally 20-25 years old. Some people say that they go to Mumbai and other places. Villages that are close to the highway have a lot of cars and trucks passing close to them. The boys stop the trucks and cars by putting big stones on the road and loot them. Or if a truck overturns they take away the tyres, batteries and money from the driver, and whatever the truck may be carrying fruits or implements or whatever. Once a tanker carrying petrol had overturned, the boys from the nearby villages made a hole in the tanker and carried away petrol in cans, in pots or whatever they could lay their hands on. Boys sell the things they take or even use them in the house. If there was an opportunity anyone would do it, one would go along.

But in our hamlet no one robs or loots. A lot of cars overturn on one part of the road which passes through our village. My father does not allow any one to touch anything. Once a truck carrying radios met with an accident near our village, my father helped the driver, and the driver gave him a radio. If I did such a thing, I would be the first to get a scolding. Even if my friends asked me to do it, I wouldn't. My friends don't do such things, we only talk. All the boys from our hamlet say, eat, drink and have fun, but don't do such things.

I remember everyone's advice. My elder brothers also say that we will never get a hamlet like this. We have grown here, we should live here. Everyone, the old and the young, all have fun and are happy throughout the year. People respect my father. I respect him too. He is doing good work. Every one tells me, you study well and do good for the people. But our family situation is such, there is no one older and working, so that I can't do the kind of work my father is doing.

We have a lot of fun in our village. We go for weddings to other hamlets and drink and dance. But we don't drink too much because we are afraid there may be fights and we might be involved in them. In our own hamlet we are very happy, we drink freely, we dance as much as we want. We celebrate festivals together, eat together. The whole village comes to our Christian festivals. We Christians don't play Holi, but we go out at night and have fun.

This Christmas my cousin and I had a party. We bought half a kilo of mutton, four litres of toddy and 10 loaves of bread. We prepared the food and everything and at night in the dark we sat out and had a nice party. Everyone had gone for the midnight mass, but we didn't go anywhere. We even slept out in the open. The other boys had gone to the church and then for a Tarfa dance. They dance the whole night, and it is a lot of fun. Sometimes there are fights also. Now my cousin had gone for sand loading and I came here. We have been together since we were young, we have never fought. We are good to each other.

From our hamlet the boys get together and go for a picnic to the forest once a year or so. Last year we took forty litres of toddy, 10 kilos of mutton and 10 litres of liquor, and put it on a bullock cart and about 40 of us went to the forest. Even four- and five-years old children also came along. We went inside a tiger's den, but of course, we didn't see it. There is a belief that the tiger attacks only outside its den, not inside. My father also says so, and he has a lot of experience and knowledge. In the village we celebrate a big festival for the Waghaya, the tiger god, he is also our village god. The older people get together and cook and drink the whole night. Then the bhagat shakes all over and kills a chicken. They have a nice time.

I like to go to the forest but I don't go much because I go to college. We chase animals, and if we kill a small animal we cook it in the forest or in the field and eat it. We get fruits to eat, depending on the season. One has to go far into the forest to get wood. People steal wood. They cut big trees in to small pieces and we carry it for them in our carts. If the forester sees us, of course, he gets angry. If we bring dry wood, he doesn't say anything.

What makes you sad?

Like that I haven't thought much about the time when I was very sad. But when I work and work very hard and take care of the house and everybody, only then will things be all right, and I will be happy. Otherwise, I don't think there will be happiness in our house because no one works. That is why we are in this condition. Only when I work, I can do something for the house.

When I was in school, I used to feel sad, and now also I feel sad. I had to walk and even miss school because there was no money. I didn't have good clothes. I feel a lot of tension. But I never steal money. There was someone in our house who used to cheat a lot with money, but I never cheat. The other day I was ill and I had no money to travel, I borrowed 10 rupees from Kamal and went home. Now I have to buy a file for five rupees, but I will not ask my father for it. Even if I can't get it, it is all right. My teachers are good to me. Even if I don't go today, he won't say anything. He scolds other children, but not me. He knows my condition.

The whole clan should be peaceful and happy. Their condition has deteriorated, that should be improved. If someone is unhappy because they don't have money, they should be given money, if someone is unhappy because they have quarrels at home, then their problems should be solved somehow. Someone should bring the hamlet together. We are all related, there are only a few outsiders. Someone should be able to say whether there is a bhutali or not. Someone should have the sense to do good for the hamlet. Our hamlet has always been united, but now there are problems. People are going in different ways.

In our pada and in the village bhutali and illness are the biggest problem. The bhutali brings disease. She has such power that no matter how much you beat her she would not die. They derive power from a copper object, my aunt has one such object so that she can be in two places at the same time, at home and at work. She can make you a mental case. She has turned her son into a mental case, because she wanted to eat his son and he didn't allow it. Bhutalis thrive on eating children. She has the power to destroy anyone in the family who is doing well. Even the doctor cannot help. The bhutali is taken to a bhagat who gives her a potion to drink. If the woman is not a bhutali, she faints and dies, but if she is a bhutali she turns ferocious, and eats whatever she can find, and then admits to whatever she has done. They don't generally affect people who are educated or well off. Even when our condition was better we didn't believe in bhutali, but now that we are affected, we believe in it.

My aunt acquired the knowledge from her mother and she taught it to my uncle. He offered his father as a sacrifice. You can practise only after you have offered someone as a sacrifice, your father, or husband or child. She has affected me mentally so badly that I can't focus on anything. I can't study, I don't feel like working. My uncle and aunt have an evil eye on our house. Our's is a better house. They are jealous that all is well in our house. Things are bad with them right now.

She knows that I know about her. She is so afraid of passing by my side that she goes far away when she sees me. In our hamlet people know who the bhutalis are. Only a woman from one's own hamlet can cast a spell, no one from outside can do it. An old woman, who was a bhutali, used to come to our school in the form of a cat. One night the boys hit her and she got injured on her leg. Next day when we saw her, her hand was broken, and when we asked her what had happened, she said she had fallen and broken her hand.

Many people in our pada say that she is a bhutali. People don't go to her house. Her son also beats her. He has now separated from them. He goes for sand work. He can drive but he has no money for a driver's licence. My uncle is paralysed. He is at home. One son is a mental case, he was in an asylum but he has come away. Her three daughters go out to work. One daughter's husband left her because of the same reason. Their condition is bad. In fact, all our relatives visit us, except them.

I don't know what it is, one doesn't know. If you see from the point of view of science, there is no bhutali, nothing is written in science about bhutali, but if you see from another point of view, she is a bhutali. I feel she has done something to me. Bhagats are able to identify the bhutali, they give the correct name. One bhagat has told me that there is someone in the family who has affected me. I hit her once. She doesn't do anything, she is scared of me. I don't speak too much. Only when I get very angry do I give a slap or two. She has affected others also. Once I told her, don't do anything again, otherwise I will hit you. She used to tell me, take me to a bhagat to identify me as a bhutali, but now she doesn't say anything.

In our hamlet the condition has become very bad. Many people have become mental cases. I don't know why. These people speak strangely, roam around at night. Something happens to them, they must be having tension. If people had work, they wouldn't have tension. But few people get jobs. In our village, there is not even one company. Most young men go for sand work, one works in a bank, and one is a Sanghatana activist.

Young people feel that we should work for the Sanghatana and do our own work also. The Sanghatana has a lot of support in our pada. We support their work, organise meetings and demonstrations for the forest plots. There are not many activists in our village, just two or three. We should oppose the government, demand our dues and fight for our rights. The Sanghatana pays attention to that. It manages to get us our dues from the government. We need to fight as well as to work. But there should be work. But no work is available in our village.

When are you planning to get married?

In our pada boys and girls don't marry young. In our village 15 and 16 year olds get married, boys of my age even have children. Even if they don't marry, the girl is brought and kept at home. The villagers are given toddy and some money according to the rules and the couple lives together. But our pada is better, it is more advanced. My father's sister's daughter got married recently. She was married to someone from the same village. Dancing was a lot of fun. This year there is another wedding in the same house, the son is getting married. He works in a bank.

My father doesn't say anything to me about getting married, my mother doesn't say anything either. She knows that I will not marry so soon. There is still time, may be even eight or nine years. I have to start working. The situation at home is not such that I can get married. In our family boys marry late, the cousin who is getting married must be around 28 years old. I think it is better to marry late, when you have a good job, so that you can have a good wedding. I have to educate my brothers and sisters and for that I have to do something. I have two sisters, if I get married, it will be difficult to look after them. I will get married only when I get a good job.

Are you proud to be a Warli?

Yes, I am proud to be a Warli. I don't feel that we have nothing. We have land, we have forests. I feel that we are going to get more respect, because Mumbai is so congested that the big people will come to the adivasi areas. If I could get a good job, I could do something for the pada, for the village, make a temple or a 'mandap', tent for weddings, or whatever my resources permitted. But I have nothing.

In our community drinking liquor and toddy is a bad thing, bhutali is bad, beating women is bad. Children are not sent to school, men sit at home and drink while women go to work, all that is bad.

There are good things also. People are honest. When someone comes to the village asking for something or begging, people don't say harsh things. They give immediately, they even ask from others and give. In the city, people don't talk, they don't even give you water when you ask for it in a hotel. When a Sanghatana person or a doctor comes to the village, our people help.

We are honest, for example, if someone gives us more money than is due to us, we return it. Warlis don't cheat. Only those whose parents haven't brought them up well, or haven't stopped them from stealing, steal when they grow up. Two or three persons like this who might steal a chicken may be there in a village. But they don't engage in big crimes or murders.

If someone really needs food, they borrow. They don't steal, they borrow from the seth, and return it by doing mazoori. People don't consider taking firewood for cooking or for use stealing. It is for use as fuelwood.

All adivasis, children as well as old persons speak nicely, not harshly or abusively. They share food. Whatever they get from the shop, they are ready to share. People say Koknas and Dhodis are a little stingy about giving and taking food. But they are good to speak to. Warlis are not stingy. They eat well, whatever they can afford. They are good natured.

We also have close family ties. Family members may be away in other villages, but they visit each other. It is good because children come to know their relatives. For example, I live in Ramubhau's house, he is related to my father. When my father asked him if I could stay with him, he readily agreed. He accepted me without any hesitation. I am happy in his house, like at home. His wife is good to me. Many young people working outside their villages live with their relatives. It is a good practice.

My grandfather's generation used to borrow money from the seth, but people of my father's generation borrow from each other, from people who work in companies or have a small business or from neighbours. People lend money to each other without interest. Even if you return the money after five years, it is all right. People take rice, kerosene, bullocks from each other for a few days, and repay by working on the field or any other way. The young help each other even more. It is going on, and it will go on. It will not disappear. People go out for a few months but they come back. Unlike the non-adivasis, who leave their own place and do business anywhere, we go and come back to our village and work honestly. It is not like this in the city. Even if you go to somebody's door, they don't bother. It is not good.

There are Warli sarpanchs, in some villages they are good, in others they are not good. They don't give the adivasis any benefits. In our village, in one year, the sarpanch has built a nice house for himself. Ever since he became the sarpanch, no houses have been provided to the destitute, in other villages poor adivasis have got houses. He was in the Congress, but now he is planning to join the Shiv Sena. When adivasis rise in status and get power, they do such things. But the poor, common adivasis don't do such things.

How will the condition of the adivasis improve? Do you have any faith in the government?

No, I have no faith in the government. It has not improved our condition. Even if it gives help, it doesn't reach the adivasis. The government people – persons in between – mess it up, eat up everything. Out of 100 per cent, we get only 10 per cent. Adivasis have to do something to set the government right. The government has to change. We have to put pressure on the government, not through violence, but by taking a morcha, by appealing to the government that what is happening is not right. If good people, who are educated, who are in high positions and know about governance, if they help the adivasis to end oppression, it will be good. We have to do things unitedly. We have to fight for our rights, but we have to be one. Although every one says so, we are divided into factions and groups, Congress, Communist, Shiv Sena, BJP. We haven't come together.

Would you go to Mumbai or to any other city, if you got a job there?

I wouldn't like to. I wouldn't like to leave home, my brothers and sisters, but one has to go wherever one gets work. Anyone would go. People go because we don't get good salaries here. But those who go out to Mumbai or other places miss the pada. They come once a week or month, on Friday or Saturday for a day or two.

There are things to see in the city, you don't get bored, but one thinks of home and one misses everyone. There are some people who work outside. They talk about scarcity of water, about not getting enough water for a bath. One has to bathe out of just one bucket of water. Things are expensive there. But of course, one would go wherever one gets a good job. Actually, if one had a vadi, one wouldn't need a job. It would be nice to be at home.

I don't think people will leave our pada and go away to live in Mumbai. Good people live in our pada. You don't find a pada like ours in the village. Everyone is good to each other. Even the old live happily. People from other villages fight with us, but we are united. Those who go out to work, return regularly. We are happy together.

I would like to get a good job for my entire life, so that I can work and look after everyone at home. Only then will there be some peace and happiness at home.

Subhash's life does not seem to have had major turning points. It has been comparatively easy so far, a happy childhood and a secure adolescence. The stable economic as well as emotional situation of the family has, in all likelihood made this possible. He has very pleasant memories of growing up, friends, cousins, fun times in school and love from everyone at home. His narration is punctuated with expressions like "it was a lot of fun".

The Christian fathers have been an important influence in his life and he views it positively. He is happy to be a Christian, and unlike many adivasis, does not see any contradiction between the Warli and the Christian religions. He has a strong Warli identity and is able to accommodate and integrate the Christian practices, beliefs, rituals within his larger Warli identity without tension.

He is very close to his family and his clan, and obviously draws a lot of emotional support from it. He expresses strong feeling for the family. But clearly, his relationship with his father is an ambivalent one, he respects his father, but also resents being dominated by him. Subhash's father is a strict disciplinarian, a principled man who wants his children to imbibe certain values. Subhash does not confront his father openly and keeps a distance, in fact, does not communicate with him at all. Subhash is scared of his father. During the course of this fieldwork, his father often came and scolded him for missing college, a fact which Subhash had not shared with me.

Behind a gentle and calm exterior there are wild fantasies of robbing, stealing and looting. He wants to fly, to have money, cars, good clothes, television and one way of getting all this is by robbing. Given the fact that a lot of young adivasi men have taken to such crime it is neither surprising nor unusual. One could also understand this in the context of Subhash's relationship with his father. But Subhash's strong family ties, his love for life in his pada, his rootedness in the Warli way of life saves him from falling over. The values he has grown up with, seem to reassert themselves and hold him back.

Like many young men of his generation Subhash recognises the need, and repeats it parrot like, to organise and collectively fight for their rights. But also like many of his generation, he is more concerned with finding a good job and earning money rather than with seeking political solutions. He does not want to become an activist, the reason given being, because his father in an activist and he must, therefore, earn for his family.

Also like many of his generation, although Subhash is proud to have some education, he knows that it does not necessarily get a good job and good money. He often talked about his friends who had finished college but hadn't still found a job. Most of them are working on their own land, of find employment in the informal sector at sand dredging or salt making. But what they and Subhash want is to earn a salary, to earn good money with which they can buy services, consumer goods, everything which makes up a good life and which they see in towns and cities. Like others, Subhash shuns mazoori of the kind in which he and his friends are currently engaged, because it is low paying, the conditions of work are poor and because it is strenuous. Given Subhash's own physical constitution, which is not strong, he is unable to sustain strenuous work of this kind.

Subhash's anger and frustration of not having what he wants is, however, directed towards his aunt whom he suspects of being a bhutali. He believes that she is responsible for his inability to concentrate on his studies or to work consistently. The hostility that he expresses towards her is quite alarming. Significantly, in a situation of scarcity, even having enough to eat can attract an evil eye of the bhutali.

It is noteworthy that all of them talk about fights between different political groups/parties as being one of the many problems they have to face. Several of them recall clashes between the activists belonging to the Congress, CPM, Kashtakari Sanghatana or BJP. Violent confrontations between them often result in destruction of house, crops or even killings. The villagers are afraid to support one or the other.

Conclusion

The foregoing life stories of the adivasis acquire an even greater poignancy when they are viewed against the background of the region, which is highly developed and resourcefully very rich. The Konkan region is known as the "food bowl" of Maharashtra. Of the five districts in this division, Thane contributes the most important share in terms of area under several important crops: almost one-third each of autumn rice, of total foodgrains and also of total food crops. In fact, it alone accounts for about 10 per cent of the total area under rice and ragi cultivation in the whole of Maharashtra, and an overwhelming 29 per cent of the state's total under the common millet and vari [Dewan, et al 1999: 48].

Thane district has the maximum area under vegetable culti-vation, 62 per cent of the Konkan division. Several fruits are grown in the district. The area under chikoo fruit constitutes over 64 per cent of all area under its cultivation in Maharashtra. Thane also ranks amongst the highest in agricultural productivity in the state. The average yield of rice per hectare in Thane is 2599 kgs, while at the state level it is 1558 kgs. Productivity levels of some pulses are the highest among all the eight divisions in the state [ibid: 50].

As compared to other talukas in the district, Dahanu taluka, from where most of the narrators happen to come, has a signi-ficant area under various food crops. All wheat in Thane is cultivated only in Dahanu. Mangoes, chillies and other spices account for 22 to 28 per cent of the district totals. Dahanu has the maximum area under cashew and the second highest under coconut. The bulk of chickoo sold in Mumbai comes from this region.

Dahanu records over 46 per cent of all electric pumps in the district (1818 of 3938), the second highest in the number of irrigation wells among all the talukas (1632 of 15,327), the third highest in the number of wooden ploughs (16,477 of 1,29,854) and the sixth in the number of bullock carts. It also has a significant share in the livestock economy, has the highest proportion of cross-bred cows and bulls over two and a half years, used for both breeding and working, and the second highest number of total local and cross-bred bulls as well as goats [ibid: 51]. It is also an important fishing centre along the coastline of the district. Along with marine fishing, intensive estuarine fishing is carried out in the large number of creeks and bays. The marine fish production of Dahanu was 10,903 tonnes in the fishery year 1994-95, 13.7 per cent of the district total. In 1996-97, it rose to 11,503 tonnes, valued at Rs 2644 lakh [ibid: 53].

The irony of the situation was striking even in the late 1970s, when I was working in the region in and around Vangaon, in Dahanu, which is popularly known as the "vegetable bowl" of the entire district. It is an important supplier of fodder to the dairies of Mumbai. Fruits and vegetables and recently flowers too, find a market in Mumbai and other cities in the country as well as abroad. But in the same village almost all my adivasi respondents were talking about hunger as their main problem. Out of nearly 100 persons interviewed, more than 90 talked about not having enough food and clothes [Munshi 1983].

With little or no land, given restricted access to an already depleted forest, absence of avenues of employment and increasing need for cash to meet the requirements of everyday life, the adivasi men and women have few options other than to migrate seasonally to salt pans, brick kilns, factories and plantations within and outside the district. Women, too, migrate, although much less than men, only to face extremely hard conditions of living, the double burden of working at home and on the work site and molestation and harassment by the mukaddam. Those who stay behind with children and the elderly while the men migrate, must bear the responsibility of the family and the field. Household work, work on own land for those with a little land, and work as agricultural labour in order to earn a cash income, constitute the burden of women who stay back [see Mehta 1999].

Life is particularly difficult for these women. Interviews with more than 60 adivasi women from several talukas of the district, Dahanu, Palghar, Talasari, Mokhada, Wada, revealed a sense of alarm over the rapid depletion of the forests, and the conversion of mixed forests into plantations of commercially valuable trees. Many of them reported having to walk for three to four hours in the forest to collect firewood. For most women, the morning is spent in the forest. Other items collected for consumption and/or sale are resin, roots, berries, fruits, leaves, leafy vegetables, seeds and mahua flowers. While roots, berries, fruits, leafy and other vegetables and firewood are for consumption, seeds, resin, a variety of leaves and also firewood are bartered for onions, garlic, fish and spices. Women are the main collectors of these items. Depletion of forest, therefore, also means a reduction in the income of women. Grazing of cattle and collection of cattle droppings now involve more time on the part of women and children. Collection of material for rab, the age-old agricultural practice in the region, has become more arduous for women and children who are primarily responsible for it. Those from the landless households need to go to the market everyday to exchange the above-mentioned produce for daily necessities. For households with some land, this not only supplements the daily diet, but constitutes a major source of food during the lean season, the "difficult months" which could last for four to eight months.

Occasionally, cash is spent on trinkets, bangles and clothes for oneself and the children. Although, going to the forest with friends is still an enjoyable activity for adivasi women, having to walk long distances with heavy loads, and being harassed by the forest guards if one is caught, takes away the pleasure. "There is no time to have fun, but sometimes we take a bottle of liquor in the basket and drink together in the forest" is the experience of many adivasi women. Forest, once a social space where women like to go in a group to collect firewood, to gossip, to eat, to sing, to roam, to bathe, and to escape from the drudgery of household chores, has become now a degraded and hostile space.

The collection of food and medicinal herbs, needless to say, requires knowledge about plants, trees, roots, etc. Most adivasi women do know something about the edible as well as medicinal plants. They often treat family members, especially children, for common ailments. Especially the suin, the mid-wife, knows a lot about medicinal plants useful for childbirth, abortion and menstrual problems. Depletion and destruction of natural forests has meant the destruction of the material basis for such knowledge. One is tempted to ask if there was a time in the Warli history when the bhagat saw women experts like the suin as a threat to his position of domination and found a way of subjugating her by denouncing her as a bhutali, the evil one.

In this context of reduced supply of herbal medicines, as well as the increased pressure on land, the phenomenon of bhutali acquires a new significance. Political organisations as well as individual researchers working in this region have reported an increase in the incidents of bhutali in recent years. One explanation offered is that the bhagat probably finds himself less effective as a result of loss of medicinal herbs. And the old conflict between the bhagat and the bhutali recurs in the new context where the bhagat must find a scapegoat in his old enemy, the bhutali [Kashtakari Sanghatana 1984: 90].

I must, however, hasten to add that the conflict between the two is an old one, which can probably be traced long back to the power struggle for domination between the genders and the ultimate subordination of women. Warli songs, for example, suggest the subordination of the dark goddess of corn, Kansari, by god Naran Dev. She is humiliated by the gods, and thrown out of their kingdom, although at the sametime the farmers and gods realise that they cannot do without her [Save 1945: 174]. In another version, the gods, the chief of whom is Indra, are engaged in a constant struggle with her to capture and attain her [Dalmia 1988: 86]. The dark goddess, Kansari, is clearly a symbol for the grain nagli, which was commonly cultivated by the Warlis on the hill slopes by shifting cultivation before the transition to plough cultivation. The supersedure of the mother goddess probably coincided with the establishment of patriarchal norms in a situation where they did not exist. Undoubtedly, contestation over land and the loss of medicinal herbs are additional reasons for its occurrence at present [for details see Munshi, 2003].

The quality of life of majority of the adivasis in Thane continues to be far from desirable, except for a small elite group which has emerged in the last few decades and which, like its non-adivasi counterpart, has appropriated economic and political benefits to its own advantage. This section, I was informed, has succeeded in establishing businesses and constructing big houses, primarily by engaging in corrupt activities. They give and take bribes for gaining and granting political and economic favours, buy and sell contracts for development projects and carry on illegal activities like trade in timber. As members of the panchayat, contractors and traders, they are able to corner the funds allocated for tribal development and dominate and terrorise the poor of their own community, especially those who belong to political parties or factions other than their own. A number of our respondents talked about the menace of factional fights, which only makes life more difficult for every one.

On the positive side, however, a number of non-party political organisations have been working in the district for the last four decades, and have succeeded in politicising and organising the adivasis, the Warlis, Kokna, Kathkari, Kolis and Thakurs, to fight for the redressal of their grievances. Organisations such as Bhoomi Sena, Kashtakari Sanghatana, Shramjivi Sanghatana, Shramik Mukti Sanghatan, Eklavya Kashtakari Sanghatana and Adivasi Ekta Parishad, spread over 10 talukas, have taken up the issues of bonded labour, indebtedness, land and forest rights, forest encroachments and wages, mostly working on their own but also coming together on specific issues. Adivasis have engaged in organised as well as spontaneous action, displaying courage and perseverance, to resist oppression and exploitation by the government officials, mukaddams, traders and employers, to protest against developments that have been to their disadvantage and to demand greater rights and justice.

A significant development in recent years has been the initiative taken by adivasi men and women in taking over the protection of a small part of the forest, a resource that is still important for their survival. In some villages, I was informed, women have emerged as leaders in the 'Jungle Bachao' struggle.

Groups of women even patrol the forest. They are keen to protect not just timber, but the forest as a whole. Incidents of women destroying saplings of teak planted by the forest department have occurred in the region earlier also.

A brief note on the experience of Jungle Bachao in Dhanau may be useful to illustrate how, in spite of internal contradictions, adivasis from some villages have undertaken the protection and management of a degraded forest, precisely because they have a stake in it. Although supported by the Kashtakari Sanghatana, the adivasis, I was told, began the programme on their own around 1991. In one village, Jamshet Shindechepada people decided to protect the forest already denuded as a result of the felling carried out by the forest department, the Forest Development Corporation of Maharashtra (FDCM) as well as the people. With a view to economise, rules regarding the use of only certain types of timber were worked out and forests were allowed to regenerate without any interference. The padas established contact with each other and the villagers decided to protect the forest on their side of the hill to stop it from becoming completely barren. Although the rules varied from one pada to another, some of them were uniformly enforced by all the padas. Decisions taken in this village were followed in other villages as well. The Kashtakari Sanghatana put forward the idea that people who cultivated the forest encroachment plots, had a right to do so only if they also protected the forest. In Shindechepada, Santoshi, Dongripada and Kamdipada, the forest protection around the plot was carried out.

Meetings were regularly held, contact with other villages made and decisions taken. Men and women both shared the responsibility, and still do, of patrolling the forest in order to keep the thieves out. The programme was adopted by other villages like Raytali, Chari and Ganjad also. In all instances, cutting of timber was regulated. In many villages, it was decided to protect teak because it is useful for house construction and seven types of trees were identified which could be used as firewood. In some villages, however, the programme did not succeed because some villagers themselves were involved in small-scale smuggling of timber and therefore, opposed those who tried to protect the forest. In others, outsiders from other villages stole timber or groups belonging to different political organisations clashed with each other over the issue of forest protection, making it difficult for a consensus to emerge.

The success of Shishne, Haladpada and Ambholi in regenerating collectively the hillside shared by them, has been a source of inspiration to others. These villages actually closed parts of the forest, no one being allowed to enter into them. Not even leaves or firewood could be taken out except with the permission of the 'gaonkari', the villagers/village elders. Fines were imposed on the offenders. In order to formalise the programme, the Sanghatana suggested that people sign affidavits stating, "I will carry out Jungle Bachao which my Sanghatana has made. I will grow trees on my plot to prevent soil erosion and if I don't, then the plot can be taken away by the sarkar". The Sanghatana surveyed these plots, mapped them, measured them and kept account of the trees on the plot, so as to be able to check the number of trees after five years. Other organisations working with the adivasis, Bhoomi Sena, Gramin Shramik Sangh, Shramik Mukti Sanghatan, Gram Swaraj Samiti and Shramjeevi Sanghatana also collected similar affidavits [Prabhu a 2001]. It may be noted that Jungle Bachao was an important factor in determining the decision of the Supreme Court to commission an enquiry referred to in Chapter II.

Adivasi women have not only opposed the traders and the forest officials, who they hold responsible for the depletion of the forest, but also their own men and women who steal from the forest. They have opposed the involvement of their own men in the illegal trade of timber, which is a thriving activity in Thane. I heard of an incident, which took place a few years ago in a village called Sukhdamba, where logs of timber had been stacked on the roadside for loading at night. Women were extremely angry to see this. They chopped the logs into small pieces and carried them away to use as firewood.

Large amounts of timber is illegally felled and transported to Mumbai and Gujarat. Adivasi men are employed to fell the trees and to carry the same to a particular spot on the road, from where it can be transported by trucks. They are, of course, paid a small sum of money as wages. But it is also common knowledge that adivasi men are engaged in relatively small-scale timber smuggling with the support of their women.

In a situation where the community is highly differentiated and unequal, and where there is a lucrative market for timber, which makes theft of timber very attractive, protection of forests by the community becomes a difficult business. But given the mutual distrust between the forest department and the adivasis, the latter want to keep the forest department out of it. This may not be the best long-term solution if Thane forests are to be protected and regenerated effectively and on a large scale. But, for the moment the adivasis are certain about their decision.

There are instances when the adivasis have committed spontaneous acts of violence to assert their rights to the resources. One such incident occurred when I was doing my fieldwork. Nearly 30 men and women, all adivasis, entered the vadi of a Gujarati vadi owner, who calls himself a Gandhian, and chopped off nearly 5000 fruit trees. Having done that, they did not run away, but stayed on in the vadi till the police arrived and arrested them for their crime. The reconstruction of the incident revealed a long history of resentment of the adivasis living in the proximity of this vadi, against its former owners. The latter had forcibly evicted their fathers and grandfathers working as tenants on the land, which was formerly paddy land, and which should legally have come to the tenants. In the meanwhile, the land changed owners twice, till the present owner acquired it. He turned it into a vadi, and in order to supply water to the fruit trees, had several electric pumps installed which effectively sucked/diverted the water from the small river adjoining the vadi. The adivasis staying close by had been using the water for a variety of purposes like washing, bathing, for their cattle, for fishing and so on. When the water level of the river started going down, the people began to get alarmed. They spoke to the owner several times but with no effect. And when the problem of water became acute, they decided to enter the vadi with sickles early one morning and fell the trees.

I spoke to several men and women who had been involved in the incident in order to find out what had led them to this violent act, and having committed it, how they felt about it. When I asked a young man if he did not feel bad destroying trees laden with fruit, he replied, "no, that vadi deprived us of water, if it had survived, we would have died. Besides, that land belongs to us, it was taken away from our elders." An older woman said, "I felt nothing cutting those trees, it didn't do us any good, in fact, it only created difficulties for us. I was not afraid of anybody, not even of the police".

In this context, it must be noted that caution has to be exercised against romanticising the adivasis' relationship with nature in general and forest in particular. There is a tendency among some scholars and activists to do so, especially with respect to women, largely to refute the view dominant in certain official quarters, which holds the adivasis responsible for the destruction of the forests, and also in order to establish their claims to resources. One can make a strong argument, for example, for a greater involvement of the forest communities in the management and use of forest resources, on which they depend, and have depended, for their subsistence and about which they have some knowledge and feelings. But for this, one does not have to impute a high ecological consciousness to them, or make a case for their being, as Hardiman puts it, "born conservationists" or repositories of superior knowledge. This kind of essentialising can have dangerous political consequences.

It is also known that not all agricultural or forest communities have the same extent of ecological sensibility. Some show greater ecological sense than others. Nor is their attitude constant and unchanging over time, independent of the broader social, ecological context. For example, regarding commerciali- sation of forest, of enhanced value of the produce of the forest and the continuing alienation of the adivasis of Thane, individuals and groups among them may show a very different attitude and behaviour at present compared to other times [For a discussion on related issues, see Shiva 1988; Agarwal 1991; Hardiman 1994; Prabhu 2001b; Prasad 2003; Parreira 1992].

As expected, people take different paths to find solutions to their problems. Many have sought and adopted non-political solutions, by turning to religious cults, which have entered the region recently and which promise happiness and 'sudhar', improvement. Young adivasi men and women adopt cults such as Malkari, Nirankari, Mahanubhav Panth, and others in the hope that it will improve the condition of their life. They give up drinking daru and eating meat and adopt new gods and rituals in order to reform their lives and fates. The converted wear a bead necklace, or sport a cap, greet each other by uttering "dandavat pranaam", look down upon their own gods, do not eat in neighbour's or relative's house because they are non-vegetarians and so on. The Hindu cults predominate although there are also Christian groups who promise liberation from poverty and misery. Apart from promised moral upliftment, they provide some actual material benefits as well, like jobs and money. Some religious organisations offer free education and even employment.

Others travel for miles in the hope of finding a treasure, gold or money, which would make dreams come true. A little security, education for the children, freedom from the perpetual grind of hard labour, from a hand to mouth existence and from want. But happiness still eludes them, because for most, as Suman says, "when there is no job, no money, what is the use of thinking of happiness". And happiness means having "enough to eat and a little leftover, a little land, a little money, a job". It also means not having to go out to labour on brick kilns, salt pans, construction sites and baloon factories, and not having to "work even when one is ill". That is the stuff of happiness.

Most adivasis, men and women, young and old, would prefer not to go out for work if work is available in the village or nearby. But "to fill ones stomach, one has to go anywhere". "There is a lot to do in the city", but the forest, the village and the pada are their familiar spaces, which provide some meaning and security. In contrast, the city and its suburbs are ugly and impersonal. "You cannot ask anyone even for a glass of water", "no one knows you", "there are no forests". Many young men told me that even when the adivasis go out, they return to the pada, "they have to return to the pada, to the neighbourhood, food and festivals and forests". Although more and more men, women and children must migrate out, it is disliked, not because adivasis in Thane are resistant to change, but because going out of the village does not mean a better quality of life for them. Informal sector employment only means a much harsher condition of existence, having to live in makeshift shanties, without even the minimum amenities available in the village, under exploitative and oppressive conditions, and without even the support and security of the family and neighbours. Change, however painful, would be acceptable if there was something to gain from it. Clearly, adivasis of Thane want "improvement" in their conditions of existence, they want to go "forward", to be free from want, to be a part of the good life that development has brought around them and to be happy. There is no nostalgia about any golden past, no desire, even in fantasy, to return to it. There is a crying need for a dignified present and a secured future.

Any serious attempt to improve the condition of the adivasis must recognise the fact that the general development of the region, the district or the taluka, does not mean an improvement in the quality of life of the adivasis. In fact, in spite of the growth of Thane, an alarming demographic change in the district is visible. While the total population of the district increased from about 1.7 million in1961 to 3.4 million in 1981 and to 5.2 million in 1991, the increase in adivasi population was only from 0.5 million in 1961 to 0.8 million in 1981. In fact, there was a sharp reduction in the percentage of adivasi population to the total population, from 30.29 per cent in 1961 to 25.40 per cent in 1971, 21.76 per cent in 1981 and 18 per cent in 1991 [DCH, 1995: 330]. Doubtlessly, poverty, malnutrition and loss of control over assets and resources are threatening the survival of the adivasi community in the face of the influx and growth of the non-adivasi population and their increasing control over the resources of the region.

The majority of adivasis must continue to struggle to get enough to eat. Although there is much less starvation now than before, food continues to be a major concern. To work and eat well is everybody's dream. Malnutrition is endemic, hunger deaths have occurred and continue to occur in Wada, Mokhada, Jawhar, Vikramgad and parts of Dahanu, where the adivasis are concentrated. The press has only recently highlighted the seriousness of the problem among the adivasis in Thane and all over Maharashtra. The foodgrains from the food security schemes do not reach the poor, given the massive corruption in the Public Distribution System. The benefits of all the schemes meant for those below poverty line are pocketed by the well-off adivasis.

A survey conducted by the Tribal Training and Research Institute in 16 tribal villages of Thane revealed that a major cause of death of 26 tribal children during April-August 2002, was malnutrition. In general, tribal children were found to be undernourished. Nearly 68 per cent of the families were in debt to the brick kiln owners, not a single family was employed under the Employment Guarantee Scheme, almost 84 per cent did not hold any land and an equal percentage worked as farm and brick kiln labourers (*Times of India* October 24, 2002).

According to the 1991 Census, at present, about 25.84 per cent adivasis of Thane are literate compared to less than 10 per cent in 1961. Many adivasi boys are educated up to 10th and 12th standards, a few have taken technical training, and a few have even become engineers and doctors, but for most, education does not guarantee a good job or a good salary. For them, even school education is a luxury not every one can afford. Although schools exist in almost all the villages, the dropout rate is very high. In fact, the distinct impression one gets at present is that there is a complete disillusionment among the adivasis with respect to education. It was very different 20 to 25 years ago when without any doubt they saw education as an essential step towards improvement. They had heard from everyone, the bureaucrat, the social worker and the local politician, that they were backward because they lacked education, but now, while the value of education is not questioned, there are doubts about its value as a means to material betterment.

Health care is better than it was in the 1950s, although it is still inadequate. Medical facility of some type is available in 15.72 per cent of the inhabited villages in the district, but it is unevenly spread, ranging from 2.34 per cent in Vada taluka to 65.85 per cent in Talasari taluka, both with large adivasi population. There has been an overall decline in medical facilities during 1981-91. Out of 1679 villages 84.28 per cent do not have any type of medical facility in their village limits. Of these, 56.54 per cent are situated at a distance of about five kilometres from the nearest medical facility, while 31.09 per cent are located at a distance of five to 10 kilometres. And in the case of 12.37 per cent villages, the residents have to cover more than 10 kilometres to reach a place with some medical facility [DCH 1991: 49]. Given that free medical care is not easily available, the adivasis often turn to the bhagat, who has become more expensive since he has to walk longer to look for herbs. The primary health care centres are most often without a doctor and even the necessary medicines. On the other hand, private practitioners, polyclinics and hospitals have mushroomed all over. In Dahanu town alone there are nearly 27 polyclinics, which give not only injections, but even glucose drips for common ailments. The lure of impressive looking modern machines often takes the adivasis to these polyclinics. As expected, they end up incurring huge costs for a treatment that is unnecessary. I was told that one important cause of indebtedness among them now is the exorbitant expenditure on medical care.

That the majority of the adivasis in India, by and large, share the circumstances of the adivasis in Thane is evident from the Sixth Report of the National Commission for Scheduled Castes and Scheduled Tribes, 2001-02, headed by Dileep Singh Bhuria. The following information is taken from that report. Commenting on the general situation of the adivasis in India, it notes,

> the tribals are living in remote, inaccessible and impoverished conditions, suffering from hunger and malnutrition and starvation deaths, particularly among the children, in some of the tribal pockets and require better attention to provide food security, at least in vulnerable seasons [GoI: 64].

In 1993-94, nearly 46.54 per cent of the scheduled tribes were estimated to live below poverty line, which is much larger than the 35.97 per cent for the rest of the society. More than 93 per cent of the tribal population lives in rural areas, as against 74 per cent of total population, almost entirely dependent on agriculture for their livelihood, supplemented by collection and sale of minor forest produce. The percentage of cultivators have decreased from 68.18 in 1961 to 54.50 in 1991, with a corresponding increase in the proportion of agricultural labour. This is so despite the existence of legislations to prevent the alienation of tribal lands and to ensure its restoration whenever alienation occurred. But the implementation of these legislations, the commission notes, is tardy and the tribals continue to lose their lands. For example, as on September 2000, the state had an alienated area of 8.55 lakh hectares, out of which, only 84.67 per cent of the cases were disposed by the courts, and only 51.21 per cent were decided in favour of the adivasis. Out of the 1,62,650 cases decided in favour of the adivasis, land has been restored in

1,58,297 cases. Significantly, in Maharashtra, only 44. 69 per cent of cases have been decided in favour of the adivasis [ibid: 119].

> The condition of landless tribals is far worse as they are more vulnerable due to lack of employment and poverty. The problem of landowning tribals is also not much different because of the small size of average holdings. A large number of tribals have to migrate to other areas/cities in search of employment due to a lack of jobs in their own areas [ibid: 115, 119].

The commission does not mince words when it says that the public sector undertakings as well as other development projects and private industries have contributed to the process of impoverishment of the tribals. "The state which is supposed to protect their interest, has immensely contributed to their exploitation". The present situation is the outcome of the location of industries and other development projects in tribal areas which are rich in natural resources. Ironically, "The poor tribals were not only deprived of the fruits of development but were also uprooted from their land and natural habitats" [ibid: 123-124].

An estimated 2 per cent of alienation of tribals has been caused by the state for mining industries and other projects. The estimate of displacement varies from nine million to 20 million. The adivasis constitute 40 per cent of the total displaced persons [ibid: 121, 124].

With respect to health and education, a significant improvement has been made since independence, but it is far from satisfactory. The commission highlights that the modern system of medicine has created additional problems for the adivasis, "as doctors and paramedical personnel are seldom available in rural areas. Postings in tribal areas for these professionals are treated as a punishment and it is generally seen that most of these posts in centres and sub-centres are generally vacant in tribal areas. The tribal women labour who actually work for at least 14 hours a day seldom visit primary health centre. Hence these women largely depend on wild medicinal shrubs, herbs, roots, etc., for their ailments. The traditional system and knowledge of medicine in tribal areas is also fading because of the advent of the modern system of medicine" [ibid: 135].

Although enrolment of scheduled caste and scheduled tribe children, it notes, has improved in schools, more than one-third dropout before completing five years of primary education, and more than a half before eight years of elementary school. Their representation in the standards 10-12 level, as well as in graduate, postgraduate and professional courses is far below their population percentages. The literacy rate among the adivasis, for example, according to the 1991 Census, is 29.6 per cent – 40.65 per cent among males, and 15.19 among female as against the national average of 52.21 [ibid: 167, 172]. And in most states the share of education at all elementary levels has declined over time.

The commission concludes that the efforts made for the welfare and development of tribals, "have become repetitive in nature". The wide gap in development indices of scheduled tribes and the rest of the population, in relation to literacy, health, income and others indicate that "There is an urgent need for a significant increase in the allocation and for ensuring its proper utilisation" [ibid].

The stories of the adivasis of Thane, India, are the stories of suffering and deprived people all over the world who have been excluded and marginalised by the processes of development and modernisation. That economic growth does not necessarily ensure enhanced quality of life for the majority, the most weak and the vulnerable, is an accepted fact now. What Nussbaum says of Gujarat, can be said of Dahanu and Thane and many other states and countries which have achieved "development", but not the development of capabilities of everyone. "If we consider each person as worthy of regards, as an end and not just as a means, we cannot in any simple way praise Gujarat's rapid economic growth, which has left many powerless people behind...." [Nussbaum 2000: 32-33].

For Jean Dreze and Amartya Sen, development is "the expansion of the real freedoms that the citizens enjoy to pursue the objectives they have reason to value, and in this sense the expansion of human capability can be, broadly, seen as the central feature of the process of development... The life of a person can be seen as a sequence of things the person does, or states of being he or she achieves, and these constitute a collection of "functionings" – doings and beings the person achieves. "Capability" refers to the alternative combinations of functionings from which a person can choose. Thus, the notion of "capability is essentially one of freedom – the range of options a person has in deciding what kind of life to lead. Poverty of a life, in this view, lies not merely in the impoverished state in which the person actually lives, but also in the lack of real opportunity – given by social constraints as well as personal circumstances – to choose other types of living. Even the relevance of meagre possessions, and other aspects of what are standardly seen as economic poverty relates ultimately to their role in curtailing capabilities (that is their role in severely restricting the choices people have to lead valuable and valued lives). Poverty is, thus, ultimately a matter of 'capability deprivation' ...." [Dreze and Sen 2002: 35-36].

The central question of capability approach, Nussbaum elaborates, is "what people are actually able to do and to be – in a way informed by an intuitive idea of a life that is worthy of the dignity of the human being. ..... Capabilities... should be pursued for each and every person, treating each as an end and none as a mere tool of the end of others......". Her approach uses the idea "of a "threshold level of each capability beneath which it is held that truly human functioning is not available to citizens; the social goal should be understood in terms of getting citizens above this capability threshold" [Nussbaum, 2000: 5-6].

Given the constraints within which the majority of adivasis of Thane and India function even after nearly six decades of independence, they do not have the freedom to choose a life that they want to live and that is truly worthy of human beings.

Is it necessary to repeat that there is a need for greater livelihood opportunities, for higher wages, and even more fundamental, for wages to be paid, for job security, for protection against oppression and extortion by the government officials, the employers and their musclemen, for better and cheaper medical care and educational facilities. Their knowledge and skills as well as the material resources of the region must be rejuvenated and used to serve the end of each and every person and not just a few.

There cannot be any legislation for restoring the dignity of a people. A commitment on the part of the state and government agencies must ensure a reasonable quality of life. So that a self-respecting, proud people are not subjected to the indignity of having to live on garbage dumps in towns and cities, to go to the employer endlessly to recover their meagre wages, to work in inhuman conditions without protection or security, to become sex workers and thieves and stand at truck nakas on highways. So that they are not deprived of the resources on which they are dependent for their survival, water sources are not polluted or just appropriated by the rich and powerful and the surrounding forests are not turned in to plantations or just taken away by the vested interests. So that development does not only mean loss of land, displacement, a disruption and disturbance to their habitat, a threat to their livelihood and forced migration. So that the life-world of a people is not disrupted without anything better replacing it. What Mendelsohn and Vicziany say of the untouchables can be repeated in the case of the adivasis that the liberation of the adivasis is "ultimately a task for themselves and that the mechanisms are political. Which does not mean that the well-meaning people from other communities cannot play an important role in this liberation. Nor does it mean that the institution of the state must be written off as constitutionally incapable of delivering crucial assistance" [Mendelsohn and Vicziany 1996: 116].

In the course of writing this book, I was often reminded of the great saga of the people of North America, immortalised by John Steinbeck in the *Grapes of Wrath*. A people who were compelled by the forces of modernisation to leave their homes and fields and neighbours in search of a modest existence. There cannot be a more appropriate end to the stories of the adivasis of Thane, so different, and yet, so similar, than by recalling Steinbeck's masterpiece on the endless quest of the poor for a dignified existence. "There is a crime here that goes beyond denunciation. There is a sorrow here that weeping cannot symbolise. There is a failure here that topples all our success. The fertile earth, the straight tree rows, the sturdy trunks and the ripe fruit. And children dying of pellagra must die because a profit cannot be taken from an orange. And coroners must fill in the certificate – died of malnutrition – because the food must rot, must be forced to rot."

References

Agarwal, Bina (1991): Engendering the Environment Debate: Lessons from the Indian Subcontinent, CASID, Distinguished Speaker Series, No 8, Centre for Advanced Study of International Development, Michigan State University, Michigan.

Dalmia, Yashodhara (1988): *The Painted World of the Warlis*, Lalit Kala Academy, New Delhi.

DCH (1995): District Census Handbook (Thane), Government of Maharashtra, Mumbai.

Dewan, Ritu and Michelle, Chawla (1999): *Of Development Amidst Fragility, A Societal and Environmental Perspective on Vadhavan Port*, Popular Prakashan, Mumbai.

Dreze, Jean and Amartya Sen (2002): *India: Development and Participation*, Oxford University Press, New Delhi.

GoI (undated): Report of the National Commission for Scheduled Castes and Scheduled Tribes, 2001-02, Government of India.

Hardiman, David (1994): "Power in the Forests: The Dangs 1820-1940" in David Arnold and David Hardiman (eds), *Subaltern Studies 8*, Oxford University Press, Delhi.

Kashtakari Sanghatana (1984): "The 'Bhutali' Phenomenon: Why Are Women Hunted Down As Witches", *Socialist Health Review*, 1 (2): 87-92.

Martyris, Nina (2001): "In Dahanu, It's the Sarpanch Not the Budget Who Matters", *The Times of India*, February 28.

Mehta, Mona (1999): Suppressed Subjects? Gender Dynamics in the Context of Agrarian Change and Seasonal Labour Migration in Dahanu Taluka, Maharashtra, Ph.D Thesis, Institute of Social Studies, The Hague, The Netherlands.

Mendelsohn, Oliver and Marika Vicziany (1996): "The Untouchables" in (ed.) Oliver Mendelsohn and Upendra Baxi, *The Rights of Subordinated Peoples*, OUP, Delhi.

Munshi, Indra (1983): Analysis of Class Structure and Class Relations in a Rural Unit in Maharashtra, PhD Thesis, Department of Sociology, University of Mumbai.

— (2003): "Women and Forest: A Study of the Warlis of Western India" in Kelkar et al (ed) *Gender Relations in Forest Societies in Asia*, Sage Publications, New Delhi/Thousand Oaks/London.

Nussbaum, Martha (2000): *Women and Human Development: The Capabilities Approach*, Kali for Women, New Delhi.

Perreira, Winin (1992): "The Sustainable Lifestyles of the Warlis in Indigenous Vision: Peoples of India Attitudes to the Environment", *India International Centre Quarterly*, 19: 1-2, Spring-Summer.

Prabhu, Pradip (2001a): "The Greening of Haladpada-Shisne", *Humanscape*, VII, Issue XI, December.

— (2001b): "In the Eye of the Storm: Tribal Peoples of India" in John A. Grim (ed) *Indigenous Traditions and Ecology: The Interbeing of Cosmology and Community*, Harvard University Press, Cambridge.

Prasad, Archana (2003): *Against Ecological Romanticism*, Three Essays Collective, New Delhi.

Save, K.J. (1945): *The Warlis*, Padma Publications, Bombay.

Shiva, Vandana (1988): *Staying Alive: Women, Ecology and Development*, Kali for Women, New Delhi.

Glossary

Abkari	Pertains to liquor
Ambil	Sour gruel from jowar/nagli/vari, considered coarse grains
Bhagat vidya	Knowledge for medicine man-cum-priest
Bhaiyas	Migrants from Uttar Pradesh/Bihar
Bhakri	Unleavened bread
Bhut	Evil spirit
Bhutali vidya	Knowledge for a witch
Bhutali	Witch/witch-hunting
Bundarpatti	Coastal plains
Dalhi	Shifting cultivation
Dargah	Shrine
Daru	Liquor
Dhandayla	Migration by men for short periods
Dhavleri	Marriage priestess
Diva	Divination
Gaonkari	Villagers/village elders
Gharorya	Man who stays in his parents-in-law's house
Halad gathi	Putting auspicious turmeric and tying blackbeads
Hali	System of pledging services in return for cash advances
Jagran	Night vigil in memory of ancestors
Junglepatti	Forested hilly area
Kaka	Father's brother
Kaki	Father's brother's wife

Kaneri	Watery gruel from rice
Kanni	Broken rice
Karbhari	Village master of ceremonies
Khand	Rent
Khatedar	Leader of a work unit on salt pans called 'khata'
Khau	Small snack
Khavti	Consumption loan of grains
Khedya	Young boy around the house to do odd jobs
Kondwada	Place where impounded cattle are kept
Kotwal	Government village revenue functionary
Kul kayda	Tenancy law
Kul	Tenant
Lagnagadi	Marriage serf
Lal Bauta	Red flag of the Communist Party
Mama	Mother's brother
Mami	Mother's brother's wife
Mandap	Tent
Mandav	An enclosure
Mann	One mann equals approximately 40 kilograms
Mazoori	Labour/wages
Morcha	Demonstration
Mukkadam	Supervisor
Pada	Hamlet
Paili	One paili equals approximately four kilograms
Pancha	Village elders
Patil	Owner/manager of salt pans
Police patil	Government police functionary
Rab	Cultivation by burning the seed bed
Raiyat	Cultivator
Raja	King
Sakhar puda	Engagement ceremony
Sansar	Life-world
Sarkar	Government
Sarpanch	Head of the panchayat
Sowkar	Landlord-moneylender-trader

Seth	Employer
Shindad	Literal meaning tree covered land
Suhasin	Married women who perform important rites at weddings
Tahal	Tree lopping
Talati	Government servant who maintains land records at village level
Tamasha	Cultural event
Tava	Frying pan
Thalawala	Storyteller
Varkas	Grassland
Veth begar	Forced unpaid labour
Veth	Forced labour
Village patil	Village headman
Vir	Ancestor
Zoli	Naming ceremony